The Story of the B-52s

Scott Creney • Brigette Adair Herron

The Story of the B-52s

Neon Side of Town

palgrave
macmillan

Scott Creney
Huntington, NY, USA

Brigette Adair Herron
Huntington, NY, USA

ISBN 978-3-031-22569-7 ISBN 978-3-031-22570-3 (eBook)
https://doi.org/10.1007/978-3-031-22570-3

This Palgrave Macmillan imprint is published by the registered company Springer Nature Switzerland AG.
The registered company address is: Gewerbestrasse 11, 6330 Cham, Switzerland

This book is dedicated to the memory of Ricky Wilson and Jeremy Ayers, and to our child, Noam Russell Creney.

Acknowledgments

At its best, Athens is a community. This book would not have been written without the support and encouragement from many people within that community. Thank you to Vanessa Briscoe Hay, Mike Turner, Christina Cotter, Dan Wall, and Gordon Lamb for their early encouragement. We are especially grateful for Jordan Stepp's intelligence, passion, and support during the writing of this book.

Lastly, Robin James at Palgrave Macmillan deserves a tremendous thank you for bringing this book into the world.

Thank you to everyone who sat for an interview, responded to an email, or shared their story with us. We are tremendously grateful to the following people who generously donated their art and photographs to be featured in this project: Curtis Knapp, Wingate Downs, Ann States, Dana Downs, Terry Allen, Keith Bennett, Chris Rasmussen, Barbara McKenzie, and Didi Dunphy at Lyndon House.

We would also like to thank the B-52s' management team for their enthusiasm, and for saying we sounded like the "perfect writers for such a project." While the band were unavailable to participate in interviews for this book because they were working on an oral history project of their own, we were able to access a vast network of primary resources and interviews, as well as conduct our own interviews with people close to the band. This book would also not have been possible without Mats Sexton. His 2002 book *The B-52's Universe: The Essential Guide to the World's Greatest Party Band* was an invaluable source, along with the generous donation he made to the University of Georgia (UGA)'s Special Collections Library of his vast collection of B-52s' scrapbooks and memorabilia. This allowed us to access nearly every article ever written about the band, as well as archives of fan-club-only interviews where the band talked more openly about their music and career than they typically do in on-the-record interviews. We also want to express our deep appreciation to the employees of the UGA Special Collections Library for their generosity and vast knowledge about the radical history of Athens.

Rather than being seen as the definitive story of the B-52s, we hope this is one of many more to come. The B-52s, both the band as a whole and the individuals within, contain multitudes. And as with rock luminaries like Prince or Bob Dylan, there is space for many different perspectives about their lives and their art, as well as illuminating stories about the band that have yet to be told. Knowing this would likely be the first critical biography of the B-52s, we have tried to be as objective and respectful as possible. This meant editing out moments when our irreverence veered into outright cynicism. It also meant limiting our discussion about the band's personal lives to what was already in the public record, irrespective of what we may have been told in interviews or stories people in Athens told us while we were writing the book.

Any one of these chapters could easily be expanded into its own book. It's impossible to tell the story of the B-52s without discussing the AIDS epidemic, the University of Georgia art department, or the late 70s/early 80s New York City art-and-music scene, among other subjects, but it's even more impossible to do justice to the depth and beauty of those stories in a book about the B-52s. We urge anyone interested to explore and document the history of these subjects further.

Contents

About the Authors

Scott Creney is the author of the poetry collection *Nation Full of Caesars* and the work of creative nonfiction *Dear Al-Qaeda: Letters to the World's Most Notorious Terror Organization*, which was a Small Press Distribution bestseller. They graduated from Emerson College in Boston, MA with a BFA in Writing, Literature, and Publishing, during which time they toured the US reading original poetry with the Guerilla Poets, who produced a collection entitled *Speak These Words: A Guerilla Poets Anthology*. They have written about music, books, and film for *Clash Music*, *The Fanzine*, *Collapse Board*, and *Ablaze!*, among others. They contributed six chapters to *101 Albums You Should Die Before You Hear* (Ed. by Everett True). Scott was also the bass player for the Athens band, Tunabunny, who released five critically acclaimed albums before going on hiatus in 2017. Most recently, Scott collaborated with Brigette Adair Herron on "You Won't Find It Online: Entering the Archives to Tell the Story of the B-52s," a chapter in *Exploring the Archives: A Beginner's Guide for Qualitative Researchers* (2022), which was a 2021 Society of Professors of Education Outstanding Book Award winner.

Brigette Adair Herron is a writer, educator, musician, and qualitative researcher from Athens, GA. She has a PhD in Adult Education from the University of Georgia and conducts research at the intersections of justice-oriented feminist pedagogy, adult learning, and qualitative inquiry. She is a co-author of the book *Philanthropy, Hidden Strategy, and Collective Resistance: A Primer for Concerned*, which won the 2019 American Educational Studies Association Critics Choice Book Award and a 2020

Society of Professors of Education Outstanding Book Award. She has authored numerous book chapters in edited volumes on qualitative interviewing, and articles in the journals *Cultural Studies <=> Critical Methodologies* and *LEARNing Landscapes.* Her writing on music has been featured in the book *101 Albums You Should Die Before You Hear* and on the websites *Collapse Board*, *Vice*, and *Eldredge Atlanta.* She is a multi-instrumentalist with a long history in the Athens music scene, including her work most recently as a guitarist, singer, and songwriter in the Athens bands Tunabunny and Mesmerized by Avon.

CHAPTER 1

Neon

I think we were original and each of us and our personalities coming together …. It was like alchemy and it propelled us into the future for a long time to come.[1]

—Cindy

They began in 1976 as five friends playing music in the small college town of Athens, Georgia, looking for a way to have fun. Before they became the B-52s, Ricky Wilson, Cindy Wilson, Fred Schneider, Kate Pierson, and Keith Strickland were five smart, charismatic individuals who knew how to make an impression. One night they decided to play some music together—as an experiment, as a lark—and something incredible happened. Call it magic, call it chemistry, call it luck, but as the B-52s, they transformed into something larger than life. The band played a show at a friend's party, and the people there lost their minds. The size of the audience has continued to change over the years, but the effect has somehow remained the same.

The band encouraged people to believe in themselves. The subsequent Athens music scene is unimaginable without the B-52s. Their arrival in New York City in December of 1977 profoundly influenced the next several years of music and art to come out of that city. Critic Michael Azerrad wrote that listeners "took the band's very existence as permission to break out of the mainstream-music rut; from there, some of them broke out of

S. Creney, B. A. Herron, *The Story of the B-52s*,
https://doi.org/10.1007/978-3-031-22570-3_1

mainstream ruts of all kinds."[2] The B-52s have made the world a brighter and more spectacular place. To borrow a line from their song Wig, everywhere they go has become "the neon side of town."

Neon is incandescent. Neon is modern and futuristic. Neon is maximum intensity. Neon is the quality of light produced by stars, and neon illuminates the illicit areas of cities around the world. Neon is rarely found on earth. Neon produces an unmistakable reddish-orange light. Sometimes neon is purple. In Miami, neon is almost always pink and often in the shape of a flamingo. Neon is a gas; neon is a noble gas. T Rex said life is a gas. Neon light became popular because it was impossible to ignore. Neon light has no stable compounds.

With the exception of that flamingo in Miami, the B-52s are all of these things. And because the band itself is unstable and always in flux, any attempt to define them in a single sentence or paragraph has fallen short of encompassing the totality of the B-52s.

The neon light on the surface of the B-52s' music can sometimes shine so brightly that it obscures the darkness that lies at the heart of most of their music. The band wrote plenty of serious songs—songs about danger and paranoia, about poverty and the environment, about loneliness and spiritual emptiness—yet too many critics have only noticed the band's more lightweight qualities. Greil Marcus wrote in 1990 that they'd "never be more than a decent joke."[3] Longtime *Village Voice* music editor and self-proclaimed "Dean of American Rock Critics" Robert Christgau damned the band with faint praise in 1980 when he called them "the world's greatest new-wave kiddie-novelty disco-punk band."[4] J.D. Considine, appraising the band's career in the 1992 edition of *Rolling Stone Album Guide*, rated none of their albums higher than 3.5 stars–and most of them 2.5 or less—dismissing them as "a party band in the truest sense of the term."[5]

It isn't just male critics who have slighted the band. In 1997, *Trouble Girls: The Rolling Stone Book of Women in Rock* was written to "gather in one place the numerous and varied talents and achievements of women," and extended all the way back to Mamie Smith and Ma Rainey. Despite this, the book only devoted a single paragraph to the women in the B-52s, and mostly just talked about their clothes. It reduced their music to "carnivalesque keyboard playing," "impressions of sea creatures," and "a virtually unintelligible rendition of the amazing line, 'Why won't you dance with me? I'm not no limburger!'"[6,7] The writer didn't mention Kate or Cindy by name, referring to them simply as "the female vocalists." Yet,

Cindy and Kate each have their own distinct singing and writing styles. Their voices are easily discernible, and it's as interesting to analyze their similarities and differences—as singers and songwriters—as it is to parse out the dynamics in other rock partnerships like Lennon and McCartney, Mould and Hart, or Foster and McClennan.[8]

Billing themselves as "a tacky little dance band from Athens, Georgia," or "the world's greatest party band," has invited people to underestimate the B-52s, even as they've said those things with a wink, and with more than a touch of false humility. But this needs to be stated clearly: the B-52s are one of the most unique popular bands in the history of rock and roll. Unfortunately, this uniqueness is so evident that it has come to define the band at the expense of their music, and ultimately, their place in the rock canon. Almost from the beginning of their career, the band's image (and subsequently, their music) has been reduced by critics, and some fans, to that of camp thrift store party cartoons. While those qualities certainly exist, they only make up a fraction of the band's aesthetic, to say nothing of their music. The B-52s didn't dress in costumes. They weren't Kiss, or Devo. Countless onstage photos and videos exist from the band's creative peak, 1978–1981, where Kate and Cindy aren't wearing wigs. The B-52s have worn whatever they felt whenever they felt like it. With the benefit of hindsight, it seems critics mistook the band's remarkable style for a uniform. Even worse, this emphasis on their clothes and style has almost always been examined on a surface level. This is unfortunate because even the B-52s' idiosyncrasies have clear antecedents in rock history. If anything, dressing up for the stage should include them in the rock canon, not exclude them.

But then the rock canon, with its endless lists and its absurdly Boomer-centric hall of fame, has never been fair. While this book's authors see the rock canon as something that should be expanded, if not outright exploded, we see the exclusion of the B-52s from that canon to be absurd, not just by our standards, but by its own.

Because no matter how original and different they were, the B-52s were also a great rock band in the conventional sense, with an abundance of strengths. They had one of the most original guitarists of his generation. They had three people fronting the band, one who wrote strange and subversive lyrics delivered in a voice that could go from playful to angry with no warning, another who sang in a soulful mix of Dusty Springfield and Bobbie Gentry,[9] and yet another who could hit incredible soprano high notes while playing two keyboards at once. They could harmonize like the girl groups, and shout like the avant-garde. All of this while being backed by a drummer who hit so hard that, 35 years later, he was the first thing their tour manager in the early 80s remembered about the band's live shows.[10]

Contrary to most conventional wisdom, the B-52s were a band that could, by anyone's definition, just flat-out rock. Songs like Strobe Light, 52 Girls, Wig, or Rock Lobster are driven by a relentless ferocity. Listen to the conviction and sheer anguish in Cindy's voice when she sings Give Me Back My Man or Hero Worship. Hear Fred's full-throated screams in Channel Z. Listen to Kate's ascending repetition of "fire!" in Wig. The ending of Private Idaho walks it home harder than any Southern rock of the 1970s, harder than Skynyrd, and harder than the Allmans.

The B-52s' music is rooted in a particularly Southern version of rock, one influenced by the ecstatic transcendence of gospel and the fierce abandon of early rock and roll. Both of these genres also placed an emphasis on visual expression and flamboyance. For all that sets them apart, the B-52s played with a passion that embodies the very nature of rock and roll, from Little Richard through Prince (a man who was known to whip out the Rock Lobster riff in concert).

With their cheap clothes and even cheaper musical equipment, the B-52s were astute practitioners of the time-honored Southern tradition of making do with limited means. When a string broke on Ricky Wilson's guitar, he just learned to play without it. In the process, he developed a method of playing that involved unusual tunings and missing strings that became its own style. Without the two middle guitar strings in the way, he found he was able to switch from playing rhythm parts on the two thicker top strings to playing lead parts on the two bottom strings faster, and with more force, than he could have done otherwise. The intricacy of his playing on Private Idaho is almost impossible to recreate on a properly strung guitar.

Like much of the band's early music, Ricky's guitar style challenged assumptions about skill and ability, as well as genius and amateurishness. There's a common idiomatic phrase use by Southerners, both Black and white alike, about "making a dollar out of 15 cents." In a 1997 essay on the nature of coolness, Donnell Alexander explained how coolness was about "living on the cusp, on the periphery, diving for scraps … being outside looking in." The B-52s, as a band that contained gay men and strong, liberated women living in the South, had plenty of experience as outsiders. Alexander also noted how limited resources could force people to improvise, and in the process come up with something new, that is, something cool:

> The real secret weapon of cool is that it's about synthesis. Just about every important black cultural invention of this century has been about synthesizing elements previously considered antithetical. MLK merged Eastern thought and cotton-field religious faith into the civil rights movement. Chuck Berry merged blues and country music into rock 'n' roll. Michael Jordan incorporated the old school ball of Jerry West into his black game. Talk about making a dollar out of 15 cents.[11]

Though Alexander emphasizes the Black experience, this approach has been utilized by poor Southerners from all backgrounds. And while there's a big difference between slave cooks fashioning delicious food from the scraps given to them by white plantation owners and a kid learning to play guitar in his bedroom, Ricky's resourcefulness and capacity for improvisation echoes this tradition. "In the beginning," he explained, "I kept breaking strings. I couldn't afford to keep replacing them all the time so I just wrote songs like that."[12]

Critics initially praised the B-52s for what they saw as an ironic or retro sensibility, but their presentation was rooted in something far more practical. Fred explained the band's approach at length in a 1993 interview:

> The reason people thought we were trying to revive the sixties was because we had no money and all the instruments were whatever Keith and Ricky had. A Sears guitar and a cheap drum kit. So people thought we wanted to be [60s surf rock band] the Ventures. We liked the Ventures, but it just so happened that was the only guitar Ricky had.[13]

The band's poverty was real enough that, according to Kate, when the band first started getting written about in New York, "We couldn't afford to buy the magazines. We'd buy one copy and share it."[14] This same impulse also fueled the band's outlandish stage costumes, which were found by digging through the thrift shops and department stores of downtown Athens. The B-52s' "trash aesthetic" that people talk about is more rooted in the culture of the South than in John Waters movies. Virginia native Missy Elliott's use of garbage bags and mirrors in her video for The Rain (Supa Dupa Fly) resembles the impulse that had Kate and Cindy putting pocketbooks on their heads and calling them wigs. Elliott talked about her iconic outfit in a 2017 interview. "To me, the outfit was a way to mask my shyness behind all the chaos of the look.... The outfit was a symbol of power.[15] The B-52s also used dressing-up as a way to get out from under their self-consciousness. Despite their reputation as a party band, Ricky and Cindy spent most of their first New York show hiding from the audience.

There's an inherent form of protest in trash art. Consider the double meaning of the word refuse (noun, accent on the first syllable) and refuse (the verb, with an accent on the second). Being excluded from mainstream society, whether through deliberate choice or being excluded by others, can give you a different perspective on that society. What mass culture deems treasure can start to look like trash, and what the culture deems trash can start to look like treasure. Seen in this light, trash art functions as a rejection of mainstream values, while also being a statement about one's alienation from those values, and a refusal to conform.

With their second-hand clothes, cheap guitars, and minimalist instrumentation, the early B-52s weren't just being different, they were making a statement.

Space Age

The B-52s sang a lot about outer space in their lyrics. While this is often depicted as one more example of the band's silliness, their portrayal of space as a place of freedom, where earth's rules no longer apply, is similar to the interplanetary vision exhibited by Sun Ra and George Clinton. Both men, along with writer Octavia Butler, are considered the progenitors of an aesthetic later dubbed Afrofuturism—defined, in the first dictionary we reached for, as

> a cultural movement that uses the frame of science fiction and fantasy to reimagine the history of the African diaspora and to invoke a vision of a technically advanced and generally hopeful future in which black people thrive: this movement is expressed through art, cinema, literature, music, fashion, etc.[16]

One can argue the B-52s perform a similar reimagining, only through a queer and feminist lens. The B-52s were fans of both Clinton and Sun Ra, as well as other Afrofuturist touchstones like Star Trek and Jimi Hendrix, long before they started the band. According to Sun Ra's biographer, the B-52s saw Ra's Arkestra "every night when they first came to

New York.[17] While there, they would have seen the bandleader direct a chant that sounds like it could have come from a B-52s song: *If you find earth boring / Just the same old same thing / Sign up for Outer Spaceways Incorporated.*[18]

Afrofuturist artists have presented themselves as being from outer space as a way to convey their (literal) alienation due to the racism of mainstream US society. In doing so, they took the otherness forced on them, and re-contextualized that otherness as a strength. Dressing outlandishly, and presenting one's self from outer space, was a grasp for personal and creative freedom, as well as a way to find protection in a dangerous and violent world. In his 1998 biography of Sun Ra, John F. Szwed called Sun Ra's depiction of space "both a metaphor of exclusion and of reterritorialization."[19] The members of the B-52s, all dealing with their own brands of otherness, likely had similar motivations.

In her overview of Afrofuturism, Ytasha L. Womack asserted the hidden depth that can be found in outlandish clothes and songs about planets:

> The space theme was more than just a kooky gimmick to play off the space age, more than an eyebrow-raising marketing ploy. The colorful, albeit shiny, costumes served as a visual tool to stimulate higher thinking and to prepare audiences for something new.[20]

Biographer Paul Youngquist describes Sun Ra's Arkestra in words that apply just as well to the B-52s when he describes "a group of intellectuals and crack musicians … womping up an alternative space program from the cultural detritus of the Space Age."[21]

None of this is to claim that the B-52s were Afrofuturists, or to equate one struggle to another. Rather, the comparison is made to suggest there is deeper meaning to be found in an aspect of the B-52s' aesthetic that is usually dismissed as mere fashion, or a goofy joke.

Party Politics

If the B-52s must be classified as a party band, then they are the sound of a party that is desperate and exploding. If they are a dance band, then they are a dance band that makes you dance relentlessly, a band that, at their peak, has made people shake the boards and strain the balconies of concert venues.

The problem has come when listeners and critics have defined them as *just* a party band, implying the band's music is somehow frivolous or shallow. For some of us, a truly great party is the closest thing to freedom we will ever experience. A party can be an expression of people's subconscious desire for revolution and anarchy. In a world still plagued by heteronormativity, consumerism, and conservatism, the B-52s' celebration of weirdness, chaos, and fun is a type of liberation, and liberation is always political.

B-52s songs often take place in liminal spaces, which cultural anthropologist Victor Turner called "an interstructural phase in social dynamics."[22] Whether it was a beach party, a nude beach, outer space, a shack out in the country, or just a chemically assisted detour through your mind, in B-52s songs these places become settings where societal norms, particularly stifling ones, become irrelevant. As Turner explained, people in these conditions, "have no status, property, insignia, secular clothing, rank, kinship position, nothing to demarcate them from their fellows. Their condition is … the very prototype of sacred poverty."[23] In the liminal spaces the B-52s sing about, everyone is welcome, and most importantly, admission is always free.

The B-52s understood the danger in being different, and so personal politics are everywhere in their music, and many of their songs tackle issue-based politics directly, with songs about environmentalism (Channel Z), vegetarianism (Juicy Jungle), animal liberation (Quiche Lorraine), and bigotry (Bad Influence). Fred stated this directly in a 2018 interview:

> We were really pretty political as a band. Rather than clothes and wigs and stuff, I'd rather talk about politics, and I know the others do too, because it's more important, what's going on in the world.[24]

The B-52s disrupted social norms, to say nothing of rock and roll norms, simply by walking onto a stage. A band with gay men, plus women who played guitars, keyboards, and bongos, was a radical concept in rock and roll in the late 70s—in many respects it still is. Their artistic and public identities were acts of rebellion against every orthodoxy you can imagine—cultural, political, social, et al. Even their well-documented Yoko Ono influence was, in the context of its time, an act of heresy in the rock world, a place where Ono's music, if not her entire existence, was considered a joke. The fact that the B-52s were still able to carve out a place for themselves—in the world, on the radio, in popular culture—can only be seen as an act of courage.

Through their music and style, the B-52s exploded conventional notions of gender and sexuality. Their lyrics discussed sex in ways rarely sang about in rock up to that point; it was playful, it was freaky, and the sex was always consensual. That they could be so disruptive, while at the same time making music that sold in the millions, is a testament to their genius. This duality, this ability to be simultaneously confrontational and accessible, strange and familiar, avant-garde and mainstream, is unusual in rock music. The B-52s have never made a record as challenging as *White Light/White Heat*, or as commercial as *Forever Your Girl*, yet they are a band that can be enjoyed by fans of both.

Fluidity Politics

In the B-52s' universe, everything—identity, sexuality, clothes, setting—is always in flux. Even the band's name is fluid. In 2008, the apostrophe was removed from the band's name, for reasons that have never been fully explained.[25] We have chosen to write the band's name as "the B-52s," since that is what they currently call themselves. However, the correct placement of the hyphen and apostrophe has proven to be a challenge for journalists throughout the band's career, something the change in 2008 only amplified. When quoting articles, we have left the band's name written the way it appeared in the original source material, as a tribute to their fluidity. We have also chosen to write the title of the band's first album as *The B-52's*, since that's what it says on the cover.

The band's fluidity is subversive because it pushes back against the idea that society and identity have to be static, that the way we live is the natural order of things. When people call the B-52s' music empowering, this is what they are talking about. The celebration of fluidity and arbitrariness, of the dissolution of borders, runs all through their music. The band may have never written a protest song in the manner of Woody Guthrie or early Bob Dylan, but Rock Lobster is, with its boys in bikinis and girls in surfboards, every bit as political. Ways of living that seem fixed to us suddenly become unmoored, and people who would normally feel excluded or marginalized are now included. They are made to feel that they, and their experiences, count. This inclusiveness is a big reason for the deep fandom and love people have for the B-52s.

There's a Moon in the Sky (Called the Moon), from the B-52s' self-titled debut album, makes this ethos plain when Fred sings, *If you're in outer space / don't feel out of place / cause there are thousands of others like you*. The lines celebrate an unabashed inclusivity—for anyone, whether they be gay, straight, pansexual, weird, clean-cut, loud, or quiet. As he continues to sing the line, Fred switches "like" from a preposition to a verb, reassuring the listener, now nearly screaming, that "others *like* you." The message is that you—whoever you are, however you identify—are accepted. You are cared for. As Fred said in a 1980 interview, "Some people write all love songs. Some people write 'life on the road songs.' We just write 'life in different space' songs."[26]

The choices the B-52s made about how to present themselves has changed lives, and in some cases even saved lives. Their music has functioned as a beacon, not just for people struggling with their sexuality, but for anyone who has ever felt like an outsider. Even if you were trapped in your bedroom, or a small town where nobody understood you—or maybe where they understood you all too well—their records made people feel less alone.

The B-52s' fluidity is a main source of their creative power. Unlike bands guided by a single songwriter, or an egomaniacal frontperson, the B-52s function more like an anarchic collective. Their music is an outgrowth of what each individual band member brings to it. Songwriting consists of lengthy collaborations, long improvisations that are later revisited in search of something that can be developed into a song. Keith explained the process in a 1990 interview:

> Collective subconscious really comes into play when everyone's improvising. Cause not one person is conceiving of this whole thing. It's coming from five—in the beginning, five different points of view. There's really no leader of the group, because we were a bunch of friends first, then we started the band. It would have been odd if all of a sudden someone had said, "Well, I'm the leader," or, "You be the leader." Friends don't do that. You all work together.[27]

Imagine the potential combinations five creative, free-spirited people are capable of forming, and you understand why attempts to narrowly define the band as "camp" or "retro" or "new wave," or even "political," feel so inadequate. Maybe the reason the band has never been properly defined is because no simple definition exists. It's no accident that Mats Sexton, someone who deeply immersed himself into the world of the B-52s, titled his 2002 book about the band, *The B-52's Universe*, as opposed to *The B-52's World*, or even *The B-52's Galaxy*.

Listening to all their albums in sequence, over the course of a day, one is struck by the stylistic breadth and emotional depth of their work. Because their music has always been a reflection of the people making it, there's an honesty at the heart of the B-52s that you can hear in everything they have ever recorded. Even less critically acclaimed albums like *Whammy!* and *Bouncing Off the Satellites* reward close listening. During this period, relationships within the band were fractured and complex, and so the music from this time is also fractured and complex. Feelings of depression, exhaustion, and confusion underpin many of the songs on these albums.

Ultimately, the B-52s' music communicates that all humans are unique and deserve a life of freedom. Many of their songs attempt to carve out new possibilities toward this utopian vision, most clearly on the *Cosmic Thing* track Topaz when Kate, Fred and Cindy sing, *Our hearts are travelling faster / Faster than the speed of love / Straight through a tear in the clouds / Up to the heavens above/ Our universe is expanding*. Their music has made the world a better place and filled it with an endless spectrum of color. The B-52s have made the world more incandescent; they have made the world more neon.

And so, we arrive at the end of this chapter in the same place where we began, on the neon side of town. Because even a planet as wild as this one still travels in a circle.

The energy of the universe must remain in balance. And so, because this story is oftentimes hilarious, it is also accompanied by tragedy. Because it is a story about people overflowing with life, it also contains a story of death. And because it is a story about failure and losing yourself, it is ultimately a story about victory and finding one's place in the world.

This is the story of the B-52s.

Notes

1. Echazabal, "Change is Good."
2. Azerrad, Liner notes, R2 78357." Azerrad also mentions artists influenced by B-52s, including Bjork, Deee-Lite, Beat Happening, Chicks on Speed, Sleater-Kinney, Dave Grohl and "literally thousands of other bands."
3. Marcus, *Real Life Rock*, 59.
4. Christgau, *Christgau's Record Guide*, 54.
5. Considine, "The B-52s," 56.
6. Dibbell, "Women and Punk," 286.

7. By comparison, Me'Shell Ndegecello, Selena, and Laura Nyro, all received their own chapters, about a half-dozen pages each. The use of the word "unintelligible" is confusing, as the line is not only clearly enunciated, but is delivered with enough force to knock over a small houseplant.
8. The latter two were songwriting teams/factions in Husker Du and the Go-Betweens, respectively, and despite their bands being far less commercially successful than the B-52s, have seen their styles compared and contrasted in biographies about their bands.
9. In a 2022 interview, Keith Strickland said of her voice, "Cindy's voice can be beautiful, but it has a primal quality at the same time. I used to tell Ricky she reminds me of John Lennon."
10. Matthew Murphy in conversation with authors, May 28, 2019.
11. Alexander, "Black People Cooler," 50.
12. Lloyd, "B-52s," 37.
13. The B-52s' United Fans Organization (UFO) Issue #10.
14. Tannenbaum, "The B-52s Say Farewell," AR-14. The article still added an apostrophe to the band's name.
15. Ghansah, "Watching the Stars," https://www.elle.com/culture/celebrities/a44891/missy-elliott-june-2017-elle-cover-story/.
16. "Afrofuturism," Dictionary.com, accessed October 10, 2019, https://www.dictionary.com/browse/afrofuturism.
17. Gross, "Sun Ra."
18. Moody, "The radical jazz activist."
19. Szwed, Space Is the Place, 140.
20. Womack, *Afrofuturism*, 58.
21. Youngquist, *A Pure Solar World*, 140.
22. Turner, "Betwixt and Between," 98–99.
23. Ibid.
24. Greenblatt, "The B-52s: The Stories."
25. There is a Facebook page, https://www.facebook.com/LogoDeface/, dedicated to the missing apostrophe.
26. Isler, "The Devil Went Down to Georgia," 24.
27. Schoemer, "Beehives and Ballyhoo," 43.

CHAPTER 2

Athens: Pre-52s

We felt like outsiders, you know, and so this whole scene kind of empowered us. We could be ourselves, so to speak.[1]

—Keith

The town the B-52s came from was every bit as unique as the band itself. Don't believe the story that Athens was a sleepy college town with nothing going on until five misfits woke it up. When the B-52s played their first show in 1977, they weren't the first incredible thing to happen in Athens. They were simply the latest in a long line of radical acts.

It took a while to develop, though. Jim Herbert would become one of the most acclaimed, as well as transgressive, artists in Athens history, and would go on to make videos for both R.E.M. and the B-52s. But when he arrived in 1962 to teach art at the University of Georgia, he recalls, "On the weekends, the campus completely cleared out. Nobody stuck around."[2]

Herbert had missed the turmoil that took place on campus a year earlier. After a federal court decision, UGA became the first Southern university to desegregate, admitting its first Black undergraduate students, Charlayne Hunter and Hamilton E. Holmes. The pair were met with hatred and vitriol from the white student population, and their presence on campus provoked demonstrations, and a near-riot outside Hunter's dormitory. Harassment of Black students and faculty would continue openly for the next several decades. UGA wouldn't hire a Black faculty

S. Creney, B. A. Herron, *The Story of the B-52s*,
https://doi.org/10.1007/978-3-031-22570-3_2

member until 1968, and wouldn't see a Black football player take the field until 1971. A Black student who graduated in 1976 recalled the university at that time as "an environment that if you were an African-American walking down the street in the spring and all of the windows were open, you would hear the ringing of ["n----r"] as you walked down the sidewalk."[3] In 1987, a Black professor could find himself mistaken for a janitor, as Robert Pratt did after he became the first Black professor in the history department and a colleague asked him to change the toilet paper.[4]

The process of desegregation in Athens was marked with ugly tragedy and violence. On July 11, 1964, Washington D.C. resident Lemuel Penn was murdered by three Klansmen who lived in Athens.[5] In 2006, the Georgia Historical Society, Lemuel Penn Memorial Committee, and Colbert Grove Baptist Church erected a marker on the spot where Penn was killed. The text reads as follows:

> On the night of July 11, 1964 three African-American World War II veterans returning home following training at Ft. Benning, Georgia were noticed in Athens by local members of the Ku Klux Klan. The officers were followed to the nearby Broad River Bridge where their pursuers fired into the vehicle, killing Lt. Col. Lemuel Penn. When a local jury failed to convict the suspects of murder, the federal government successfully prosecuted the men for violations under the new Civil Rights Act of 1964, passed just nine days before Penn's murder. The case was instrumental in the creation of a Justice Department task force whose work culminated in the Civil Rights Act of 1968.[6]

While the racism in Athens was typical of the rest of the South (and persists in new and old ways to this day), a politically progressive culture of protest and liberation rose up in Athens around this time.

There wasn't much of a music scene during the 60s and 70s, but the University of Georgia was on fire. In some instances, literally. Vietnam War protesters tried to burn down the Reserve Officers' Training Corps (ROTC) building on five separate occasions between 1969 and 1972. The incident at UGA on February 10, 1969, was only the second case of arson involving a campus ROTC building in the entire country.[7] In August 1970, one student even threw a Molotov cocktail into the building.

Other Southern universities had chapters of Students for a Democratic Society (SDS), but UGA's chapter went to greater extremes, going so far as to stage an "Anti-Military Ball" three years in a row.

In 1967, members of SDS also helped successfully integrate a popular off-campus bar for students. The group then began "peace vigils" in 1968, openly demonstrating against the war. During one protest, anti-war demonstrators covered the ROTC building in graffiti, spray-painting the memorable slogan "Che Lives."[8]

On April 10, 1968, several hundred students participated in the "March for Co-Ed Equality," a protest organized by SDS demanding an end to gender-based discrimination. The students occupied an administration building for three days. Two weeks later, the student body overwhelmingly voted to eliminate the separate set of rules that existed for women students, and it was approved by the university in July. A *New York Times* article that month referred to UGA as "one of the most liberal universities in the South on student privileges."[9]

In 1968, Robert Croker joined Jim Herbert as a teacher in the art school. They had been recruited by Lamar Dodd, a Georgia native who had spent time studying in New York City. He returned to the South in 1937 when UGA hired him as an artist in residence. The following year he was appointed head of the art department, a position he would retain through 1972. When the art department received increased funding in the 1960s, Dodd used his position to hire a series of radical teachers who would serve as mentors and catalysts for a burgeoning creative scene, one that encompassed visual arts, sculpture, film, and ultimately music. In his article "Why Athens?" sociologist Arthur Jipson wrote, "This art community was clearly (and visibly) distinguishable from the remainder of the community through their party behavior, adventurous lifestyle, and artistic and fashionable dress and demeanor."[10]

One of the most radical hires was William D. "Bill" Paul, who became the director of the Georgia Museum of Art (GMOA) in 1967. "I thought our job was to supply questions," says Paul, "and students could find the answers, aesthetic answers. And my other charge, I thought, was to give the art museum a physical, national presence. And we really did that." The first exhibition Paul curated was titled "The Visual Assault," and featured NYC artists like Andy Warhol and Robert Rauschenberg, among others. According to Paul, "It got press as the largest show of contemporary art ever held in the Southeast, so we started with a good time."[11] A year later, the museum put together an exhibition titled "American Painting: the 1960's." It included work from Jasper Johns, Roy Lichtenstein, Cy Twomby, as well as Warhol's famous Campbell Soup Can and Marilyn paintings. When the B-52s—a band that has received its share of pop art comparisons—were coming of age, some of the most iconic pop art works in the world could be found on display in their hometown.

Athens had other connections to Andy Warhol and New York City. Jeremy Ayers was an Athens native whose father was a religion professor at UGA. Ayers graduated from Athens High in 1966 and briefly attended classes at UGA, so briefly that Jim Herbert couldn't remember whether he was an official student, or just someone who hung around the campus.[12] Bill Paul confirms Ayers was a student in one of his classes ("He wore a suit and tie to class .... He hated me because I used to say his name 'Germ-y'"[13]), but notes it was common for people to attend classes at the art school who weren't formally enrolled. So much so that he was surprised none of the B-52s' members were art students. "I thought they were all in the art school," says Paul. "Well, some of them were hanging out in the art school."[14]

Either way, Ayers soon left for New York City, where he became part of the Warhol crowd. Adopting the name Silva Thin (sometimes written as "Sylva," or "Thinn"), Ayers/Thin penned a column in Warhol's *Interview* magazine for a couple of years in the early 70s. Rumors of Ayers' involvement in the NYC scene grew to legendary proportions back in Athens. Vanessa Briscoe Hay, future member of Athens band Pylon, recalls meeting Jeremy in 1975:

> He was quite beautiful at that point. You would practically fall over looking at him. He was so sweet, and so soft-spoken and everything. After that, I heard rumors about him. I heard rumors he was on John and Yoko's wedding plane. I heard rumors that he brushed John Lennon's cats when he lived in New York. I heard rumors that he knew Andy Warhol, and was a famous cross-dresser called Silva Thin. And I think all of those might be true.[15]

Ayers also appeared in "Vain Victory," a drag musical penned by Warhol cohort Jackie Curtis, that the *New York Times* called "unabashed trash, the quintessence of camp."[16] Co-star Holly Woodlawn told stories of the cast, including Silva Thin, "getting bombed in our dressing rooms" and then "going out and acting like crazed banshees." One night Thin threw a lit cigarette on stage that landed on a cast member's costume and started a fire.[17]

During the 1972 debut of *Women in Revolt*, a film directed by Paul Morrissey and produced by Warhol, *Interview* editor Bob Colacello recalled an editor at *Women's Wear Daily (WWD)* standing outside the theater door shouting for her photographer to "Get her! It's Silva Thin!" Colacello wrote, "Silva Thin is WWD's favorite drag queen, the only one permitted at Candy's party, though at the last minute Holly Woodlawn's name was put on the list."[18] That same year, Warhol sent Thin in his place to an art opening sponsored by Yoko Ono, along with Woodlawn and Curtis.[19]

Ayers wasn't the only Athenian hanging out in New York. By this time, Bill Paul had established art connections there, often spending time at Max's Kansas City, the restaurant/music venue favored by the Warhol crowd. While it's fun to imagine him running into Silva Thin and shouting "Germy!" Paul has no recollection of ever seeing Ayers in NYC.

Bravery in the Classic City

Many people in Athens did courageous things around this time in ways that extended beyond the art scene. John Hoard and Bill Green were two UGA freshmen who arrived on campus in 1968. They came from Savannah and Albany, respectively, and met at a fall leadership retreat for UGA students and formed a quick friendship. Hoard and Green were both gay, and had become aware of their sexuality while still in high school. In the wake of the Stonewall Riots in 1969, they began discussing the idea of forming a student organization for gay people on campus.

Their efforts remained purely hypothetical for the next couple of years, though both men cited the Kent State shootings as a catalyst for their own activism. In May 1970, the US National Guard killed four unarmed students in Kent, Ohio, during a protest against the expansion of the Vietnam War into Cambodia. The student deaths sparked protests all over the country, including Athens. The following day, 3000 people marched on UGA's campus waving black flags and breaking windows while chanting "one-two-three-four, we don't want your fucking war." The university suspended classes for two days, and issued restraining orders against SDS, along with 500 students.[20]

A few days later, the National guard in Augusta, Georgia—an hour-and-a-half drive southeast of Athens—murdered six unarmed black men after allegedly being given the order by Governor Lester Maddox to shoot any protesters on sight. The people in Augusta weren't protesting Kent State, however. They were protesting the murder of a 16-year-old Augusta boy named Charles Oatman who had been beaten to death by police in a jail cell the night before.[21]

The Augusta riot, along with the lingering anger over Kent State and the Jackson State killings that same month,[22] prompted a May 15th march in Athens led by Jesse Jackson and Rev. Hosea Williams. An uncredited campus flyer promoting the event urged white students to participate in the march. "We same people who opposed the killings at Kent State must stand alongside our black brothers in their struggle to fight against this wrong. The blacks in Athens are mobilized …. It is now time for students to join the struggle."[23] That night, 300 protesters showed up at the Ebenezer Baptist Church. Nearly a third of the group consisted of white students. Chanting "Soul Power!," they made it a few blocks before they were arrested by "a wall of policemen and National Guardsmen."[24]

The bravery on display in Athens that spring—and take a moment to imagine the terror of marching into a group of National Guardsmen who had killed six protesters only a week earlier—inspired Hoard and Green to take action. Hoard explained, "You can't hide and live somebody else's life, you've got to live your own life."[25] In November 1971, they announced at a campus meeting that they were forming the Committee for Gay Education (CGE), to help "promote understanding between gay people and straight people" and "help society adapt to changes in sex roles."[26] If approved, it would be the first such club at a college in the South.

Flyers went up around campus announcing the first CGE meeting, and campus newspaper *The Red and Black* ran an article about the group. Reaction among the UGA administration was swift. A professor called the Provost and asked, "What the hell is going on here?"[27] Another official called for the Dean of Student Affairs to immediately return to the campus. After much debate, the group was allowed to have their meeting, and approximately 70 people attended. The next day, a university representative met with three students to discuss the future of CGE. One of them was a law student named Maureen McLaughlin, who many years later would become the B-52s' first manager. Not only was Maureen a CGE member, but she put her legal knowledge to work helping the group prepare the necessary materials to be recognized as an official student organization. As CGE attempted to navigate the process, some members began addressing fellow students in classes and demonstrations, attempting to raise awareness and dispel prejudices about homosexuality. One student asked them if speaking about their sexuality in public made them afraid.

"Yes," answered Hoard, "but we have faith in society. We think it has the potential to change, and we think it will."[28]

The publicity surrounding CGE in local newspapers meant that the group's founders were effectively outed publicly. For Bill Green, this meant going home to Albany and telling his family he was gay. While his mother and siblings were willing to accept him, his father was not. They wouldn't speak for several years. As 1972 began, an openly gay University of Minnesota student visited the campus and addressed CGE. He challenged the group to be more public, prompting a UGA student to concur, asking, "At what point do we stop laying low and start making ourselves known?"[29] The group decided to stage a public dance for gay and lesbian students, and quietly reserved Memorial Hall for the evening of March 10th.

However, John L. Cox, the Director of Student Activities, immediately canceled the group's reservation, which prompted a sit-in at Cox's office. O. Suthern Sims, the Dean of Student Affairs, told the group their dance was illegal because it would violate state sodomy laws, and so CGE went looking for legal counsel. The American Civil Liberties Union (ACLU) declined to represent them, but they found two local lawyers who were willing to take the case. As the issue headed toward the courts, CGE continued planning their dance. They asked a local Athens band called Ravenstone if they would be willing to play the event, and the band was more than happy to oblige.

Ravenstone's music was a mix of Lou Reed- and Iggy Pop-inspired glam rock, but the band were just as notorious for their politics. An early photo shows the band in a cemetery, the drummer leaning against a cross-shaped tombstone dressed in a military uniform, while the bass player wears a gas mask and a tuxedo t-shirt. A Mickey Mouse doll lays at their feet. Ravenstone specialized in provocation. Singer Michael Simpson often wore a t-shirt featuring an upside-down cross and the number 666. When Simpson wasn't penning thoughtful columns in *The Red and Black* calling for the legalization of marijuana, or amnesty for draft-dodgers, he was singing songs like "Off a Pig," a pro-vegan anthem that was often misinterpreted as being anti-police—not that Ravenstone minded. When the police threatened to arrest them for playing the song during a campus performance, the band's response was to play louder.[30] Asked why a band of straight guys would play a gay dance, Simpson said, "Our answer was 'why wouldn't we?' For us it wasn't about sexual orientation. It was a human rights issue. Why shouldn't everyone be allowed to dance?"[31] To round out the bill, CGE chose Diamond Lil, an Atlanta area drag performer, and another band, Break of Day.

On March 9th, one day before the dance, CGE filed a suit claiming their rights to freedom of speech, association, and privacy had been violated, along with their equal protection under the law. A hearing was scheduled in Clarke County Superior Court the following day at 3 p.m., mere hours before the dance was to take place. Dean Sims and John L. Cox testified on behalf of the university, as President Fred Davison—the named defendant in the suit—chose not to attend. Sims and Cox presented a less-than-compelling case. Under cross examination, they admitted the university's motivation was almost entirely political. Though Cox cited student safety as the driving force behind the ban, he admitted that the Ku Klux Klan had almost certainly spoken at on-campus events without any objections from the administration.[32]

Less than two hours before the dance was scheduled to begin, Judge James Barrow ruled in favor of CGE. Everyone rushed to get ready. "My recollection is they called the band house and said it's on!" said Ravenstone singer Michael Simpson. "And then we had to run around, and we called Jimmy Ellison, one of our roadies, and said 'you gotta come over here and help us pack up all our equipment quickly!'"[33]

The event drew people from all over northeast Georgia, including news crews from Atlanta and curious onlookers. While some people showed up to express support, others did not. Ravenstone were tuning up when Michael Simpson stepped outside to get some air. He was approached by a man who asked him, "Is this where the queers are holding the dance?" The man then asked if Simpson was in the band playing the show. When Simpson told him he was, the man replied that the Klan "was not happy about the dance," and made some veiled threats before walking off.[34]

Nearly 500 people attended the dance. Before the music started, Bill Green addressed the audience and urged them to dance freely. Afterward, Diamond Lil performed a wonderful rendition of Stand By Your Man. A student was quoted in the local newspaper saying, "This is the greatest thing that's ever happened on campus."[35] Though the future, both for CGE and for LGBTQ+ people in Athens, would be filled with setbacks, disappointment, and continued prejudice, for one night they had triumphed.

The Space Queen

The Red and Black wrote about the dance in the clumsy wording prevalent at the time. "Most of the gays were dressed in regular street clothes. One notable exception was the Space Queen, a student who was attired in silver blouse and slacks and a long white scarf."[36] The Space Queen wasn't a UGA student at all, but an 18-year-old high school senior from Athens named Keith Strickland. He was attending the dance with his best friend, Ricky Wilson, who had graduated from Athens High the year before. Keith talked about that night over 40 years later:

> I actually remember what I wore. I feel like I had some sort of long cape on, but I'm not sure. I remember the silver pants and blouse. My friend Lucy, she used to wear this long velvet cape a lot. She always had a velvet cape on, so she was probably wearing that. I'm not sure what Ricky was wearing. Ricky would put together really amazing outfits .... We were very defiant in our look.[37]

Keith had been born in Athens, but he grew up about 20 miles north in a small town called Comer. It was a dreamy country existence. Keith would sit outside with his brother, marveling at the vastness of the night sky, wondering if tonight would be the night a UFO appeared. "I have a vivid memory of being at a playground when I was about five or six," said Keith, "and questioning, 'What is the point of all of this?'"[38] Music was a huge part of his childhood. A cousin had turned him on to Little Richard, Elvis, and James Brown at a young age, which was quickly followed by a love for The Beatles and the Rolling Stones. Keith moved to Athens his freshman year of high school (1968, give or take a year), after his dad got a job running the Greyhound bus station.

Ricky Wilson had lived in Athens his whole life. Before Keith arrived in Athens, Ricky and his close friend Roy Bell were forced to walk to school after another student told them "no two long-haired queers are going to ride the bus that I'm going to be on."[39] Roy was a year older, and lived across the street from Ricky. They went everywhere together. They both got jobs working at the Georgia Fairgrounds, and spent two years washing dishes at the Athens Country Club. They hung out at The Looking Glass, Athens' first head shop, opened by two arrivals from San Francisco, just to look at the black lights. Roy was the first person that Ricky came out to. "Ricky told me he might be in love with me," recalled Bell. "At first, I didn't know how to accept it, and then I realized Ricky's my best friend and I love him like a brother, so it doesn't matter. For a while, I even wished that I could be gay. But I just couldn't."[40] Ricky asked Bell not to tell anyone at school, and they remained best friends. One summer, they got jobs working for the city as garbage men because "that was the only place you could work if you actually had long hair."[41] Ricky, an aspiring guitarist, worked there to buy a reel-to-reel player so he could record his music.

By that time, Ricky and Keith had met and became close friends. When Ricky was 16, he sat Keith down on the sofa to tell him something important. Keith recalled that day in 2011 for *The Washington Blade*, a D.C. LGBTQ+ paper:

> One afternoon Ricky sat me down on a sofa. He said, "I want to tell you something." I said, "What?" He said, "Ricky Wilson is gay." I can't remember, really, how I responded but I mean I wasn't shocked. I knew that I was at the time, but it was hard for me. I wasn't ready to say it. I couldn't really articulate it.[42]

A week or two later, Keith told Ricky he also was gay. In telling the story, Keith acknowledges that even after the band started, they weren't "publicly out," and wouldn't be "for many years."[43] Keith touches on an important distinction here, one that is often misunderstood. The idea of "outness" is incredibly complicated, and both politically and emotionally volatile. Not only are there degrees of outness—being out to one's friends, one's family, one's employer, to the general public—but there are also multiple closets. Should one feel obligated to announce one's queerness or non-heterosexuality to everyone they talk to? One of the inevitable products of living in a society that assumes heterosexuality as the norm, is that anyone identifying outside of the mainstream is automatically "re-closeted" in ways that are constant and exhausting for LGBTQ+ identifying people. This puts the burden on the marginalized, then blames them if they fail to perform their non-heterosexuality "correctly." These ideas of purity only serve to perpetuate and reinforce systems of oppression, while absolving straight people from having to do anything to improve the situation.[44]

Keith and Ricky were out to their friends, and to some of their family, in the early 70s. They were out with people who they could trust. To be completely and publicly out at the time would have been dangerous—it can still be dangerous today, even in Athens. Keith talked about it in 1993, a year after he had finally come out publicly himself. "When someone makes the decision to come out about being gay," he said, "they're putting themselves in a [situation] to maybe receive a lot of flak about it, negative reaction ... that's just a fear that you kind of grow up with."[45]

Ricky and Keith had the good fortune to be two young gay men coming of age in Athens, which thanks to the university had a small, supportive gay community. Still, it was a long way from being a utopia. Athens was also a place where *The Red and Black* could publish letters and editorials from students that said things like "I feel that to be gay is to be sick." During a 1975 awareness day, when CGE asked gay students to wear blue jeans to identify themselves, one student responded by wearing a handwritten t-shirt that read "Faggot Killer."[46]

By the time CGE held their dance at Memorial Hall, Bill Green, one of the group's two founders, was receiving death threats on a nightly basis, including a man who would call Green at his job and tell him he was going to shoot him. Afraid to stay in his apartment, he began sleeping on the couches and floors of his friends. When the semester ended, he left school and moved to Atlanta for a while, before eventually moving to Florida with a boyfriend.

Walker Harper designed the poster for the CGE dance and recalled both the incredible freedom of being gay in Athens in the 1970s and the clear limits on that freedom. "The gay scene was all about coming out and a growing pride in identity." But he added, "Even so, that expression was mostly just among us gays."[47]

Keith expressed a similar sentiment in a 2008 interview. "We had friends who were older and who were out and gay, and we'd hang out and go to their house for parties. There was a gay community in Athens but it was fairly closeted. It depended on who you knew."[48]

A Radical Feminist Professor and Her Mom's Counterculture Bookstore

The gay community in Athens also included women. Julia Penelope Stanley arrived at UGA in 1968 to teach Comp Lit, Grammar, and Linguistics. Her mother moved up from Florida shortly after Stanley arrived in Athens and opened The Hobbit Habit, the town's only non-university bookstore at the time. John Seawright, an Athens writer, remembered the store as having "good literature, but also every kind of possible political psychedelic manifesto and leftist writings. That was an education for a lot of kids."[49]

In the fall of 1972, Julia Stanley attended an organizing session of the Southeastern Gay Coalition in Atlanta. Though still closeted, Stanley felt she had to "put up or shut up" when one of her students nominated her as a coordinator. She was elected, and the following Monday, *The Red and Black* ran an article about her new position, effectively outing her. Recalled Stanley, "Someone told me that one of my colleagues quipped, 'Well everyone knew but did she have to have it on the front page?'"[50]

Stanley had good reasons to protect her privacy, having been kicked out of two different colleges while a student for being a lesbian. Despite her secrecy, she said "All of the gay and lesbian students were signing up for my classes."[51] Certain signaling through dress and speech can communicate a person's sexuality to those who "know," while their silence allows those who don't want to know to feign ignorance. This phenomenon, the dubiously titled "open secret," ultimately controls and functions as a restriction on gay expression in public.

Stanley's sudden public outing resulted in other women faculty members telling her of their own homosexuality "at the rate of one a day."[52] As always, there is strength in numbers, and the power of a community standing together should not be underestimated. Elizabeth Knowlton was a PhD student at Duke who came to Athens to attend a lesbian caucus meeting in February 1973. There, she met Julia Stanley. According to Knowlton:

> Athens was the most notorious place in Georgia, and Julia Stanley was the most notorious person in Athens. She did what she wanted; she looked like a diesel dyke. There was no hiding! Women would migrate over to Atlanta after they finished at the University of Georgia and talk about her in awe. Gays in that era could walk around campus holding hands at a time when nowhere else was that going on. It was because of her; she provided a nucleus for that atmosphere.[53]

Nevertheless, Julia Stanley soon felt compelled to leave Athens, and headed to New York City in 1974, then spent time working on a commune in middle Tennessee. Finally, she dropped her last name, became

Julia Penelope, and headed to the University of Nebraska, where she taught one of the first Women's Studies classes in the country. After being passed over for full professor, she eventually settled in Lubbock, Texas, where she continued her writing until her death in 2013.

"Germy" Returns

By 1975, Jeremy Ayers had grown tired of the city. "Where are you now, Silva Thin," wondered New York Doll bassist Arthur Kane in his 2009 posthumous memoir. Silva had gone back to Athens. No longer Silva Thin, no longer Jeremy. Now he wanted to be called Jerry.

If Ayers had picked a great time to move to New York, he also chose a great time to come back to Athens. It still didn't have much of a music scene (Ravenstone had come and gone), but its art scene was quickly becoming world class.

Jeremy Ayers became an essential part of that scene, as well as the LGBTQ+ community. Ricky and Keith met him while they were still in high school, and Keith recalled Jeremy years later as "a big inspiration and … a mentor to Ricky and me."[54] Ricky and Keith even drove up to visit him in New York City in 1972. Roy Bell remembered Ayers as "a worldly, thinking individual. He taught us about theater, music, art and fashion, but mostly he taught us about being who we were and who we wanted to be."[55]

In the evolution of the Athens music scene, The B-52s are less an outlier than a link in a long chain. They bridged the outrageousness that came before them with the outrageousness that came afterward. The audacity of the B-52s' music, aesthetic style, and politics all had clear antecedents in the community they came from. These conditions in Athens made it different from other college towns in the South. Before the B-52s played a single note—before Pylon, the Tone-Tones, and the Method Actors came charging into the space the B-52s had opened up and solidified the nascent music scene—Athens already had nearly everything necessary to make it happen. Jeremy Ayers would serve as mentor to all of it. As Vanessa Briscoe Hay recalls, "He had very good taste. I'll say that. He liked the B-52s, Pylon, and R.E.M. right from the beginning."[56]

It would take an act of creative spontaneity to shape music out of the artistic and political freedoms being explored in Athens. But as we have seen, the town had already provided the B-52s with countless examples of courage and radical self-expression to build upon.

Notes

1. Bartunek, "Dance Revolution," 72.
2. Jim Herbert in conversation with authors, April 20, 2019.
3. Holland and Sicurella, "Confronting UGA's History."
4. Ibid.
5. Bill Shipp's book *Murder at Broad River Bridge* is essential reading for anyone wanting to know more about this story.
6. "Lt. Col. Lemuel Penn and the Civil Rights Act," Georgia Historical Society, Accessed October 12, 2019, https://georgiahistory.com/ghmi_marker_updated/lt-col-lemuel-penn/.
7. Hewitt, *Political Violence and Terrorism*, 30–39.
8. Huff, "Student Movements of 1960s."
9. The *New York Times*, "U. of Georgia Eases Rules."
10. Jipson, "Why Athens?" 21.
11. Bill Paul in conversation with authors, May 19, 2019.
12. Jim Herbert in conversation with authors, April 20, 2019.
13. Bill Paul in conversation with authors, May 19, 2019.
14. Ibid.
15. Vanessa Briscoe Hay in conversation with authors, April 25, 2019.
16. Gussow, "Stage: 'Vain Victory.'"
17. Warholstars.org, "Jackie Curtis' Vain Victory."
18. Colacello, *Holy Terror*, 115.
19. Colacello, *Holy Terror*, 147.
20. "WSB-TV Newsfilm Clip of Governor Lester Maddox Blaming His Generation For the Current Social Unrest as Students Protesting Kent State, Georgia, 1970 May 13," WSB-TV newsfilm collection, reel 1639, 7:54/09:03, Walter J. Brown Media Archives and Peabody Awards Collection, The University of Georgia Libraries, Athens, Ga, as presented in the Digital Library of Georgia, http://dlg.galileo.usg.edu/crdl/do:ugabma_wsbn_59642.
21. Chandler, "Race Riots Explode in Georgia."
22. Eleven days after Kent State, city and state police in Jackson, Mississippi killed two students, and injured 12, when a group of 100 black students gathered after hearing rumors that a civil rights leader had been assassinated.
23. University of Georgia Ephemera Collection, UA85-001, Box 77, Folder 42, University of Georgia Libraries Special Collections.
24. The *New York Times*, "200 Seized in Athens."
25. Bartunek, "Dance Revolution." Bartunek tells the full story in the detail it deserves, and it's well worth your time to read in its entirety.

26. Ham, "Gay Students."
27. M. Louise McBee from the Office of the Dean in UGA Division of Student Affairs to Dean O. Suthern Sims, November 11, 1971, Box 1, LGBT Resource Records, UA17-009 University of Georgia Libraries Special Collections.
28. Bartunek, "Dance Revolution."
29. Ibid.
30. Southerngaragebands.com, "Ravenstone."
31. Ibid.
32. Testimony in Court Case Re: Dance, March 10, 1972, Box 1, LGBT Resource Records, UA17-009 University of Georgia Libraries Special Collections.
33. Bartunek, "Dance Revolution."
34. Ibid.
35. Hunt "Gays Hold Dance," 1. The photographs accompanying the article feature black rectangular bars over the faces of the dancers to protect their identities.
36. Sanderlin, "Diamond Lil Highlights Affair."
37. Bartunek, "Dance Revolution."
38. Ferrise, "Interview: Keith Strickland."
39. Bell, "Athens Art & Music Scene," Rabbit Box Storytelling, Mixcloud.
40. Ibid.
41. Ibid.
42. YouTube, "Keith Strickland on 'It Gets Better.'"
43. Ibid.
44. Our thinking on the subject of outness was shaped by the following books: Eve Kosofsky Sedgwick, *Epistemology of the Closet* (University of California Press, 1990); Rosemary Hennessy, *Profit and Pleasure: Sexual identities in Late Capitalism* (Routledge: New York, 2000); Darryl W. Bullock *David Bowie Made Me Gay: 100 Years of LGBT Music* (Overlook: New York 2017); Richard Smith, *Seduced and Abandoned* (Cassell: London, 1995).
45. Sexton, "B-Hive Fanzine," 5. Excerpt of unpublished interview conducted by Liesl Dano for her fanzine "The B's Connection" in 1993. Dano originally edited out the parts of the interview where she asked about Keith's sexuality when the interview ran in issues #12 through #15.
46. Hogan and Pace, "Student React to Jeans," 1.
47. Bartunek, "Dance Revolution."
48. Dagostino, "Keith Strickland, The B-52s."
49. Gumpert, *The American College Town*, 200.

50. Sears, *Rebels, Rubyfruit, and Rhinestones*, 111.
51. Sears, *Rebels, Rubyfruit, and Rhinestones*, 37.
52. Sears, *Rebels, Rubyfruit, and Rhinestones*, 111.
53. Sears, *Rebels, Rubyfruit, and Rhinestones*, 113.
54. English, "Friends Remember Jeremy Ayers."
55. Ibid.
56. Vanessa Briscoe Hay in conversation with authors, April 25, 2019.

CHAPTER 3

Deadbeats

We formed our own group of crazy individuals: eccentrics and artists just having fun together and creating our own fun.[1]

—Kate

In addition to political activism and a thriving art scene, by 1975 Athens finally had something else it had been missing—Kate Pierson. Born and raised in New Jersey, Kate came to Athens with her husband, the improbably named Brian Cokayne. As a former member of the White Panther party, Kate had seen her share of protests, even moving to England after the Kent State shootings because she "had had it with America."[2] She met Brian while over there, and now they were two hippies determined to live off the land in Athens. In 1990, Kate recalled her early years in the town with fondness:

> I had a big organic garden and canned my own food and raised milk goats. The place I lived was six miles out of town, and I used to ride my bicycle back and forth every day .... This place was $15 a month. It had no running water.[3]

Kate spent her free time checking out exotic music from the Athens and UGA libraries. Favorites included "Perez Prado and Kai Winding, and soul music, and B-movie soundtracks and Nino Rota."[4] To help make

S. Creney, B. A. Herron, *The Story of the B-52s*,
https://doi.org/10.1007/978-3-031-22570-3_3

ends meet, she worked for the *Athens Banner-Herald* doing paste-up. It didn't take long for Kate to start meeting people around town. Her farmhouse turned out to be a great place for parties, and for growing psychedelic mushrooms:[5]

> We had eclipse parties. We'd play pygmy music and all the cows in the field would gather 'round, 'cause they were curious and mainly 'cause they thought we'd have food, and nod their heads. One night they all dropped their heads in rhythm to the music; it was real eerie. A cow cult.[6]

Fred Schneider had come to Athens in 1969 to attend UGA as a forestry major, but a couple of years later he switched to journalism. "I thought by taking wildlife management, I'd be doing conservation," he said, "and let's just say I was wrong."[7] He took a creative writing class, began writing poetry, and then stopped going to college. Fred worked for a while coordinating meal deliveries for the Athens Council on Aging. He also waited tables and spent time working in a used record store. This pattern of moving to Athens to attend UGA but later dropping out to pursue creative projects while working service industry jobs continues to this day. Fred met Keith at a show on campus where Keith saw him wearing a Hawaiian shirt and, legend has it, poured feathers all over him.[8]

Cindy Wilson was born in 1957, four years after her brother Ricky. "Cindy was a hood girl," according to Keith:

> The first time I met her I went over to Ricky's house and she was coming out as I was going in and she had all this white powder all over her face. Her hair was red Ann-Margret style and she had white go-go boots and a little mini-skirt and earrings and pink lipstick and she just went out and got in the car and shut the door and fixed the rear view mirror to where she could see herself and just pretended she was driving.[9]

Ricky included Cindy in his home recording experiments, employing her as a singer. "We would layer tracks," said Cindy, "and have the best time. Our voices blended really well together, and it was great fun."[10] Keith and Cindy eventually got thrown out of high school for taking part in a demonstration. "They were trying to cut back the lunch hour," explained Keith.[11]

Fred met Ricky through Keith, and then later met Cindy. In 2017, a journalist asked Fred about his first impression of Cindy:

> Oh, [she was] fabulous! I kept asking Ricky for years, "When am I gonna meet your sister?!" And there'd be no response. [Laughs] Not that he was ashamed or anything like that, but it was just like [feigns eye-rolling tone], "Oh, my little sister," you know. But we hit it off right away.[12]

Radical Athens in Decline

In 1975, following the US withdrawal from Vietnam, the town was becoming less politicized.

The Committee for Gay Education (CGE) found itself besieged by problems both inside and outside the group. A conservative campus group called Union of the American People (UAP) formed at UGA in 1973. Their platform in a 1974 student election called homosexuality "a grave social and mental illness."[13] That same month CGE published a newsletter in which a member wrote, "The Gay community in Athens and at the University of Georgia is currently undergoing a period of severe stresses and strains." The newsletter responded to charges of elitism, and bemoaned the splintering of CGE into three separate gay organizations in Athens. The letter wearily concluded, "Unfortunately, CGE has never been able to tap more than a fraction of the gay strength in the community for active support."[14] By 1980, an article in *The Athens Observer* about being gay in Athens would state, "Political activity heading into the 80s is considerably less than it was five or 10 years ago." The writer looked back on the gay dance as something that "was one of the big events on campus until interest faded."[15]

Art Attack

At the time, with artistic and personal freedoms expanding by the minute, political activism may have felt unnecessary. The UGA Art Department had become a progressive hotbed that resembled the experimental environment at Black Mountain College in the 1950s. Art student Michael Lachowski made the comparison explicit when he compared Robert Croker's teaching style to Black Mountain professor John Cage:

> If anything, [Croker] was the biggest radical as far as his teaching techniques and personal interests. His own art was based on coming up with these schemes ... all based on the way that people like John Cage made music. In his case, heavily influenced by that kind of experimental music, things like using chance and establishing systems that let the system determine the outcome. And that resulted in the painting.[16]

In addition to Robert Croker, the art school was staffed in the 1970s with iconoclastic, forward-thinking professors like Jim Herbert, Richard Olsen, Judith McWillie, and many more. They created an environment of artistic and social freedom, both on campus, and at their homes where some of them hosted parties inspired by the "happenings" of the 1960s. They threw parties that lasted 24 hours, parties where people dressed like their favorite character from a Fellini movie, parties where people got naked and painted each other. According to Bill Paul, GMOA director during this period, the irreverence wasn't always appreciated by the administration:

> We had some really awesome people in art education, but they all got fired quickly. Elizabeth ... I forgot her last name ... made art from huge mounds of junk, from trash and stuff. We used to have these stuffy art history lectures every Tuesday night, and she filled up this long corridor, gallery, in the visual arts building. People had to walk on all kinds of stuff, bed springs, all kinds of unstable things through this tunnel to the lecture—and she was out of there in no time .... Then Joe Schwartz was a faculty member, and there was a faculty show in the art department and [he] did a portrait of a naked man, kind of obese, and he did a styrofoam penis the size of your thumb, and Lamar [Dodd) made him take it down.[17]

Everything was process oriented. The art building was open 24 hours a day, and students were encouraged to draw everywhere they went. In Croker's class, students were expected to produce 100 drawings a week. Olsen demanded seven. Bob Nielsen would turn out the lights and have his students draw in the dark. Jim Herbert recalls the UGA art department of this time as "a short, like 5 to 10-year period where it was really the place to go to see some freaks, to see some interesting things. It was an arty art department."[18] Lachowski says, "Those teachers like Croker and them were like pied pipers."

> All of these young northeastern and midwestern people coming down into Georgia, and not just in our department, but for sure in the art department. And that was the fuel. It was a rare combination for a state and a university in the south, or anywhere really, to have such a robust art department, and then bring in all this talent. Then we all come in, having just barely escaped getting drafted for Vietnam, and we were all influenced by the hippies in the late 60s.[19]

It wasn't just the classes. In his position as museum director, Bill Paul continued to bring cutting-edge exhibitions to GMOA that received national attention. 1970 saw a Philip Pearlstein show that made the cover of *Art News* magazine. Paul also brought Alice Neel, who he describes as the "doyen of the feminist art movement in the 1950s and 60s," to Athens in 1975.[20]

He recalls, "Alice did lots of portraits of pregnant naked women. One of her most famous paintings is a nude self-portrait when she had her show in 1975." According to Paul, the students "adored her," but Neel was less appreciated by UGA's administration. Hubert Owens, the dean of the School of Landscape Architecture, compared her student followers to "a cult," and called her art obscene. Lamar Dodd also disapproved of Neel's work, as well as her feminist joie de vivre. Paul recounted a lecture she gave about her portrait of two counterculture legends from the Warhol scene:

> So Alice gave a lecture and it was packed. She was on the cusp of being a superstar. She told a story about Rita Red and Jackie Curtis. She was talking about one of them … deciding to have a sex change. She used very explicit language …. Lamar got up in the middle of it and started muttering in a very loud voice, and he snarled all the way out of the building. He should have bought the painting—it was $5000—instead of raising hell about it. About three years ago, the Cleveland museum paid about $1.5 million for it.[21]

In 2021, the Metropolitan Museum of Art featured a Neel exhibition in its prestigious Tisch galleries, the first female artist to appear there. A *New York Times* critic wrote that the show "confirms Neel as equal if not superior to artists like Lucian Freud and Francis Bacon and destined for icon status on the order of Vincent Van Gogh and David Hockney."[22]

Downtown

GMOA and the art school were both located on North Campus, right along the border of downtown Athens. As a result, it was common for people, both students and non-students alike, to wander freely through the art buildings. Jim Herbert recalls that during this time, "It was really a cultural center for activity. It was a place where some people, students on campus, would come over and just sort of sit down in the hallways and stuff, and watch people go by."[23]

If it was common for non-students to wander over to the art school, it was just as common for the artists to explore downtown. When a fire broke out at the Athens Fish & Oyster Company, Croker took his class to go draw the scene. When questioned, he replied, "I didn't 'let my class out' to come here. We are having class. This is better than anything we could have done in the classroom."[24] Michael Lachowski recalls walking across the street to browse local hardware stores looking for art materials. Bill Paul says, "After I was done at the art museum, I'd go for lunch with my paper bag and I'd pick up trash off the street and make artworks out of it."[25]

Downtown also had a bunch of record stores. Kate and Fred briefly worked at a couple of them—Kate at Wuxtry Records, and Fred at Ort's Oldies. Chris Rasmussen moved to Athens in 1974 to attend UGA, and almost immediately got a job working at Schoolkids Records, where he put the Roxy Music records front and center. "And it was probably playing," recalls Rasmussen. "We were playing … Sparks, off the wall stuff, the Eno stuff, John Cale, and the Velvet Underground."[26] Schoolkids was run by his sister, Alba, and brother-in-law, John Underwood, whose families soon lent them the money to purchase the store, which the kids renamed Chapter III. As an English art-rock obsessive growing up in Atlanta, Rasmussen had established contacts with foreign distributors around the country before he left high school, so when punk rock happened in the UK, especially the artier post-punk that came in its wake, he already had the contacts to bring the records into Chapter III:

> We bought the NME and Melody Maker every week from Barnett's, and they had the absolute current information on what was going on in England and what was hot and what to get …. It turns into Buzzcocks, Wire, Siouxsie and the Banshees, and we start ordering those things as they come out. On top of that, we were ordering from people in the States who were putting

> out their own things, people like Devo, the Shoes, the Residents, Pere Ubu. We were ordering that stuff directly from the bands, because you couldn't get it otherwise.[27]

Crucially, Chapter III was located at 229 Broad Street, right across from North Campus, and a well-struck baseball's distance from GMOA and the art school. Rasmussen says:

> All the art students would come and hang out, and if they had any kind of event going on—an art show, a band they were in was playing—they'd have a flyer, and they'd come in and hang it up in the store. And we had air conditioning, which a lot of stores didn't. It was kind of a hangout spot, and you could meet somebody there, say "Hey, I'll be at Chapter III. I'll meet you there after class."[28]

Years later, Michael Lachowski singled out Chapter III for impacting this period in Athens. "We were listening to music from Manchester and Leeds and Cleveland and New York."[29] And according to Lachowski, they were listening closely:

> If you were in possession of records, you could come and deliver new information, new experiences, to people at a party. Sometimes it would be that people would drop by with a 12 pack and they'd bring two singles and you would just play them like seven times, hang out, and talk about it.[30]

Boredom

After high school, Ricky and Keith settled into a pattern of post-graduation ennui. Ricky briefly attended classes at UGA, even enrolling in a music theory class so that Keith, a non-student, could attend in his place. This ruse lasted several weeks before the professor found out. Keith worked for his dad at the bus station, and the two friends would save up money and travel around Europe during the summer, Ricky briefly taking classes at a university in Germany.

They were also deeply involved in music. Keith ordered Patti Smith's independently released single Piss Factory in 1974, out of the back of *Rolling Stone*.[31] Chris Rasmussen recalls, "Ricky and Keith were pretty advanced with their music taste."[32]

Part of the B-52s' creation myth is that the band members were musical neophytes, unschooled and untrained amateurs who could barely play their instruments. Leaving aside the idea that the ability to listen is an important musical skill, every single member of the band had been fanatical listeners of music since childhood, and they all brought their own musical experiences to the band.

Keith and Ricky had played in multiple bands, dating back to high school. One was called Black Narcissus, likely named after the art film, that lost a high school battle of the bands. Another early Keith/Ricky band was called Loon (song titles included "Venetia" and "Pissing on the Grill"). Kate had been in an all-girl "folk-protest" band in high school called The Sun Doughnuts, and occasionally played acoustic songs around Athens. Fred played a show in 1975 with Keith and some other people that was more akin to John Cage than Elton John, as they played the same four songs for three hours:

> We had like fifteen people on stage, including three violins. I don't know where we got so many violins. I don't think we had a drummer, but Keith played guitar.[33]

That project was called Nightsoil, and featured a slideshow projection of Canada, as well as people onstage in drag.[34] Keith and Fred also made recordings under the name Bridge Mix, basically Fred reciting his poetry while Keith poked around on the guitar. Several of these songs would be mined for future B-52s songs, including one about a poodle named Quiche Lorraine. A venue called The Station briefly opened in Athens around 1975. Fred was invited to do some poetry, but instead formed a band with Ricky, Keith, and a few other people. Song titles included Bush Hog and Dead Mink. Neither the band nor the venue lasted much longer.

Keith also sometimes filled in on drums with The Zambo Flirts, another glam-influenced Athens band that never quite made it. One night in 1973, Jeremy Ayers took his new friend Kate Pierson to see the Zambo Flirts, where she met Keith. There were also other, less formal performances. Jim Herbert recalls seeing some B-52s members playing at a house party:

> Just off the kitchen, the B-52s got together to play some music for just six or seven people. I mean it was just like really the beginning sort of thing, and they were just sort of testing out the waters. I'm not even sure that all of the members that subsequently became the B-52s were there at that time. I think it was Keith and Ricky, and you know, just maybe four people. Fred wasn't there, I don't believe, at that time. You could tell right away that

> there was a very original energy there. I remember thinking, "Wow, this is really exciting and intense." [35]

Note the indeterminacy. We see, over and over in this story of Athens, people from different backgrounds crossing boundaries and bravely exploring unfamiliar spaces. Other towns had cheap rent, a university, even a decent record store, but the close proximity of Athens' latent strengths meant that you had people coming into contact with each other who came from different classes, different genders, different sexualities, and different aesthetics all exchanging ideas and learning from each other. Even Cindy, a local teenager with a GED, was using the university to educate herself:

> You could go to the library and they had this periodical section that had old Vogue magazines from the sixties, which was amazing to see. So you had a good concept of the world through that. Also they brought in foreign films which was great, and strange art films.[36]

By 1976, everything was coming together for what would become the B-52s and The Athens Music Scene. Maureen McLaughlin, the former CGE member, was now a UGA law grad living in Atlanta. Her friend, Moe Slotin, left the city to roadie for Blue Oyster Cult and ended up working for Patti Smith's management in New York City. He invited Maureen to fly up and visit him. She took a taxi from the airport to a Times Square that had yet to be gentrified into the neoliberal shopping mall it is today. Maureen described a scene where "shabby offices could be rented for a song, since utilities and elevators were usually in dubious condition."[37] In that office she met some of the pillars of the artistic side of the NYC punk scene: Tom Verlaine, Patti Smith, Smith's manager Jane Friedman (who was dating John Cale at the time), and others. Maureen made such an impression that the NYC crowd would ask her to return to the city whenever the Patti Smith Group had "something big" coming up. As a result, Maureen would soon play a prominent role for bands in Atlanta and Athens.

For nearly a decade, Athenians had been going to NYC for inspiration. Now, people from NYC were beginning to find inspiration in Athens. Elaine de Kooning, a legendary artist tied to the New York abstract expressionists, arrived in Athens as the first Lamar Dodd Visiting Professor of

Art. During her time at UGA (1976–1978), she painted the first in her famous Bacchus series, marking the first time she had used acrylic paint.

The year 1976 was also the year that Georgia native, and former governor, Jimmy Carter was elected president. He had made a big impression on *Rolling Stone* journalist Hunter S. Thompson in 1974 when Thompson accompanied Ted Kennedy to Athens to attend UGA's Law Day. Part of the ceremonies included the unveiling of an oil portrait of Dean Rusk, former Secretary of State, and then UGA international law professor. Rusk, a native Georgian, had been one of the architects of the Vietnam War, and Thompson spent the day wondering out loud why Rusk's portrait didn't have any blood on the subject's hands.[38] Thompson had never heard of Jimmy Carter before, but when the governor started speaking, Thompson ran out to the car to get his tape recorder. He later wrote that Carter's speech, in its denunciation of injustice and abuse of power, was "the heaviest and most eloquent thing I have ever heard from the mouth of a politician."[39]

After Carter's successful 1976 campaign, a group of 30 artists in New York City asked to donate some of their works to a museum in Georgia in an exhibition called "Open to New Ideas" to support the new president. Les Levine, a spokesperson for the group, explained, "Throughout the campaign and since his election, he's conveyed to us a similar openness to new ideas."[40] Bill Paul got in touch, and worked out a deal. GMOA would fund a convention to bring the artists to Athens, where they would draft a manifesto for the future of art under the new Carter administration. The event took place on January 7, 1977, and included such renowned artists as Gordon Matta-Clark and Laurie Anderson. Bill Paul says, "There's never been so much pot smoke in the Georgia Center before or since."[41] A CBS Evening News crew showed up and devoted nearly four minutes of national coverage to the exhibition. Paul adds, "Lamar was fuming. He could put almost as much smoke in the air as the pot smokers!"[42]

Bohemia

For all the excitement happening in Athens it could still be kind of boring on a day-to-day basis, but you could always make your own fun. Band friend and writer/photographer/chef John Martin Taylor recalled, "We lived simply .... But we also lived wildly, seldom conforming to anyone else's sense of fashion or decorum."[43] Their lives were their art. As Fred put it, "You could get away with things in Athens … a lot of it was performance."[44]

Fred published a book of his poetry called *Bleb*, which he gave away to friends. Some of the poems, like "There's a Moon in the Sky (Called the Moon)," would inspire future B-52s songs. In 2017, an interviewer asked if the book had inspired the band, and Fred replied, "I think everyone read the book and liked it. I don't know if it inspired them." Cindy chimed in, "I think we inspired each other." Fred agreed. "Yeah. We all had a lot of similar tastes. We liked a lot of the same music, movies. We had a similar sensibility about a whole lot of things."[45]

Cindy was out of high school now and had moved into an apartment with Ricky and Keith. She worked as a waitress at the Whirly Q luncheonette, a diner in the Kress department store. Cindy liked painting, and quickly became part of the art/party/music crowd. Kate would come in, and Cindy would serve her cups of coffee with "whipped cream stacked so high it'd fall all over the counter." Kate would later joke that, "Legend has it there's a plaque on the Whirly-Q wall inscribed with the words, 'At this point worked Cindy Wilson of the B52s, 1977–1977.'"[46]

The people in the scene were a club of sorts. They made up names for themselves. Cindy told an interviewer about it in 1979. "There was the Waitress Club, The Waiters Club, The Roller Skating Society, The Laundry Club …. There was a Laundromat that had a jukebox and everybody could get together and go dancing while they did their laundry."[47]

The story goes that one day someone called them deadbeats on account of their sustenance-level career ambitions. It could have been affectionate, or tongue-in-cheek, or (knowing Athens) tongue-in-ear. But there was never a formal deadbeat club, with t-shirts or secret handshakes.

Athens may have been a bohemian paradise of sorts—the living was easy; rent was around $60; you could eat at Taco Stand for a couple of bucks; hit Allen's on quarter beer night—but it wasn't always fulfilling. Fred moved to Atlanta for a while, though he still came back to Athens regularly to see his friends. Kate was still on the farm, and still working odd jobs. Keith and Ricky were still working at the bus station while saving up money to bum around Europe playing music on the streets. Cindy was considering going with them next time. On some level, they all knew the fun and party life couldn't last forever. Sometime around Halloween 1976, the five friends decided to go get some Chinese food.

They met up with Owen Scott at Hunan Chinese Restaurant over on Baxter Street, where they consumed a flaming volcano. Less dramatic than it sounds, the flaming volcano is essentially a variation on the scorpion bowl, that is, a large bowl of alcohol (rum, brandy, sometimes gin) and fruit juice served with multiple straws for everyone to share. Afterward, they all went back to Owen's place. A former Zambo Flirt, his basement was filled with music instruments, so they pulled them out and everyone started to jam, except for Owen, who went upstairs to catch up on his mail. Ricky and Keith drove the music while the others traded off vocals. It clicked immediately. "We had lots of great ideas, and we were rolling on the floor just laughing," said Cindy. "It was just so much fun. We kind of knew something was going on, something was happening."[48]

They wrote a song that night called Killer Bees. It would only last a few shows before being phased out, but Ricky's description of the song gives some idea of the creative energy that night. "It's about a bus being chased by killer bees," he explained in a 1980 *Rolling Stone* interview. "It runs off into a river, and all the people get eaten by piranhas. And then the killer bees swarm into a theater, where these people are watching a movie, and they attack them." Ricky then added, with a hint of mischief. "It's a true story."[49]

The spirit was highly collaborative from the start, and they had a perfect mix of energy and experience. Keith's account of playing music in high school gives us an impression of how he might have approached that first practice:

> I learned how to listen. We all realized at the same time that there was almost a psychic kind of thing happening, where you would almost know what the other person was going to do. And it was free-form yet there was this flow to it. You could just sense it. I felt like in those days, that's when I really learned to listen to other players, which allowed me to be comfortable with just picking up an instrument and playing it. Everybody has something unique and individual to offer, and it's really about being yourself and being comfortable with who that is, and not seeing your limitations as limitations.[50]

They continued to get together and play. Sometimes they would meet out at Kate's house. "Everybody came from a different place," recalled Cindy, "but everything was very creative and open-minded. Also, everybody had probably taken acid at one time or another, so we were kind of in the same stream."[51] Fred added that "Sometimes pot would help too." [52]

Fred was now back in Athens, washing dishes and waiting tables at the El Dorado. UGA art student Sean Bourne said, "He would wear a hard hat with a flashing light and come out with your food—always saying funny, ironic stuff."[53] Fred also got his job back at Athens Council on Aging. "They made me a Meals on Wheels coordinator. So I had a sort of career for a while,"[54] he said.

The band set up a practice space in a building behind the El Dorado in the former bloodletting room of an old funeral home. "It was awful," recalled Cindy. "It had these drains in the floor ...."[55] Fred remembered the room being filled with pigeon feathers. "We never saw the pigeons, but there were feathers all over."[56] There was no heat either, and they had to wire in the electricity from the El Dorado.

In such a small scene, word quickly spread about this new project. A Valentine's Day party was coming up at a house on Milledge Avenue where Julia Stimpson and Gray Lippett lived, and it was decided the band would make their debut. The week of the show, Keith Strickland had a dream. "There was this lounge group ... and this woman with a big bouffant was playing the organ in this little club."[57] The group in Keith's dream was called the B-52s. When he suggested the name to the others, they unanimously agreed. Still, he worried that people might associate them with the US military bomber. Knowing that B-52 was Southern slang for a bouffant hairdo, Keith wondered if maybe Kate and Cindy could wear their hair up for the show.

There turned out to be an easier solution. "Keith and I found the girls these fake sheepdog-fur pocketbooks and muffs downtown at the Diana Shop," said Fred. "So we told Kate and Cindy and they went and bought them."[58] Though their wigs would become more elaborate over the years, Cindy and Kate's trademark style began as fuzzy pocketbooks placed upside-down on top of their heads.

So on February 14, 1977, a mere five weeks after the "Open To New Ideas" conference, the B-52s made their public debut. That night, the B-52s were closer to performance art than a traditional rock band. The only live instruments were Ricky's guitar and Keith playing the bongos. Everything else was pre-recorded on a reel-to-reel tape machine (except for a gong, apparently there was also a gong). Cindy, Kate, and Fred stood up front and sang.

They opened with Planet Claire, and also played Rock Lobster, Strobe Light, and Killer Bees. Cindy recalled, "I hid behind the curtains. Ricky played with his back turned. We all talked between songs. Once, the tape came unplugged."[59]

The performance art vibe suited the gig perfectly, given that most of the audience consisted of the band's art friends. Barbie dolls were hung from a chandelier by photographer and UGA art student Kelly Bugden. Zeke Addison, a painting student working on his MFA, supplied the PA. John Martin Taylor had a B-52s t-shirt made at a county fair, an "awful airbrush painting of a woman with a bouffant hairdo with 'B-52' sprawled across the back."[60] Sally Stafford wore a curtain from the 1950s as a skirt. Keith Bennett was another UGA art student, and close friends with Chapter III's Chris Rasmussen. Bennett attended the show, and was immediately impressed by the band's "really, really good ideas." He told the story back in 2014. "They played their five songs, and everybody went nuts. Then they came back out and played them exactly the same way. I thought, oh my god it's rehearsed. This is not just some fluke. Who are these people?"[61] Sean Bourne recalled, "The first time I saw them play was like a mystical experience," adding, "I didn't go to sleep that night because the show was such a weird experience."[62]

Cool things were also happening an hour west of Athens. The Fans were an Atlanta band heavily influenced by the artistic side of 70s rock—Roxy Music, Eno, Sparks, and so on. They even featured a former UGA student, synth player Mike Green, who had ties to the art school. One of the Fans biggest supporters was Robert Croker. Maureen McLaughlin was also friends with the band, and started trying to get them a show at Max's or CBGB's, the two important NYC venues at the time. It was the Fans manager, Felipe, who had the brilliant idea to fly Hilly Kristal, proprietor of CBGB's, into Atlanta so he could see the band play at the Great Southeast Music Hall. "He courted him hugely," recalls Fans guitarist, Kevin Dunn. "Provided other blandishments of one form or another, I suspect. I have no direct evidence of that, but it *was* 1976."[63] The Fans ended their set with a cacophony of screaming and instrument abuse. The "vast huge noise-fest," as Dunn recalls, made such an impression on Kristal that he booked them to open some shows for Talking Heads in January 1977.

John Rockwell, critic for the *New York Times*, saw one of their shows at CBGB's, and raved about the band in the next day's paper, concluding, "One suspects the Fans will be heard from in the future."[64] Kevin Dunn read the review while getting breakfast at an NYC deli, and recalls, "We were fairly sure we were going to be famous."[65]

Theresa Randolph was part of the Athens crowd who hung out with the Fans. An Athens High graduate who had gone to school with Ricky and Keith, she was also a childhood beauty pageant winner who became the inspiration for the girl on Sunbeam bread. Theresa accompanied the Fans on another trip to New York, this time to play Max's Kansas City—a gig set up for them by Maureen. Curtis Knapp, a young illustrator, was a regular at Max's who had been commissioned to paint a mural on the wall that he describes as "almost Aubrey Beardsley goes punk." He stopped working on it when he realized he wasn't going to get paid. "I didn't stop going to Max's," says Knapp. "I just stopped painting the wall."[66] Knapp was also a big Brian Eno fan, and was blown away by the Fans' cover of Baby's On Fire. He was also blown away by Theresa, who invited him to come visit Athens.

Shortly after arriving in town, he was brought to the El Dorado, where the B-52s were practicing next door. Knapp recalls the scene:

> All I can say is, I wish I had a photograph when I first opened that door, just great energy. They were sitting on vegetable boxes, and turned-upside-down cans, and Fred had a toy piano. It was like a ballroom in Paris from the Dada people, you know?[67]

Theresa lived with a bunch of people, including the owner of the El Dorado, at a two-story house in Five Points, known colloquially at the time as "the old Jewish country club." The house featured an enormous party room, where the band was scheduled to play their second show. Nearly 200 people showed up. According to the account in *Party Out of Bounds*, the show was "pandemonium," with girls on roller skates, cold showers, screaming, and "magical illicit sex."[68] A power cord got tripped, and again stopped the band mid-set, but it didn't dampen the enthusiasm. Toward the end of the night, Kate recalled, "Theresa was getting pretty wild. She was up on somebody's shoulders and was screaming, 'I can't believe this is happening in Athens, Georgia.'"[69]

Neither could Curtis Knapp. He went up to the band after their set and told them they should be playing Max's. "I knew the B's would be cool for New York at that moment," recalls Knapp, "and New York good for them. New York was in a wear-black slump kinda thing. There was a huge gap in the music world in New York at that moment."[70]

The show galvanized the band, and they began to practice even more intensely. Kate remembered those early days in a 2018 interview with *People*:

> Sometimes we'd all swap instruments. We had Brian Eno's cards, Oblique Strategies. We used those in the studio sometimes. But mostly Keith and Ricky did the instrumentation, and Fred and Cindy would jam on vocals. And because I played keyboard I wound up playing the bass parts and the keyboard parts.[71]

"They practiced four or five days a week for months," recalled Keith Bennett. "Rehearsal was a sacrament. They had no gig, no prospect of a gig. They just knew they had something."[72] The songs the band was coming up with were also complicated, and required a lot of practice. As Cindy explained, "They were unconventional songs, and an unconventional way to write. So we had to rehearse to learn when to come in and nail down the vocal melodies."[73]

Keith Bennett had seen Cindy at the first B-52s show and developed a bit of a crush. After a few weeks, mutual friend Jackie Slaton arranged for Keith to drive Cindy home from The Last Resort. Bennett says,

> She lived with Ricky in Five Points in a house behind a house with no phone. I asked her if we could go out sometime. She said, "Yeah. We don't have a phone, but just come by," She was never there. I went by five times. Ricky was always there. He was painfully shy. I didn't know that. I'd go, and the door would be open. He's reading. "Is Cindy here?" "No." "You know when she's coming back?" "No." "Could you tell her Keith came by?" "Okay."[74]

Their first real date was that spring, before Bennett had gone home for the summer. "I hauled ass up from Macon in my Ford Maverick," he says, "and we went and took pictures of all the glass bricks around town that she knew about. Her favorite glass bricks!"[75]

Bennett's car died shortly afterward, stranding him in Macon, but Cindy mailed him a letter with copies of photos they had taken that day. "The University of Georgia had the only color xerox machine in the Southeast at the time, and you could go there and use it. She used it mercilessly."[76] They reconnected once Bennett returned to Athens in late summer, and they are still together today.

New York City

That summer, the Fans had another show in New York. This time, Ricky, Keith, Cindy, Theresa, and Curtis decided to go up with them and try to get a gig. They brought along a demo tape and some photos. CBGB's turned them down, but Curtis took them to Max's and played the tape for Tommy Dean and Peter Crowley, the club's owner and booker, respectively. Tommy and Peter wouldn't commit either way, and the band left without a gig. The Fans show was pretty good though.

Meanwhile, the B-52s also reached out to Maureen McLaughlin to help get them a show in NYC. She was working as a lawyer now and traveling around the country, but had helped out the Fans. She told the B-52s they "needed to have more than six songs before they went to New York,"[77] but the band insisted. While they continued to hound Maureen, Curtis would call Max's from the bus station where Keith and Ricky were working. I said, "Tommy, they're gays in plaid shirts from the thrift store. The girls have these fab hairdos, and everybody's dancing. Trust me."[78] After the fourth call, Tommy relented, and gave the band a Monday night show on December 12th.

While Maureen has also claimed to have set up the band's first NYC show, it's possible she and Curtis each played an important part. Knapp believes Maureen got them their first gig at CBGB's, two months after the December gig at Max's, but acknowledges, "I think the two of us bombarding Tommy Dean and Peter Crowley together, that got them the gig."[79]

Keith Bennett heard about the show when he went to Cindy's parents' house one day to pick her up:

> Her room was one of those little Scottie trailers in the carport. I never knew what she was going to be wearing. Sometimes 60s mod. Sometimes it would be like one of my aunts, with a pocketbook and a scarf. You just never knew. Anyway, she comes out and she's like, "Guess what, we're gonna play New York City!" I was like, "You've got to be kidding me."[80]

That November, Talking Heads played Atlanta with Elvis Costello. The Fans and the B-52s were in the audience that night, and invited the bands to the Fans' house after the show. Talking Heads drummer Chris Frantz later said the B-52s "reminded me of a bunch of Southern RISD [Rhode Island School of Design] kids. They were not like any of the other bands.

I felt that before I'd even heard any of their music; you could just tell."[81] None of the B-52s members had gone to art school, but Athens provided them with an education that allowed Frantz to assume they were art students. They had learned from the record stores, the art department, the library, the university, the other creative people in town, then they filtered all of these influences through their own distinct personalities. The result was an aesthetic so strong that Frantz, a graduate from one of the most prestigious art schools in the country, and whose band had already come up through the NYC punk scene, was fascinated before he heard a single note of their music.

A week before their NYC debut, the B-52s played a warm-up gig in Athens at a house out on Atlanta Highway. One of the residents was Curtis Crowe, who would go on to make his own mark in Athens history as the drummer for Pylon. But his biggest contribution this night was letting the B-52s set up their drums on his kitchen table. This marked the first B-52s show to feature live drums and keyboards. Keith played the former, with Cindy taking his place on bongos. Kate played the latter, using her left hand to play the basslines while she played melody lines with her right. Kate and Cindy also picked up guitars occasionally. Fred played a walkie-talkie and toy piano, and also helped out on keyboard bass when Kate played guitar. "I didn't know which keys I was supposed to hit," he said, "so they put black tape on the keys."[82] There were no egos. All that mattered to the five band members was getting their songs across. For their first several years, the B-52s operated as a kind of Marxist utopia—each member contributing whatever they could, based on what the band needed.

Danny Beard was in the audience that night. He had gone to UGA, but moved to Atlanta in 1976 and opened a record store called Wax 'n' Facts. He loved the band and offered to go with them to New York. "I asked them if they had somebody to do sound or help carry equipment. They didn't have anybody so I did it."[83] The show at Max's Kansas City would be the fourth show they had ever played, and only their second as a full band.

If the idea seems preposterous—a band that was barely a band playing their fourth show at one of the hippest venues in New York City—it shouldn't be. The five members of the B-52s had a long history behind them, a history of creativity, of ambition, and of dreaming. Whether the band was ready or not, Kate, Fred, Keith, Ricky and Cindy had spent years preparing for the moment.

Notes

1. Hann, "Everyone."
2. Carlin, "The B-52s Kate Pierson."
3. Moore, "Southern Comfort," 17.
4. Hann, "Everyone."
5. Malins, "Shiny Hippy People," 34. In the profile, Kate recalls "buckets of psychedelic mushrooms in fields full of cows."
6. Goldstein, "Do You Dig." The goats were named Angie and Sappho.
7. Rotter, "The B-52s at 40."
8. Brown, *Party Out of Bounds*, 16.
9. Lloyd, *NY Rocker*.
10. Simadis, "Cosmic Thing."
11. Sexton, *The B-52's Universe*, 29. The story sounds unlikely, but we confirmed it with Keith Bennett, who informed us she eventually got her GED.
12. Reyes-Kulkarni, "The B-52s' Reflect."
13. The Red & Black, "SGA Election Extra," 2.
14. CGE Mouthpiece, April 14, 1974, Box 1, LGBT Resource Records, UA17-009 University of Georgia Libraries Special Collections.
15. Shearer, "Life Uncertain."
16. Michael Lachowski in conversation with authors, May 16, 2019.
17. Bill Paul in conversation with authors, May 19, 2019.
18. Jim Herbert in conversation with authors, April 20, 2019.
19. Michael Lachowski in conversation with authors, May 16, 2019.
20. Bill Paul in conversation with authors, May 19, 2019.
21. Ibid.
22. Smith, "Right Where She Belongs," C-1.
23. Jim Herbert in conversation with authors, April 20, 2019.
24. Lamb, "Art Rocks Athens."
25. Bill Paul in conversation with authors, May 19, 2019.
26. Chris Rasmussen in conversation with authors, July 29, 2019.
27. Ibid.
28. Ibid.
29. Bennett, "Pylon's Michael Lachowski."
30. Ibid.
31. Phipps, "Random Rules."
32. Chris Rasmussen in conversation with authors, July 29, 2019.
33. Morgan, "Interview: Fred Schneider."
34. Ware, "Freak Beat." Some people say it was three songs in four hours.
35. Jim Herbert in conversation with authors, April 20, 2019.
36. Simadis, "Cosmic Thing."
37. maureenmc2000, "Athens, Ga./NYC Axis."

38. Having seen the painting in person, it truly is profoundly ugly. Though as an architect of a war that killed approximately 2,000,000 Vietnamese civilians, the painting's ugliness does an excellent job of capturing Rusk's essence.
39. Thompson, *The Great Shark Hunt*, 47.
40. Glueck, "Far-Out Art."
41. Bill Paul in conversation with authors, May 19, 2019.
42. Ibid.
43. Taylor, "The B-52s and Me." This post on Taylor's website is a must-read for anyone interested in the story of the B-52s. The writing and the photographs are incredible.
44. Ware, "Freak Beat."
45. Reyes-Kulkarni, "The B-52s."
46. Ellen, "B-52's," 34.
47. Rambali, "The B-52s."
48. Runtagh, "The B-52's."
49. Henke, "Interview."
50. Hodgson, "Interview: Keith Strickland."
51. Runtagh, "The B-52's."
52. Pennock, "The B-52s Rock Lobster."
53. Sullivan, *R.E.M.*, 6.
54. Shapiro, "Fred Schneider."
55. Henke, "Interview."
56. Ibid.
57. Brown, *Party*, 36.
58. Ibid.
59. Rambali, "The B-52s."
60. Taylor, "The B-52s."
61. Bennett, "RB 24."
62. Sullivan, *R.E.M.*, 6.
63. Kevin Dunn in conversation with authors, May 26, 2019.
64. Rockwell, "The Fans Rock."
65. Kevin Dunn in conversation with authors, May 26, 2019.
66. Curtis Knapp in conversation with authors, April 17, 2019.
67. Ibid.
68. Brown, *Party*, 38.
69. Brown, *Party*, 39.
70. Curtis Knapp in conversation with authors, April 17, 2019.
71. Runtagh, "The B-52s."
72. Bennett, "RB 24."
73. Reyes-Kulkarni, "The B-52s."
74. Keith Bennett in conversation with authors, November 8, 2019.

75. Ibid.
76. Ibid.
77. maureenmc2000, "The Athens, Ga./NYC Axis."
78. Curtis Knapp in conversation with authors, April 27, 2019.
79. Ibid.
80. Keith Bennett in conversation with authors, November 8, 2019.
81. Frantz, *Remain*, 280.
82. Tannenbaum, "The B-52s Say Farewell," AR-14.
83. Brown, *Party*, 50.

CHAPTER 4

NYC

In Georgia, we tried to be as outrageous as possible just to see what kind of reaction we got. In New York City they were doing the same thing but in black leather, trying to shock, but in a different way.[1]

—Cindy

From a distance, the whole thing sounds like a fairytale. A band full of weirdos from a small college town in the South gets a gig at one of the most iconic venues in New York City and blows away a small crowd of people with their original music and style. They get invited back to play again (and again), and a year later, sign a contract with one of the most prestigious record labels in the world. And yet, that's exactly what happened.

On December 12th, almost exactly ten months after their first show, the B-52s played Max's Kansas City. They weren't the first Athenians to set foot in there—Jeremy Ayers and Bill Paul had spent time in Max's nearly a decade earlier. The Fans had played there only a few months ago, but none of them had made an impression on the city like the B-52s would.

The band piled into the Wilson family station wagon, strapping their equipment to the roof of the car ("like the Beverly Hillbillies," recalled Cindy)[2] and drove 20 hours north.

The cover charge was $3, and the other two bands on the bill were Gizzom and Nylon. The first band (spelled "Gizzmo" on the Max's

S. Creney, B. A. Herron, *The Story of the B-52s*,
https://doi.org/10.1007/978-3-031-22570-3_4

marquee) is lost to history, but the second involved Judy Nylon, a collaborator with 70s art rock icons Brian Eno and John Cale, possibly playing that night with her band Snatch. There are stories out there that Teenage Jesus & the Jerks also played that night, but Lydia Lunch was in England at the time, and the two bands wouldn't play together until June.[3] Kate said 17 people paid to get in, so the bands split the $51 three ways.[4]

"We were *so* nervous," recalled Cindy. "We kept our backs to the audience the entire time, and I stayed behind the curtain."[5] The band may have all been intimidated, but Fred was the least intimidated. "The curtain didn't open," he said, "so I had to throw it open .... All the other bands were dressed in black and we were like a rainbow congregation."[6] Cindy's reticence (and new role on bongos), coupled with Kate's new position behind the keyboard, placed Fred front and center. To most observers, that made him the band's de-facto frontperson.

The band went over well, despite huddling together after each song to "figure out what to do next," said Kate.[7] To the New York audience, the B-52s' lack of polish must have seemed refreshing, with NYC being such a densely populated crucible of self-awareness and mass media. After the B-52s finished their set, Lux Interior, lead singer of The Cramps—a band then trafficking in a kind of perverse horror rockabilly—stopped one of the band members to say the B-52s were his new favorite band.[8] Danny Beard recalled, "I don't think anyone in that audience, or in the B-52's, knew what had just happened. A dance band from nowhere Georgia suddenly became the talk of the town."[9] As everyone was getting ready to leave, Beard ran back inside to ask if the band could come back and play again. The person he talked to enthusiastically told him yes.

The City

The B-52s' success involved a lot of talent, but it also involved a lot of luck. The band arrived in NYC as it was on the cusp of a cultural renaissance of sorts.

Centered around the Lower East Side of Manhattan, CBGB's and Max's had already nurtured bands like Television, Patti Smith, the Ramones, Blondie, and Talking Heads, helping to create the punk scene. The musical styles of the different groups, aside from the Ramones, bore little resemblance to what most people today consider punk. As Thurston Moore and Byron Coley wrote, "The genuine tradition of New York bands was art rock, with punk merely just one of its aspects."[10] Along with lesser-known, but no less influential groups like Suicide, Richard Hell, and native Georgian, Wayne (later Jayne) County, NYC had one of the most vital and best-known underground scenes in the United States. The B-52s often presented themselves as overawed bumpkin outsiders adrift in the big city, but they had already seen the Ramones and Talking Heads in Atlanta when they played their first show at Max's.[11] They were acutely aware of what was happening in NYC and longed to be a part of it.

Crucially, the city had been hit hard by a financial crisis in 1975 spurred by white flight and deindustrialization, and rent was unimaginably cheap. A typical Lower East Side resident paid about $150 a month for their apartment, or the equivalent of $500 today.[12] The rent was cheap for a reason—most people didn't want to live there. Lydia Lunch poetically described NYC during this period as "a beautiful, ravaged slag—impoverished and neglected after suffering from decades of abuse and battery. [The city] stunk of sewage, sex, rotting fish, and day-old diapers. [It] leaked from every pore."[13]

But if you were able to handle the crime and squalor, you could gain access to the largest media center in the United States. This meant that at the tail end of the 1970s, a window briefly opened in NYC that made it accessible to anyone who had the nerve to live there. Artists and musicians flocked to the city, and the sparks created from all these people constantly bumping up against one another—painters & guitar players, entrepreneurs & performance artists, gallery owners & kids from the Bronx—triggered revolutions in music and the arts that are still being felt today.

The B-52s would play a major role in this. The band's aesthetic was so strong that they helped shape the direction of New York City's music and art scene for the next several years. As Steven Hager wrote in his 1986 book about early 80s New York, *Art After Midnight: The East Village Scene*, the B-52s were responsible for "swinging the pendulum in a completely different direction."[14]

Recording Rock Lobster

The B-52s made it back from Max's in time to catch the Sex Pistols' first US show, in Atlanta on January 5th of the new year. "It blew me away; it was so much fun," Cindy said years later.[15] The following week the B-52s played their first Atlanta show. Afterwards, Danny Beard suggested they put out a single.

Bearing his initials, "DB," as the name of the label, Beard intended the record to be a one off. He just wanted to "get their name around so they could play in New York more and get a manager and a label and do what they needed to do."[16] So in February, the band headed into Stone Mountain Studios in Atlanta to record two songs—Rock Lobster and 52 Girls. Beard brought in Kevin Dunn from the Fans to help with production, since the Fans had already recorded a seven-inch of their own. Unfortunately, theirs played at 33 RPM, so when CBGB's put the single in their 45 RPM jukebox, the record sounded, in Dunn's words, "like we were ants with horns."[17] Dunn functioned mostly as a liaison between Bruce Baxter, who ran the studio, and the band. "I basically existed to make sure there were no misunderstandings between what was going on out in the studio and in the control room."[18]

The single versions of Rock Lobster and 52 Girls are completely different from what would surface on the band's debut album a year later, and are marked by their sparse production, particularly the lack of reverb. Dunn said, "The aesthetic back then was for dry drums. It was, like, to do as little to the rhythm section as possible."[19] Any ideas he might have had about experimenting in the studio were abandoned after the band overruled Dunn about putting a ring modulator effect on the "down, down" section of Rock Lobster.[20]

Fred's delivery on the single is more restrained than on the album version. In fact, there's a stiffness in his delivery and the band's playing that suggests the self-consciousness of a band's first time in the studio. Given that both songs are in faster tempos and higher keys, one can't help wondering if the recordings were sped up, either in the studio or during mastering.

Rock Lobster is also missing its third verse. The "underneath the waves" section that appears on the album version was performed at a May 1978 show, so it was likely cut here for reasons of length, as anything over five minutes on a vinyl seven-inch would create mastering problems. The DB version runs 4:35 compared to the album's 6:49. The third verse also got chopped when Rock Lobster was eventually released as a single by Warners and Island.

Regardless, they completed the recording in 11 hours spread across two days.[21] "I was sitting there in the studio listening to the playback when the session was over," recalls Dunn, "and going, huh, that's something new under the sun."[22]

Back to New York

It would take a few months to get the recording pressed onto vinyl, packaged, and shipped. In the meantime, the band returned to New York to play some more shows. The band climbed back into the station wagon, now nicknamed "Croton," armed with the Strickland family credit card. This time, the band played twice at Max's, February 24th and 25th, followed by two shows at CBGB's on February 26th and March 1st. It was unusual to play both venues so close together, but Fred explained, "We were one of the only bands they would allow to play both Max's and CBGB's, because we said, 'Look, we can't be driving 800 miles on alternate weekends.'"[23]

By now, the band had a strategy to break through the icy New York crowd. Kate said, "Our friends who came up with us broke loose on the dance floor and people just started dancing and all of a sudden there was a dance craze!"[24]

Word about the band had spread in their absence. When Cindy walked into Max's she noticed, "John fucking Cale was sitting at the bar. I was in shock!"[25] Maureen told a story from this period that showed how big things were getting, and how fast:

> Judy Wilmot's boyfriend came up and told me that Ivan Kral from Patti's [Smith] band had personally called every music critic, rock star, novel writer, journalist, and photographer in the place. Later on, I realized that Judy's boyfriend was Lester Bangs: the same writer whose articles I had been clipping from Tiger Beat, Creem Magazine and Rolling Stone.[26]

Courted by Sire

Seymour Stein, head of Sire Records, was the first major label executive to try to sign the B-52s. He wrote extensively about his courtship of the band in his 2018 memoir *Siren Song: My Life in Music*. Stein heard about the B-52s after Sire employee Michael Rosenblatt, whose father was head of marketing and sales at Sire's parent company Warner Brothers, came into the office raving about the "wildly original party music he'd seen the night before." Stein tried phoning the band, only to find the number they had given to Rosenblatt belonged to "the Greyhound Bus Station in Atlanta [*sic*], where two of the musicians worked." Stein marveled, "The B-52's were so broke they didn't even have a telephone."[27]

Sire was already home to the Ramones, Talking Heads, and Richard Hell, and at the forefront of new wave, a more commercial strain of punk. New wave was as much marketing strategy as music genre. The phrase had been bouncing around since punk began, but Seymour Stein employed it to counteract the stigma surrounding punk at the time, even going so far as to place advertisements in magazines that read, "Don't Call It Punk, Call It New Wave."[28] The strategy was beginning to work, as 1978 saw the more accessible artists in the NYC punk underground cross over into the mainstream. Patti Smith, Talking Heads, and Blondie, all had their first hit singles, with the latter reaching #1 with "Heart of Glass." Along with acts like the Police and the Cars, Talking Heads and Blondie were considered to be at the forefront of new wave.

As the B-52s are often called a new wave band, it's worth noting that the genre has proven especially tricky to define. The Allmusic description of new wave runs nearly 400 words before the writer finally concedes, "By the early '80s new wave described nearly every new pop/rock artist,"[29] probably after realizing that Elvis Costello and The Human League, while both considered new wave, have nothing in common.

Unable to reach the B-52s by phone, Stein flew all the way to Atlanta to catch the band's next show on March 29th at the Downtown Club. A reporter for *The Athens Observer* saw Stein after the show with his arm draped over Fred's shoulder. The two went outside to discuss "the possibility of a Sire contract," with Stein "muttering things like 'amazing … really amazing.'"[30]

That May, the B-52s played the Georgia Theatre in Athens, where they unveiled two new songs, Running Around and 53 Miles West of Venus. A representative from Virgin Records was in attendance, and Keith told an *Athens Observer* reporter after the show, "We haven't decided not to sign with Sire. We just decided to wait for a bit and see what happens."[31]

In the meantime, Ricky checked out a book from the Athens library about contracts, and according to the story in *Party Out of Bounds*, "By the time [the band] pieced sense out of the jargon, they realized everyone was trying to rip them off."[32]

Rising Stars

A week after the Georgia Theatre show, the band headed back to NYC for a four-night stand at Max's. Befitting their new status, they were supported each night by a different local luminary, including power-pop

CBGB's vets Marbles, new wave up-and-comers Nervus Rex, and the aforementioned Teenage Jesus & the Jerks, featuring Lydia Lunch. An audio recording of the final night can be found on the internet. Even as the band still struggles with a lot of dead time between songs, the audience is loud and enthusiastic.

The final night at Max's proved to be important when Richard Cramer, an assistant art director at Andy Warhol's *Interview* magazine, invited photographer George Dubose to come see the band. After the show, Dubose invited the band to come to his photo studio. Longing for Athens and Keith Bennett, Cindy had already left, so Maureen, now acting as the band's manager, decided to stand in for Cindy.

Dubose was so taken with the band that he offered Maureen the extra room in his apartment whenever she came up to NYC. Soon afterward, Dubose was vacationing on Long Island when he called back home to check his messages, only to be surprised when Ricky answered the phone. Duobse realized, "The whole band had moved into my apartment."[33] Thankfully, they turned out to be wonderful houseguests, and Dubose was delighted when he returned home. "Cindy had obviously spent several hours," he writes, "scrubbing and bleaching the bathtub and it never looked so white."[34]

While Cindy supposedly cleaned George Dubose's apartment, the New York press had begun to take notice of the band. Kate recalled, "We were in a vacuum, because we were always driving, so we didn't really have a sense about how our audience was building."[35] Within weeks of their Max's engagement, reviews appeared in the *New York Times* and the *Village Voice*. NYC critic Tom Carson recalled seeing *Times* critic John Rockwell at one of these shows, "lurching around in a black leather jacket with day-glo racing stripes on the sleeve, clutching a broken bottle of Lowenbrau and bellowing, 'Fan-fuckingtastic! I'll fight anybody in the house who says no!'"[36]

In the June 3rd edition of the *Times*, Rockwell's language was more sedate, but no less enthusiastic. "Anyone who thinks the CBGB's-Max's underground-rock club scene in New York has stopped introducing exciting new bands hasn't heard the B52's."[37] Rockwell was a smart critic, and one of the first journalists to take note of the fledgling punk scene back in 1975,[38] but his review anticipated how the band would come to be defined. He writes extensively about the band's clothes, and uses words like "amusing" and "kookiness" when talking about their music. Still, Rockwell draws attention to qualities that other critics often miss. He cites the band's musical power, especially the "sheer, driving danceability" and notes the band's physicality, how they were "gyrating furiously" onstage. Rockwell also mentioned that the band was planning to move to New York and were "already talking with record companies."[39]

A week after the *Times* article appeared, Tom Carson raved about the B-52s in the *Village Voice*, calling them "the best new music to have come out of the CBGB-Max's Kansas City circuit in months if not years."[40] Carson goes even deeper than Rockwell, focusing on the band's intelligence, using words like "surrealism" and "intellectual" to describe the band:[41]

> The pop-culture frame of the B-52s' music doesn't have any of the coyness of an ironic pose. To people who grew up in the '60s … pop art and camp are the only artistic tradition they've got …. Even the B-52s' most willful—or potentially cloying—conceits are given an enigmatic intensity by the band's respect for them.[42]

The *Village Voice* was home to some of the most respected music writers in the country, if not the world. Bands dreamed of getting a review of this caliber. Carson's was published only six months after the band's first New York show, and it concluded with a paragraph that suggested the city needed the B-52s as much as the band needed the city:

> Now, particularly, with the New York rock scene in a jaded and complacent interlude, and dozens of young bands hunting through the debris of punk rock/new wave/power pop for some shred of character they can call their own, a band as inventive and energetic as the B-52s is almost incredibly refreshing.[43]

Though both writers talked about the B-52s in terms of their clothes and hair, and their retro sensibility, neither writer dismissed the band as mere camp, or kitsch. That would come later.

Lobster Released

The write-ups were followed by the release of the Rock Lobster single. Different sources place the release date anywhere from May to November, a range that—given the haphazard nature of putting out your own single—is more plausible than it might sound. The single was a homemade, do-it-yourself labor of love, with the cover printed by Athens local Rick Hawkins (known around town as "Rick the Printer") in his Oconee St. studio. The whole thing cost Danny Beard $400.[44] The back cover featured a photo of the band taken by friend and photographer Ann States. Nobody in the band is wearing wigs in the picture, or anything outlandish, ironic, or tacky. They just look like sweet Athens bohemians. The band had a record release party at Wax 'N' Facts in Atlanta, then another at Chapter III in Athens, where co-owner Chris Rasmussen recalls:

> They came and signed seven-inches for people. It was cute because Cindy and Ricky's parents came, and they bought a ton of stuff. They were very big supporters of the band, and everything that came out they'd come in and buy stacks of them. They would give them out to their friends, and I think [Cindy's] Uncle Bill still has stacks of everything in his house that he has stockpiled.[45]

Reviews of the single appeared throughout the year in various underground magazines, which, coupled with the band's continued presence in New York, helped the record sell nearly 20,000 copies, unheard of for a small independent label putting out its first record. Danny Beard recalled, "We'd make 5000 records and they'd be gone. That's what it seemed."[46] A write-up in UK music paper *Melody Maker* early the following year called Rock Lobster "one of the best and best received independent 45s released [in America]."[47]

The Rock Lobster single managed to sound original by virtue of pulling from so many disparate touch points in the history of rock music. Musically, it combines elements of surf music, girl groups, and the avant-garde, powered by a series of riffs that classic rockers like Jimmy Page might have killed for. The song is so catchy that it's easy to miss how complicated it is. After the final verse (*Motion in the ocean*), the song starts changing sections so quickly it's hard to keep up. The structure is closer to prog-rock, or Brian Wilson's "pocket symphony" Good Vibrations, than anything typically found in new wave.

The band continued to play shows. Kate recalled, "We blazed the path between Athens and New York for months. Each time we'd come back [to Athens], we'd write more songs, rehearse like crazy and go back up."[48] They began to form relationships with some of the biggest bands on the scene. Debbie Harry and Chris Stein of Blondie made daiquiris for the band in their loft and offered to produce their album. The members of

Talking Heads also became friends. "Bands were very supportive of each other during this period," said Keith. "We were like outsiders coming from Georgia so it was really great."[49]

It wasn't long before George Dubose invited them back to his studio for another photo session, this time to make some posters the band could use to promote their shows. When Dubose saw fans tearing the posters down as fast as he could put them up, he began selling them for 52 cents each, or two for a dollar. *Interview* would use Dubose's photo when they ran a feature article on the band early the next year.

Downtown Club

September 2nd found the B-52s playing a show in Atlanta at the Downtown Club. Filmed by a crew of students from Georgia State University, it remains the easiest video to find from this period.[50] The show is noteworthy for the tightness of the band's attack—it's obvious the constant playing has turned them into a machine. They launch into opener 52 Girls at full speed, Kate playing the lead riff on guitar while Fred plays the bass part on the keyboard. It's surprising to see the singers playing so many instruments throughout the set. As the band progressed through the years, Kate, Fred, and Cindy would gradually give up their instruments to other, more "virtuosic" players.

The band seem completely comfortable with each other. Between songs, Cindy places a gentle hand on Fred's shoulder. Kate switches over to keyboard for Devil in My Car as Fred takes center stage, unshaven and clad in a white tank-top style undershirt. In this instance, there's nothing camp about his performance. Fred dances wildly, and when he shouts *I don't want to go to hell*, there's a desperation in his voice that contradicts the band's reputation as tongue-in-cheek purveyors of irony.

At the end of their set, the band leaves the stage for a minute to mingle among the crowd before hopping back up for an encore. Before they start, Fred introduces the band. "On lead guitar we have Snapper. On drums we have the former Pebbles. On vocals and tambourines we have Cinderella. On organ and guitar we have Swoop Bagnell, and I'm Slack Thompson. This is called Rock Lobster." The performance continues to build in intensity, until Fred shouts "Let's rock!" and the song reaches the kind of hedonistic peak that defines great rock and roll. The entire room appears to be floating. "Thank you," shouts a gasping Fred as the song ends. "We'll see you tomorrow night."

Y'all, I Just Don't Know What to Do

The band was young and beautiful. They sounded like nothing else on earth, and they were clearly in love with what they were doing. It's easy to see why New York City was falling at their feet. The B-52s' watershed moment in New York City came at the beginning of October with a two-night engagement at Hurrah that was completely sold-out. Fred remembered Ricky looking out the windows of the club the first night and wondering, "What are all these people doing out there?" Fred then realized the line around the block was people waiting to get in the club to see their show.[51] Kate commented on this stunning realization saying, "That was the first moment I was like, 'Oh my god, we're rock stars.'"[52]

In the October 23rd issue of the *Village Voice*, editor Robert Christgau wrote, "In this one year I've seen more of the B-52s, a 'tacky little dance band from Athens, Georgia,' than I've seen of John Prine and Sonny Rollins combined in my entire life." Christgau then added snippily, "Not that I think that the B-52s are better than Prine and Rollins, who are geniuses. It's just that I'm basically a rock and roller."[53]

By now, the Rock Lobster single was "selling like hotcakes" at cool New York record stores like Gem Records and Bleeker Bob's, the latter of which was also selling them to overseas distributors.[54] Influential UK DJ John Peel got a copy and began playing it on his BBC show.

Labels continued to court the band. Keith Strickland recalled Maureen walking into a room around this time with a contract in each hand shouting, "Y'all, I just don't know what to do!"[55] The band and their manager were in over their heads. On one hand, they wanted to hold out for the best deal possible. As Ricky confided, "We think a lot of New York groups have made mistakes with their contracts."[56] Fred also pointed out, "The basic contracts record companies offer new groups are insulting."[57] At the same time, the band wasn't sure what a good contract would look like. "It was real strange because we were handling all the business ourselves," recalled Fred. "Someone from one of the record companies would call us up at Kate's farm, and we'd have to take turns doing the business. We bought these law books, and they'd send us contracts and we'd try to look them up."[58]

It's also possible the B-52s felt ambivalent about taking the next step. For a group of amateurs, choosing to go professional wasn't as straightforward a decision as it might have been for other bands. Signing a contract was serious business, and it would mean losing some of the autonomy and freedom they were clearly enjoying.

Art After Midnight

Two clubs opened around this time, Club 57 and the Mudd Club, that would influence the next several years of NYC art and music. "These symmetrical crossings [of punk and new wave art and music] peaked at the Mudd club," writes Bernard Gendron, "a nightclub that combined punk/new wave music with 'art after midnight.'"[59]

Mudd Club owner Steve Maas (sometimes spelled Mass),[60] got so excited when he first saw the B-52s play that he invited them to perform at the club's opening night on Halloween even though the stage wasn't finished being built. DJ David Azarch recalled the evening as "just an amazing night. The downtown arts scene mixed with the rock and roll scene from a little bit north. It was just a magical mix."[61]

Their opening act, a solo performer called Animal X, recalled the B-52s' performance:

> They were introduced by their manager, who came out wearing a bathing suit, a swim cap, and a rubber ducky. The band came out dressed in girdles from the fifties. On the first song they held a laugh box to the mike after every chorus. They were the only band around with a sense of humor.[62]

One fan showed up dressed in a giant lobster outfit, wanting to dance onstage with the band. "We told him there wasn't any room," remembered Fred, but as soon as the band started Rock Lobster he jumped on stage anyway, only to disappear through a hole in the unfinished stage.[63] After the show, Maas asked Fred to throw a theme party at the club, and Fred chose a Hawaiian luau. Theme parties, already common in Athens, would become a defining characteristic of both the Mudd Club and Club 57, described as "highly conceptualized events that would eventually rival the be-ins and happenings of the sixties."[64] The B-52s suddenly found themselves at the center of one of the coolest scenes in the country, influencing and being influenced, and attracting visual artists as well as musicians. Gendron describes the Mudd Club scene:

> The B-52s soon became the unofficial "house" band, performatively alternating with the DJ-driven musical stream. The artists soon joined in with their own spectacles .... The new wave of young artists turned increasingly to the accommodating Mudd Club as the site where, in Warhol's words, "mistakes" could be called "experiments."[65]

A week after the Mudd Club opened, "New Wave Vaudeville" debuted at Irving Plaza, a 2000-capacity ballroom owned by a Polish immigrant named Stanley Stryhaski. Featuring a series of cabaret and performance art acts, the engagement only ran six nights, but Stryhaski was so impressed with what he saw that he asked the organizers—Susan Hannaford, Tom Scully, and Ann Magnuson—to curate events in a space he had opened back in February called Club 57. Located in the basement of a church over on St. Mark's, it would become the band's spiritual home, with many of the key people involved described as "a gang of B-52's groupies."[66] Artist Kenny Scharf, who designed the Club 57 logo, was known for "dragging in debris off the street ... to glue together and paint,"[67] an aesthetic that would have fit in perfectly at the UGA art school. Scharf, along with Magnuson, performance artist John Sex, and painter Keith Haring, brought presents to the band's early shows. Scharf recalled Haring "[giving] them plastic fruit once and they *loved* it."[68]

The affection was mutual. In a 2018 interview Kate said, "That was such a fun scene. Lots of downtown artists ... were mixing with musicians, and it was just a very cross-pollinated scene."[69] In 2017, nearly 40 years after they first met, Kate inducted West Virginia native Magnuson into that state's Music Hall of Fame. In the announcement, Pierson said, "Ann is an actress, innovator, performance artist, musician and wild child who helped define the New York post-punk art and music scene. And she blasted through it all with some serious fun and madness!"[70]

That madness continued with the Nova Convention, a three-day event at the end of November to celebrate William Burroughs' return to NYC. The convention featured readings and performances, and drew such luminaries as Patti Smith, Allen Ginsberg, John Cage, Philip Glass, Laurie Anderson, Kathy Acker, and of course Burroughs himself. Poet Eileen Myles and a friend audaciously came out on stage and performed a reenactment of the "William Tell Routine" where Burroughs had shot and killed his wife, to mixed reaction.[71]

The convention was conceived and organized by Sylvere Lotringer, founder of Semiotext(e), a hyper-intellectual journal and press that would publish some of the earliest US translations of seminal French theorists like Jean Baudrillard, Gilles Deleuze, Jean-François Lyotard, and Michel Foucault. Still operating today, Semiotext(e) boasts a history of producing books that have, in their own words, "famously melded high and low forms of cultural expression into a nuanced and polemical vision of the present."[72]

Experimental poet John Giorno enlisted the B-52s to perform at Irving Plaza for the convention. According to one observer, the band drew a crowd "far beyond what the organizers could handle and almost entirely eclipsing the theoretical context and the political dialogue that had first motivated Lotringer's project."[73] This description does a disservice to the band, who "melded high and low forms of cultural expression" as well as anyone at Semiotext(e). Furthermore, a flyer for the convention featured a Burroughs quote, "A new mythology is possible in the Space Age," which sounds right in line with the B-52s' aesthetic. Gary Indiana, one of the great writers and critics to come out of this time in NYC, wrote that Burroughs "has always written for the Space Age. His work addresses readers who want OUT of present slave-planet conditions."[74] In that light, the B-52s were a perfect choice to play the convention.

Kate noticed a famous guest at the Irving Plaza show. "I remember Cindy saying 'Oh my God! David Bowie's here!' He was standing right in back of us, and we were laughing because he overheard us. And he was so nice."[75] Bowie also spent part of the night deep in conversation with Ricky.

Bouffant Bop

The band were moving in heady company now. Even the UK press had begun to notice. *Melody Maker* ran a live review of the Irving Plaza show calling the band "without question … the most promising new group I've seen this year."[76] The review compared the band favorably to Blondie and Talking Heads, acknowledged Captain Beefheart as an influence, and concluded with the statement, "The B-52's are ready to take off; a mission over the Atlantic would be in order."[77]

Two weeks later a photo of Cindy Wilson appeared on the *Melody Maker* cover in the lower right corner with the headline "B-52s' bouffant bop: this year's Blondie?" One of the two largest UK music papers putting an unsigned American band on the cover was almost unheard of. The two-page feature inside was accompanied by that now-ubiquitous George Dubose photograph. The writer's introduction was a full-throated gush:

> More than any group since the Ramones, they project the bottom-line fun that rock 'n' roll music is supposed to be all about. They do it by looking funny, by having a goddamned good time onstage, and by playing a selection of songs that are intended to free the mind enough to let the ass follow.[78]

The article ends with an entertaining Q&A that includes their "manager-friend Maureen McLaughlin." At the end of the conversation, the writer asks the question on everybody's mind—when the hell was the band going to sign to a label? Fred, Ricky, Maureen, and Kate all take turns avoiding a direct answer until Fred finally concludes, "We can wait."[79]

And why not wait? The B-52s were having the time of their lives. In less than a year, they had gone from playing Max's to 17 paying customers, to being the coolest band in the coolest city. But they couldn't wait forever. If the adventure was to go any further, the B-52s were going to have to sign one of the many contracts they were being offered. That meant making a commitment. It meant making hard decisions.

The band was right to be hesitant though. As William Burroughs once said, "Paranoia is just having the right information." And despite their vigilance, the B-52s would end up having their worst fears confirmed. It turned out the music business was a lot more about business than it was about music.

Notes

1. Sexton, *The B-52's Universe*, 39.
2. Simadis, "Cosmic Thing."
3. Fromthearchives.com, "Teenage Jesus Chronology." Lunch confirmed this in an email to authors on June 15, 2019, adding "this is a mistake people make often." Lydia Lunch rules by the way.
4. The B-52s' United Fans Organization (UFO) Issue #9.
5. Henke, "Interview."
6. Grow, "Love Shacks."
7. Henke, "Interview."
8. Brown, *Party*, 51–52.
9. Sexton, *The B-52's Universe*, 6.
10. Moore and Coley, *No Wave*, 6.

11. Lamb, "Beyond."
12. Sokol, "Club 57."
13. Lunch, introduction to Moore and Coley, *No Wave*, 4.
14. Hager, *Art After Midnight*, 60.
15. Crawford, "B-52s' Cindy Wilson."
16. Hutcherson, "Producer Danny Beard."
17. Kevin Dunn in conversation with authors, May 26, 2019.
18. Ibid.
19. Pennock, "The B-52s."
20. Ibid.
21. Sexton, *The B-52's Universe*, 41.
22. Kevin Dunn in conversation with authors, May 26, 2019.
23. Pennock, "The B-52s."
24. Brown, *Party*, 51.
25. Crawford, "B-52s' Cindy Wilson." Cale was a founding member of the Velvet Underground before moving on to a solo career. His 1974 album *Fear*, featuring contributions from Brian Eno and Judy Nylon, is a career high point, though he's probably best known for his version of Leonard Cohen's "Hallelujah" as featured in the hit movie *Shrek*.
26. maureenmc2000, "Athens, Ga./NYC Axis."
27. Stein, *Siren Song*, 155.
28. Helmore, "They Wanted to Be."
29. Allmusic.com, "New Wave."
30. Haines, April 13, 1978, 10-B.
31. Haines, May 18, 1978, 4-B. In the forthcoming year, the band rarely played Runnin' Around, and never played 53 Miles West of Venus, suggesting these songs may have been tried out because the show was in Athens. According to Kate, the latter song was finished in the studio while recording *Wild Planet*.
32. Brown, *Party*, 92.
33. George-dubose.com, "The B-52's."
34. Ibid.
35. Biography, "Kate Pierson."
36. Carson, *NY Rocker*, July 1979, 4.
37. Rockwell, "B-52's, Rock Band" 11.
38. Rombes, *Cultural Dictionary of Punk*, 236.
39. Rockwell, "B-52's, Rock Band," 11.
40. Carson, "Take Off," 49.
41. Ibid.
42. Ibid.
43. Ibid.
44. Hutcherson, "Producer Danny Beard."

45. Chris Rasmussen in conversation with authors, July 29, 2019.
46. Sexton, *The B-52's Universe*, 41.
47. Sigerson, "B52s on Target," 5.
48. Grow, "Love Shacks."
49. Sexton, *The B-52's Universe*, 41.
50. https://www.youtube.com/watch?v=7evMUowv4sc. Back before all the Vision Video stores closed in Athens, you could rent the bootleg DVD for $1.
51. Martens, "Fred Schneider."
52. Biography, "Kate Pierson."
53. Christgau, "Ain't Got No Home," 49–50.
54. Sexton, *The B-52's Universe*, 41.
55. Brown, *Party*, 92–93.
56. Mieses, "Bouffant Bop," 19.
57. Ibid.
58. Henke, "Interview."
59. Gendron, *Between Montmartre*, 7.
60. The *Washington Post* has spelled it "Maas," while the *New York Times* has spelled it "Mass." We've gone with "Maas" because it is a more common last name. Consider this one more example of the fluidity and chaos that surrounds the B-52s.
61. Lawrence, *Life and Death*, ix.
62. Hager, *Art After Midnight*, 60.
63. Ibid.
64. Hager, *Art After Midnight*, 58.
65. Gendron, *Between Montmarte*, 300.
66. Reynolds, *Rip It Up*, 264.
67. Sawyer, "Public Has a Right."
68. Reynolds, *Rip It Up*, 264.
69. Runtagh, "B-52s at 40."
70. Harrison, "B-52s Singer."
71. Dangerous Minds, "Frank Zappa, John Cage." We considered adding the word "accidentally" to describe Burroughs' shooting of Joan Vollmer, but the incident is too shrouded in mystery to definitively say one way or another exactly what happened.
72. "About" page, accessed August 2018, http://semiotexte.com/?page_id=2.
73. Cusset, *French Theory*, 68.
74. Indiana, *Utopia's Debris*, 71.
75. Paulson, "The B-52s."

76. Mieses, "Caught in the Act." The review says they played at Club 57, but it's far likelier the writer saw the Irving Plaza show at the beginning of December, as there's no record of the band ever playing the tiny club. Irving Plaza events were often credited to Club 57 because the Club 57 crowd booked events at the larger venue. Understandably, this has created a lot of confusion over the years.
77. Ibid.
78. Mieses, "B-52s," 19–20.
79. Ibid.

CHAPTER 5

The B-52's

One day I was washing pots and pans at the vegetarian restaurant I worked at, and the next I was flying to the Bahamas to record an album.[1]

—Fred

The band opened 1979 with two shows at Atlanta's Agora Ballroom in January with the Brains. Then in February, a feature appeared in Andy Warhol's *Interview* magazine, written by Glenn O'Brien. A former member of Warhol's factory, O'Brien lived his life as "a social fixture in the downtown Manhattan art, music and fashion world for a half-century."[2] He had begun hosting a cable access show called TV Party in December 1978 that featured high-profile guests from the New York music and art scene such as David Byrne and artist Jean-Michel Basquiat. Steven Hager wrote that TV Party "set a standard for infantilism, chaos, and insanity that will probably never again be equaled on television."[3] During broadcasts, O'Brien often quipped, "Welcome to TV Party, the show that's a cocktail party, but which could also be considered a political party." Within the year, Fred would appear as a guest.

Glenn O'Brien wasn't much different from the B-52s' friends back in Athens, and they had no trouble bantering with their genial interviewer. You can see the closeness and comfort within the band during this time, and with Maureen, by the way they complete each other's thoughts in the following exchange:

S. Creney, B. A. Herron, *The Story of the B-52s*,
https://doi.org/10.1007/978-3-031-22570-3_5

O'BRIEN:	What do you think about flying saucers?
SCHNEIDER:	They're up there.
O'BRIEN:	Have you ever seen any?
SCHNEIDER:	No. I wish I had.
MCLAUGHLIN:	But we look for 'em.
B-52s:	We look for 'em.
PIERSON:	I was depressed we didn't see any on this trip.
SCHNEIDER:	Ontario's a terrific state to see 'em.
PIERSON:	In Michigan they sit on the road.
CINDY WILSON:	Listen, we were driving down this road and it was real dark and I saw this real eerie light, it looked like something from another world. And we got closer and it was a lit motel.
SCHNEIDER:	There are a lot of funny motels. There was one motel in the middle of nowhere, it was real plain, but it had a gigantic green monster, something like the Creature from the Black Lagoon, standing next to this lake.
CINDY WILSON:	We went to the Mystery Spot.
O'BRIEN:	Is that where things roll uphill?
CINDY WILSON:	Yes, they defy gravity. But it's just an illusion. But did you know that Minneapolis is really sideways? The gravity is off.
MCLAUGHLIN:	We read it in their newspaper. When you're standing up straight you're not really standing up straight, you're leaning towards Texas.
O'BRIEN:	I'd think you'd be leaning the other way, towards Alaska.
STRICKLAND:	Is it the curve of the earth or is there a dip?
O'BRIEN:	It must be the Minnesota Dip. Do you have any saucer theories? Who do you think is in them?
SCHNEIDER:	People.
O'BRIEN:	What color, do you think?
PIERSON:	Oh, green for sure. I think they're benevolent.
STRICKLAND:	They could be from another dimension, not necessarily from outer space. They could be from under the ocean.[4]

As the Minneapolis anecdote suggests, the band were now playing outside of Georgia and New York. Buoyed by the modest success of Rock Lobster and their glowing write-ups in the New York press, they were able to draw crowds in the bigger cities—no small feat for a band that still didn't have the financial support of a big label. "In the van," says Keith Bennett, "they had the equipment. They had the driver, the passenger, two lawn chairs. And then the fifth person had to lay on top of the equipment, so they would take turns doing that."[5]

Sire Records boss Seymour Stein was still intent on signing the band. Feeling they needed more professional management than Maureen was providing, he introduced them to Talking Heads' manager Gary Kurfirst. "I wanted to make sure they had a manger, the plan being—like all our new-wave bands—to keep them touring and developing professionally."[6] Keith Strickland, on the other hand, has said Kurfirst was suggested by Chris Frantz and Tina Weymouth of Talking Heads.[7] Both stories could be true, as Kurfirst had working relationships with both Stein and Talking Heads at the time, and each were involved with the B-52s. Regardless, Kurfirst accompanied Chris and Tina to a B-52s show in Washington, D.C. at the end of February to check out the band.

Gary Kurfirst was already a music industry veteran when he met the B-52s. Born in 1947, he grew up in Queens and started out promoting rock shows in the mid-60s, including the first east coast shows for The Who and Jimi Hendrix.[8] Kurfirst got his first real education in the cut-throat nature of the music business from west-coast promoter Bill Graham. After Kurfirst established the Village East as a viable rock venue, Graham took it over and changed its name to Fillmore East, where it became an iconic venue often referred to as "the church of rock and roll." After that, Kurfirst decided to move into management, representing Mountain, a band best known for their 1970 classic rock hit Mississippi Queen.[9] Through Mountain, he formed a close relationship with Chris Blackwell, head of Island Records, a UK label that was an early exporter of reggae music from Jamaica. Island released records by important artists like Bob Marley, Peter Tosh, and Toots and the Maytals—the latter two managed by Kurfirst. But it was the label's involvement with early/mid-70s art-rock titans like Roxy Music, Brian Eno, and Sparks that would have given Blackwell, as well as Kurfirst, the context to appreciate the B-52s.

By this time, the band's relationship with Maureen had grown complicated. Kate later said, "It seemed that she didn't know the next step ... when we were being approached by record companies."[10] A story in *Party*

Out of Bounds alleges, "Tension and hard feelings bred as the band began to feel that Maureen was using them to enhance her own position in the New York City club scene."[11] After seeing the band's D.C. show, Kurfirst offered to co-manage with Maureen as a show of diplomacy, but when Maureen refused, the band felt they had no choice but to fire her. Keith explained:

> It was a difficult split with Maureen. We really hated doing it. But it was a decision we had to make. Gary was saying he would work with her if we wanted to do a split deal, but it was all getting crazy and we thought for the long run it was best to make a clean break. It was very emotional.[12]

The decision wasn't popular in the NYC scene. Lester Bangs ran into Maureen at the Mudd Club and tried to cheer her up. First he bought her an expensive beer, then he called the band "a string of epithets" before solemnly telling Maureen that "justice would be done."[13] Tom Carson wrote about the split in a July 1979 feature on the band:

> Maureen seemed like an indispensable part of the band. Everyone adored her, and she was probably more responsible for the band's early success than any other person outside of the members themselves. Gary Kurfurst [*sic*], on the other hand, is almost exactly the opposite: a smoothly professional manager.[14]

Fred talked about the decision in the Carson feature. "We agonized over it, you know—but we just had to take control." Fred then added, "We haven't really discussed anything with her, except we hear bad things that she says about us."[15]

By most accounts, Kurfirst was an excellent manager who worked hard for his bands. In 2014, Frantz and Weymouth called him "brilliant," and credited him for helping Talking Heads build their following.[16] Still, Kurfirst had some red flags in his past that should have raised questions. From 1976–78 Kurfirst ran Island Artists, a management company he formed with Chris Blackwell to manage the artists on Island Records.[17] This is hugely unethical, which may be why Island Artists only lasted a couple of years. The situation made contract negotiations absurdly easy for Blackwell—one pictures him in his office comically switching back and forth between chairs as he negotiated contracts, one minute as the band's manager, the next as the band's label.

Kurfirst was a professional though, and he instantly improved the B-52s' touring situation. He enlisted Steve Ralbovsky, a college student who booked their show in Buffalo, to tour manage the band for $200 a week, a position he would hold until 1981.[18] Maureen's old friend Moe Slotin joined the crew, but they still needed one more person. Cindy suggested her boyfriend, Keith Bennett. He had accompanied the band on some of their New York trips, but Slotin was skeptical about his qualifications. Bennett wanted the job badly, and so he did the sensible thing—he lied. He also said he would work for free. This clinched the deal for Kurfirst. Bennett recalled, "Sure, cheap labor, keeping one of the singers happy, two for one motel room, you're hired."[19]

Davitt Sigerson reviewed a March Mudd Club show for *Melody Maker* and noted "a record deal is imminent."[20] It sure was. That April, over a year since Seymour Stein first expressed interest, the B-52s finally signed a contract. To Stein's eternal regret, they rejected Sire, and instead chose Warner Brothers, Sire's parent company, to handle the US and Australia. For the rest of the world—in what was probably a complete coincidence—they would be signed to Chris Blackwell's Island Records.

Compass Point

The band almost immediately headed to a studio in the Bahamas owned by Chris Blackwell, who would also be producing the album. Built in 1977, Compass Point Studios would become one of the most important studios of the 1980s, hosting AC-DC, the Rolling Stones, Grace Jones, James Brown, and Sade, just to name a few. Talking Heads were the first band to record there, crafting their 1978 album *More Songs About Buildings and Food*. Tina Weymouth recalled apartments "right behind the studio. We could swim in the morning, clear our heads, and then in the afternoon and evening we could start working in the studio. It was an amazing situation."[21]

Paul Rambali from the *New Musical Express* (*NME*), the UK's largest music paper, visited the B-52s during the recording sessions, and told stories of Kate making gumbo for everyone while the band grooved to some "Native African Top 40 music" on one of Keith's cassettes. Rambali wrote about their living quarters:

> On the table are copies of National Enquirer, OMNI, and a book of Dylan Thomas' stories, offering between them: frontier technology, mystical

> anointment, and the real truth behind Charlie's Angels. Piled in the corner is some black snorkeling equipment, and some pink snorkeling equipment; a big gaudy beach ball is slowing deflating on the sideboard. The only casualty is the sofa, which has collapsed at one end, and the only luxury is Keith's portable compact tape system, still going strong.[22]

The B-52s had more songs than would fit on one album, and Blackwell helped choose which ones to include.[23] Runnin' Around, Devil in My Car, Private Idaho and Strobe Light would all have to wait until the next album. The band remembers engineer Robert Ash handling most of the actual recording work. Kate said of Blackwell, "He basically put his feet up on the console and smoked pot. I mean, he *directed* the whole thing but he was very 'mellow.'"[24] Kate elaborated about Blackwell's methods in a 2012 interview:

> He's really a genius, the way he produced the first album, because he wanted us to sound exactly like we do live .... He said, "Whatever you play onstage is what I want you to play on the record." So that's what we did.

Cindy and Kate shared a vocal booth, with Fred in another.[25] Like most first albums, particularly during the punk and new wave era, few overdubs or studio effects were added. One exception was the treatment on Kate's voice in Planet Claire:

> I think Keith wanted to come up with a more formalized melody, so he came up with that sort of Fellini-esque, Nino Rota-inspired melody line on the keyboard. I sang along with it, but ... the only thing that I was disappointed about was that the engineer, Robert Ash, he decided to really put a lot of effect on my voice, which made it sound like a synthesizer. Some people don't even realize I was actually singing that part.[26]

The band enjoyed the process, though they were a bit taken aback when they heard the finished product. Fred has used the word "rinky-dink" several times to describe the thinness of the production. Keith added, "I mean to me, to my ears, we never sounded that way ... it always sounded much bigger to me when we played live."[27]

Compared to live recordings from this period, the album does sound more restrained, particularly on Lava, which seems to drag sonically and sounds less inspired. But that may not have been Chris Blackwell's fault. The band attacked the songs in concert with a sharper intensity than they do on the record. It's possible the more controlled, sterile atmosphere of a recording studio simply created a more controlled, sterile recording. Also, because the early B-52s had such a sparse sound, even the slightest adjustment in the studio would have a massive impact on the finished result. Ricky's guitar sounds substantially cleaner on the album, and it lacks a lot of the distortion and grit that came across live. Perhaps the more polished guitar tone played a role in creating the smaller sound Keith was hearing.

To his credit, Blackwell made sure to include the band in the decision-making process. While mixing Lava, he asked them, "Are you all sure you're happy with that? Because if you aren't happy, now is the time to speak up. Once the record is made it'll be too late. That's it. It will always be the B-52s first album."[28] Kate, who Rambali described as having "the most diligent interest in the protracted and distracting mixing process," responded by asking Blackwell to raise Cindy's voice in the mix.[29] Keith then asked for the guitars to be turned up. It's interesting that both Kate and Keith asked for someone else's part to be louder. This exemplifies how the band saw themselves at the time as being part of a single organism. As Blackwell said, "It's strange, but they don't have an obvious leader. Most bands have someone who seems to become the spokesman. But not them."[30]

Over time, the band came to appreciate the album's sound. Kate is already on record calling Blackwell's production "genius," but even Keith eventually was able to, if not love the album's sound, at least accept it. "Now, I get it," he said in 2018, "and I like it, it's a document."[31]

The album was finished in either two or three weeks (accounts vary), and cost only $10,000 to make,[32] a pittance by major label standards at the time. This suggests Gary Kurfirst got a good deal for the band, and was able, for now, to avoid any accusations of impropriety.

Warner executives flew in during the recording session to discuss the album art. They paid Keith Bennett $200 for the rights to the band's logo he had designed—the same logo that had earned him an F in his UGA art class.[33] To date, that logo has adorned every album the band has released.

For the album cover, the label wanted to use the photo George Dubose had made into posters. Tony Wright, Island record's creative director, was editing the photo with Dubose when Wright offered him $750 for the rights. Dubose "quickly calculated [the offer] as five weeks of my present pay," and said yes. According to Dubose, Wright "hated the band," which is why he was credited under the pseudonym "Sue Ab Surd."[34] The album cover is now part of the collection at the Museum of Modern Art, credited to Wright with no mention of George Dubose at all.

Back in New York

While the band was recording at Compass Point, things in NYC continued to move fast. An Atlanta friend of the B-52s named Anita Sarko showed up at Mudd Club asking for a job as a DJ. After she gatecrashed an uptown party for The Who and introduced herself to Steve Maas, he put her on Monday nights.[35]

Club 57 began hosting its own theme parties that suggested a B-52s influence. According to critic Simon Reynolds, the parties "distilled a whole new sensibility from elements of pop art, drag, the trash aesthetic, and performance art."[36] Events such as reggae miniature golf, punk rock game shows, female wrestling, and The Model World of Glue (an excuse to sniff it, basically) gave the club a reputation around the city for kitschy goofiness. "The Mudd Club was a business, and Club 57 wasn't," recalled Haoui Montaug, a doorman at Hurrah. "It was more like a fun, drug-crazed clubhouse."[37] Added Kenny Scharf, "One of the things that strikes me about the club … is that there were no fixed identities. People were so fluid."[38]

Klaus Nomi was all the rage that year, having made a stunning debut at one of the New Wave Vaudeville nights at Irving Plaza the previous November. Originally from Berlin, Nomi combined opera with new wave, and his stage presence blurred the boundaries between man/woman and earthly/alien. His singing voice, an otherworldly falsetto, was so astonishing that people had to be reassured it wasn't a recording. The B-52s invited George Dubose to attend a Nomi show at Max's Kansas City, and he was blown away by what he saw. "Klaus belonged on a big stage. He was larger than life."[39] The singer appeared on TV Party, and backed up David Bowie on *Saturday Night Live*, before signing with RCA.

Athens

Back in Athens, people were following the B-52s' lead and starting to form their own bands. One of them was Pylon, started by UGA art students Randy Bewley and Michael Lachowski, who began the group as a sort of conceptual art project. Their goals were to form a band, play New York, get written about in the *New York Rocker*, and then break up.

Lachowski had been reluctant at first, feeling the "whole idea had been explored" by that point, but Bewley insisted. "The argument that he made," recalls Lachowski, "is that [the B-52s] had left town. And he said somebody has to step it up."[40] The pair enlisted drummer Curtis Crowe, who had hosted the B-52s' third show at his old house. Said Crowe of the band, "They went to New York and became instant successes. It looked so fun and easy. It was like, 'We can do this.'"[41] They got fellow art student Vanessa Ellison (nee Briscoe, later Hay) to sing. While the B-52s were back in town, visiting Athens before their album came out, they saw Pylon play a house party out in Oglethorpe County. "It was maybe our fifth show," says Vanessa. "I think they were all there. I'm pretty sure they were. Keith remembers it. Kate and Fred, though, were the ones that talked to us and said you have to go to New York. We'll help you."[42]

Pylon hastily recorded one of their practices on a boombox and gave a cassette to the B-52s, who brought the tape to Jim Fouratt at Hurrah. He flipped when we heard the tape, and asked a question many others would ask over the next several years about Athens, "What is it down there?"[43] He gave Pylon a list of bands that were coming to the club and asked who they wanted to open for. The band chose Gang of Four, an arty UK post-punk band whose records hadn't yet been released in the US but were huge in Athens thanks to Chapter III stocking import copies. Pylon borrowed a van for the long drive to NYC. Old B-52s friend, Glenn O'Brien, attended the show and raved about the band in *Interview*.

The success of the Rock Lobster single meant Danny Beard could continue putting out records. In 1979, DB Records released singles by Kevin Dunn and Pylon. A year later, Pylon didn't just appear in *New York Rocker*. They were on the cover. The B-52s may have left Athens, but as Vanessa says, "They had a lot of help themselves, so they were just passing it on down the line."[44]

Around this time, Bill Paul staged a GMOA exhibition of Michelangelo Pistoletto's work. The Italian artist came to Athens in February and fell in love with the town, particularly its thrift stores. "He was supposed to be here for two weeks," recalls Paul, "but he didn't leave for six months. He got involved with the community, students, and everybody. The longer he stayed, the madder everybody got." Pistoletto staged public art happenings in Athens, practicing his own version of the "trash aesthetic" by dumping junk and trash on the steps of the Clarke County courthouse. "The county commissioners voted to condemn the artwork and haul it off to the city dump," says Paul. However, Mayor Upshaw Bentley intervened, and announced Pistoletto could relocate the installation to City Hall, where he would be given the key to the city. Pistoletto's detritus art happenings culminated in a June trash parade. Paul remembers, "We got permits to march with poles of trash and people clamoring and making noise from Lyndon House all the way to the museum steps."[45] The parade went past Chapter III Records, where Chris Rasmussen recalls seeing a young art student named Michael Stipe in the crowd.[46]

Album Release; Critical Reception

On July 6, 1979, the band's first album, simply titled *The B-52's*, was finally released. Critics praised the album. John Rockwell raved about it in the *Times*, concluding, "This is an original musical experience, and will be fascinating to follow as it evolves."[47] Stephen Holden praised the "tense, post-primal" vocals in the *Village Voice*, as well as the songwriting. He also noted the band's Southern-ness, "a locale which probably accounts for their funkwise rhythm section,"[48] and finished his review by comparing them to Little Richard. "Their trash rock anthem squirming with animated sea creatures belongs squarely in the tradition of 'Tutti Frutti.'"[49]

But when critics attempted to define the B-52s, they spent most of their time emphasizing the ways the band was different from most rock bands. And in a rock world that valued qualities like authenticity, strength, and sincerity, the B-52s were more likely to be misunderstood and underappreciated. The qualities that had made the band unique and contributed to their stratospheric rise now began to marginalize them. Holden called *The B-52's* "a superb exercise in camp nostalgia." And though he quickly added, "I think it's more than that,"[50] most critics didn't look any deeper. Every article about the band used variations on camp, retro, and trash to describe them. Because Fred's voice didn't fit the archetype of a classic rock & roll front man, and because Kate and Cindy were two women playing instruments, the B-52s didn't look like a traditional rock band. Therefore, critics concluded, they must not be. Even in 2018, Fred still seethed about these early reviews:

> People were saying, "They're camp" and shit like that. It's like, hello, camp means you don't know what you're doing, that you're funny 'cos you're ridiculous. All our stuff, we knew what we were doing. We were a band with a sense of humour, and a lot of uptight, probably straight, white guys didn't get it.[51]

One can't help wondering if the "straight, white guys" Fred was talking about might have felt uncomfortable, consciously or otherwise, dealing with some of Fred's more overtly sexual lyrics (*Put on the lifeguard*, indeed), and the open secret of the band's diverse sexuality. Homosexuality was still considered taboo in the public sphere, which limited how openly writers could talk about it and what kind of language they could use. As a result, words like camp and kitsch functioned as a kind of code, signaling the existence of non-heteronormative elements within the band without explicitly acknowledging them. Regardless of a writer's intentions, the result simultaneously painted the band as different while not allowing them the full power of that difference. Even worse, this kind of thinking took away the band's agency. Some reviewers were even openly contemptuous of the band. A writer at *Stereo Review* called the band fey, before concluding, "I think I prefer my *Ride the Wild Surf* straight."[52]

The retro tag was often unfairly applied as well. Writing in *Creem*, Billy Altman compared the B-52s to the Ramones, but only noting that both bands wrote about the beach.[53] It's a shame Altman didn't pursue the comparison further, because the two bands are less different than he assumes. Both dressed in retro clothes rooted in late 50s/early 60s America. In fact, the Ramones adhered even more rigidly to their uniform of leather jackets, jeans, and converse sneakers. Both bands wrote funny absurdist lyrics about pop culture and suburbia, and both bands' music was rooted in an energetic minimalism. In "53rd and 3rd," the Ramones even had a song on their debut album about male prostitution that was far more explicitly homosexual than anything the B-52s were singing about. Yet, even as the Ramones dressed like Fonzie from Happy Days, they were allowed to pass as an authentic rock band in ways the B-52s couldn't—the first band's idiosyncrasies perceived as a reason to take them seriously, the second band's a reason to not take them seriously at all.

Critics also struggled with the B-52s' combination of high and low art. Though the technique is a fundamental tenet of postmodernism, the term postmodern wouldn't come into popular usage until after the publication of Jean-François Lyotard's *The Postmodern Condition* in 1979, the same year that the B-52s' debut album came out. Yet, the band members were all familiar with Andy Warhol, whose pop art paintings in the 60's had deliberately blurred distinctions between high and low art. Although they weren't the first artists to do so, the B-52s exemplified aspects of postmodernism before such a term was common currency. The B-52s' postmodernism was instinctive; it was felt, or maybe received, by growing up in an era that was, in many ways, already postmodern without calling itself as such. Instead, most critics settled for describing the band's aesthetic as trash.

Theo Cateforis discussed the embedded classism in the use of the word trash in his 2011 book *Are We Not New Wave?*

> The trash aesthetic hinted at a social inequality, one that amplified the trash appearances and culture of the lower classes. It is telling, for example, that critics commonly imagined Cindy Wilson's and Kate Pierson's costumes as some part of a working-class parody, describing them as "manicurists" and "waitresses."[54]

Critics assumed the B-52s couldn't be part of the working class, but two members of the band, Cindy and Fred, had waited tables for a living. Ricky and Keith worked at a bus station, and Kate and Cindy also worked in a factory. Of the five, only Kate had a college degree. Fred and Ricky were college dropouts, and none of the band had much in the way of career options. Shortly after the release of the first album, when Fred was asked about the band's motivations, he expressed a typical working-class definition of success. "We want … financial security. We've all had terrible jobs, bumming around."[55]

Cateforis also observed how the band members were "more connected with Athens's local working class than its transient collegiate culture."[56] While this ignores their social connections to the art school, those connections may have also bred an inferiority complex within the band members. In early interviews, they were quick to shut down writers who wanted to ascribe an intellectual interpretation to their music, even if doing so meant denying the very real self-awareness and brainpower that had gone into creating it.

If the B-52s didn't want to play the role of serious artists, critics were happy to take them at face value, even going so far as to infantilize the band. Carson talked in his *Rolling Stone* review about teenagers and pajama parties, Holden deemed the band "defiantly nonserious" and dropped the phrase "kiddie-show space travel" into his discussion of There's a Moon in the Sky.[57] Even Rockwell described Kate and Cindy as "cute," and the music as "innocent, bouncy."[58] Critics picked up on the early 60s beach party movie references in Rock Lobster and lazily applied the sexlessness in those movies to the band itself. Altman went so far as to imagine the band's mom—he apparently believed they all had the same mother—giving them "plenty of lemonade and tuna fish sandwiches."[59] But *The B-52's* was an album made by adults, filled with overtly sexual lyrics and written from an adult perspective.

Fan Response

Critics may have struggled to fully understand the B-52s, but ordinary listeners understood the album perfectly. *The B-52's* struck a chord with disaffected adolescents of all kinds, but particularly with people navigating their own sexual awakening.

Aaron Fricke was a high school student in Rhode Island when the album was released. After his school refused to let him and his boyfriend attend prom, he decided to sue the school. Fricke won the case, and it is still considered a LGBTQ+ milestone.[60] In 1981, he titled his coming-of-age memoir *Reflections of a Rock Lobster*.

To a sizeable number of listeners, the science-fiction themes running throughout the album didn't make the band wacky or kooky. It reflected their actual lives. Ideas we associate with science-fiction or space travel—isolation, loneliness, alienation, disorientation—apply equally well to adolescence. Science-fiction writer Ursula K. Le Guin once said, "What I do in my fiction is talk about the so-called future. But it's really a way of looking at the right-now .... It is just looking at the present from a different angle."[61] The same applies to the B-52s. The B-52s used the subject of outer space to comment on social hierarchies and the feeling of difference here on earth. In doing so, they were able to make political statements, but in a way so subtle that most critics missed it entirely. The fact that so many fans heard the band's subversiveness clearly and connected so deeply with *The B-52's* on an emotional level that escaped critics, speaks volume about the limits of music criticism in the late 1970s.

The Album

Planet Claire fades in slowly. The gradual increase in volume feels like a signal from a distant planet slowly being tuned in. A Morse code pattern on Kate's keyboard implies a message is being communicated, but what is the message? What is this planet called Claire? We learn that the citizens of Planet Claire are immortal (*no one ever dies there*), and that they value the body over the intellect (*no one has a head*). The song is about the difficulty of communication and the frustration of being misunderstood. The most dramatic moment in the song happens after Fred lists off the false things people say about the song's protagonist, then screams in his angriest voice *WELL SHE ISN'T!* It's no wonder misunderstood adolescents connected so strongly with the album.

The B-52's then slams into its fastest song. The lyrics of 52 Girls are breathtakingly straightforward. These are the girls of the USA. They can be found in one of two places, either at the beach or in New York City. That's it. The lyrics were co-written by Athens legend Jeremy Ayers, who explained, "There were never actually 52 girls in the song. It was really long and went on and on, so it had to be shortened."[62] The song only mentions 23, or 24, depending on whether you count "Tina Louise" as two separate entities or the name of the actress who played Ginger on Gilligan's Island. The first name in the song, Effie, was likely chosen in honor of Effie Matthews, who presided over Athens' most notorious brothel until the town closed it in 1974. It makes more sense to imagine the title referring to a club, or a gang, The "52" Girls.

52 Girls is the first of several songs that contain lists, the others being Dance This Mess Around (a list of dances), Rock Lobster (underwater sea life), and There's a Moon in the Sky (planets). The themes of exploration on *The B-52's* are countered by specific examples of scarcity and limits. A decade earlier, Wilson Pickett had sung of a land of 1000 dances, but in 1979 there are only 16 dances. In an era with gasoline in short supply, the low-mileage Plymouth Satellite driven by the unnamed visitor from Planet Claire feels almost like an act of rebellion, if not outright decadence.

52 Girls is also the first of two consecutive songs on the album that speed up as the band heads into the second verse. Rather than being a weakness, it's a strength in the band's playing, and demonstrates how well they listened to each other. During their 1979 sessions for *London Calling*, producer Guy Stevens famously told the Clash that "all great rock and roll speeds up."[63] Rolling Stones songs are notorious for their changes in tempo, what Bill Janovitz, in his examination of *Exile on Main Street*, called "a looseness, a human element that makes them sound funky."[64] Because the Stones are rock and roll legends, their sloppiness becomes part of their story, one more aspect of the band's charm. Despite playing a tighter and faster version of that "looseness," the B-52s are almost universally regarded as inferior musicians. Even though both bands filtered similar influences (mainly Southern, mainly Black) through their own sensibilities, the Stones' pastiches of mid-60s soul are considered more

authentic than the B-52s' Motown/Stax-infused Dance This Mess Around. Is it just because the B-52s song mentions a type of cheese?

Dance This Mess Around's power is rooted in its slow buildup, the way Cindy takes her time before she explodes. When she appends the *think it over* line with her own *roll it over in your mind*, it's the first line in the song that doesn't sound borrowed from an old 60s song. The break from tradition seems to spur her vocals from traditional soul a/la Dusty Springfield into a broken screaming place that few singers had reached at that point in rock or soul. More than one critic compared her performance in this song to Patti Smith, but there is more vulnerability and heat in Cindy's voice than the cooler, tougher Smith brought to her songs. The third time she sings *Why don't you dance with me?* Cindy breaks the melody into something simultaneously more raw and melodic. It's an audacious choice, and Fred and Kate appear to suddenly turn the heartbreak into a party. They don't even have time to do all 16 dances before Cindy starts to feel better.

Rock Lobster shatters the vibe. It opens with a scene right out of *Un Chien Andalou*, with a man's ear lobe falling off into the ocean. Or maybe it's a David Lynch movie, though his film *Blue Velvet*, which also used the image of a severed ear to set the mood, wouldn't come out until 1986.

The party happening in Rock Lobster is a very different party from Dance This Mess Around. It's impossible to tell whether people are enjoying themselves or are terrified. In an interview, Aaron Fricke said he saw the song as "a metaphor for growing up gay: being isolated and under pressure at the bottom of the abyss and hiding under a hard shell. And rock lobsters have no claws, so they have no way to fight back."[65] Fred's aggressive disruption of language is one means of fighting back, and the song, right down to its title, contains a series of free-associative puns that wouldn't be out of place in *Finnegans Wake*, or a Marx Brothers routine. In their 1978 examination, *Upon the Pun*, Hammond and Hughes observed the liberating quality of wordplay, how "puns that free language free the man."[66] Because puns demonstrate what is unstable in language, they also destabilize our ideas about what is fixed in society.

Rock Lobster describes a liminal space, a blurring area where traditional notions about identity and hierarchy become unfixed. The song's setting is a beach, a place that is neither entirely water nor entirely land. This chaos causes everything to be thrown into flux. This can be frightening, but it can also be a means of liberation. Victor Turner wrote extensively about how liminal spaces function in societies, and observed how, "One's sense of identity dissolves to some extent, bringing about disorientation, but also the possibility of new perspectives."[67] Turner added that these environments bring participants "into close connection with deity or with superhuman power, with what is, in fact, often regarded as the unbounded, the infinite, the limitless."[68] One can hear all of this happening in the chaotic ecstasy of Rock Lobster's closing minute.

Nothing in the world of Rock Lobster is what it seems. The perspective switches back and forth from sand to ocean seemingly at random. Gender boundaries dissolve (*boys in bikinis/girls in surfboards*). Animals no longer behave according to the laws of nature—jellyfish are walking, sea robins are flying. There's a catfish chasing a dogfish, an inversion of the standard dog-chases-cat scenario. Suddenly a bikini whale shows up—or as it's written on the album's lyric sheet, a BIKINI WHALE!—and the song explodes into yet another layer of intensity. All that's left now is for Fred to chant the words *rock lobster* over and over as Kate sings a siren song in the distance.

As we will see going forward, the B-52s seem to have a fascination with these kinds of liminal spaces. Even Planet Claire mentions *3:30 in the morning*, a time that is neither night nor day, when the barrier between individual days becomes permeable.

Lava has an over-the-top sexuality that is—like so much sexuality in rock and soul—completely ridiculous and yet somehow not ridiculous at all. Cindy's verse takes the song into a darker, more disturbing direction. *My love may be as high as the highest volcano* is a sexuality brag worthy of the greatest bluesman, but Cindy's man has the power to give her a mean look and make her feel so cold that the only thing able to make her feel better is his "hot lava." Kate, on the other hand, has her own lava to deal with. *I gotta lotta lava love locked up inside me.* Taken with Fred's line *My love's a lava bomb / Knock you in the head*, it's hard not to interpret the song as being about both male and female ejaculation. In fact, taken at face value, Lava turns into a song about a hyper-ejaculatory ménage-à-trois. Five years after the release of *The B-52's*, UK radio would ban Frankie Goes To Hollywood's Relax in part for placing an emphasis on the word *come*, but nobody seemed to notice the lyrics of Lava. However, the song was clearly understood by fans, which speaks to a certain genius for subversion that is quintessentially B-52s. But then, as nonconformists living in the South, the ability to communicate their sexual desires through subtext and metaphor would have been necessary for their pleasure *and* their survival.

Following his eruption, Fred says he's going to go jump in a crater. The girls, nonplussed, simply say *See you later.* What do they care? They still have each other.

After a song about outer space (Planet Claire) and two songs about parties (Dance This Mess Around and Rock Lobster), we finally get a song about a party in space: There's a Moon in the Sky (Called the Moon). The party in outer space also becomes a liminal zone, populated by guests both real (the Van Allen Belt) and not (Kryptonite). The song is one of their most generous, a song of reassurance that cemented the band's connection to their fans. It contains what may be the key message of the album, that there are others like you. Novelist Clifford Chase chose to write about *The B-52's* in *Heavy Rotation*, an anthology of writers on the albums that changed their lives, and focused on this song in particular. Chase wrote, "Fred assured me that if I felt like a misfit, there were, in fact, 'thousands of others like you! Others like you!' and since he didn't specify what those others were, I didn't have to be afraid."[69]

After two mid-tempo songs, the intensity of Hero Worship arrives with a shock and a rush. Keith's kick drum sounds massive. The lyrics were written by Athens friend Robert Waldrop, who met Keith and Ricky at a Captain Beefheart concert back in 1971. Yet the decisions Cindy (who sings the song unaccompanied by Fred or Kate, the only solo vocal on the album) makes to emphasize certain words and phrases does as much to create the song's meaning as the words written on the paper.

Hero Worship refutes every claim critics have ever made about the band. It's their darkest song, one that tells a story of power and obsession.

The story is relatively clear. There is a "he," a hero who has died, and an "I" who worships him and tries to revive him. It could be the tale of a groupie, or maybe just a fan. But what is straightforward on paper becomes chaos in the performance. Cindy's singing explodes any semblance of meaning as she refuses the role that's been written for her as the victim. Instead, she chooses to strut through the song with a confidence and cockiness that negates the lyrics as she sings them. By singing with anger, with mockery, with resentment, and with rapaciousness, the intensity of her desire reduces the hero until he almost ceases to exist.

Punctuated by staccato bursts from Ricky, Kate plays the main ascending riff on guitar increasing the tension to almost unbearable levels. There is no time for the listener to contemplate anything. Every time Cindy sings a line, the ground shifts underneath your feet. By the time she screams,

God give me his soul, Cindy doesn't sound like a fan; she sounds like Mephistopheles, coming to collect her debt.

Cindy's shout of *I deserve it!* doesn't even appear in the printed lyrics. In the last minute of the song, Cindy and the band ascend into glossolalia, to a place where desire becomes primal and all language is inadequate. Hero Worship is the kind of song that, when it ends, the listener sits there dumbfounded, wondering what just happened.

After the drama of Hero Worship, 6060-842 feels like a chance for the listener to catch their breath. The song follows in a long line of "phone-number" songs such as Wilson Pickett's "634-5789 (Soulsville)" and the Marvelettes' "Beechwood 4-5789." 6060-842 takes the genre in a smuttier direction though, placing the phone number on the wall of a bathroom. We all remember the apocryphal playground story about a number written in a bathroom stall that a boy could call "for a good time," presumably with a female. Here, the band inverts the gender norms of that story in every direction. In 6060-842, a woman named Tina calls the number on the wall, with the gender of the person on the other end of the line going unmentioned. In the gay community, bathrooms have long played a prominent role in cruising, including people's phone numbers being written on walls. When Tina doesn't get an answer, she calls the operator who informs her the number's been disconnected, which the singers repeat in unison. This serves as an extension of the theme of connection running through the album. It isn't enough to leave your phone number, you also need to be there when the person reaches out to you.

The album closes with a cover of Petula Clark's 1965 hit Downtown. "Cindy just came up with it and started to do it one day at practice," said Ricky of the song's origin. "It was an instant song."[70] They don't so much cover the song as use it as a jumping off point, not unlike Patti Smith's "Gloria" on her 1975 album *Horses.* The B-52s' version omits entire verses and adds or changes words as Cindy sees fit. She doesn't bother with the lines in the original about worries and gentle hands; she's already imagining all the cool stuff *she's* going to do. Unlike Petula, Cindy's friends are coming with her (Fred can be heard in the background shouting *I want a beer!*). After so many songs about disconnection, the album finally ends with an affirmation of friendship, and the idea that you can do anything you want if you have your friends beside you. This had been the story of the B-52s, and with Downtown closing out the album, it also becomes the story of *The B-52's.* Despite whatever misgivings the band had about the production, they had made an album that accurately, and thrillingly, told their story.

European Tour

Just three days after the album came out, they were in London to start a month-long European tour. Legendary British critic Nick Kent raved about their show in the *NME*, opening with praise for the two musician boys in the back:

> The B-52s are, above everything else, a dance band; a great dance band. This factor in their aural blitzkrieg is supplied by Keith Strickland—who is up there with Charlie Watts for straight ahead hyper-drive rock drumming—and Ricky Wilson, a superb rhythm guitarist utilising several different tunings but still slicing riffs and chord progressions that sound like Keith Richards on four-wheel drive crossed with former Magic Band guitarist Zoot Horn Rollo. They provide a beat so fearsomely gorgeous that if your feet fail to respond, then you're dead.[71]

He goes on to compare the band to their beloved Captain Beefheart three more times, before concluding, "the sheer unfettered joyous ingenuity of the B-52s sound had everybody on the dance-floor. It's hard for me to recall leaving a concert more elated."[72]

Jon Savage, his *Melody Maker* counterpart, was less impressed. Divorced from many of the band's US cultural touchstones, Savage could only helplessly wonder about the album, "Why do all these new American groups come on like cartoons?"[73] A *Melody Maker* feature that same month suggested Fred had read the review and wasn't pleased. "Fred becomes mildly tetchy about being called a 'Cartoon.' He regards the term as meaning 'something totally fake—an interpretation that I'd never intended. I wouldn't call it a cartoon—that's sort of insulting.'"[74] Fred preferred the word surreal. It seemed like no matter how hard the band tried to explain themselves, they were still being misunderstood. The band played shows in Paris, in Amsterdam (Cindy wore a Mondrian-inspired dress for the occasion), in Hamburg (just like The Beatles!), in Liverpool (even more just like The Beatles!). They played all over the UK, including the one-day-to-be-famous Factory club in Manchester.

The album reached #22 in the UK, higher than that year's Talking Heads album *Fear of Music*, and Rock Lobster reached the UK Top 40, again eclipsing the commercial success of Gary Kurfirst's other band. The B-52s were beginning to, in the parlance of the industry, cross over. No less a rock icon than John Lennon—then five years into a self-imposed retirement from the music business—had his life changed when he heard

Rock Lobster. "I was at a dance club one night in Bermuda" said Lennon, telling the story a year later. "I suddenly heard 'Rock Lobster' by the B-52's for the first time. Do you know it? It sounds just like Yoko's music, so I said to meself, 'It's time to get out the old ax and wake the wife up!'"[75]

In October 1980, Lennon would release a new album, a collaboration with Ono called *Double Fantasy*. Tragically, that December he would be shot and killed by a deranged fan. One has to wonder what Lennon thought of Hero Worship. More ominously, one wonders if Lennon's assassin heard the song, and what he—someone who, at least in part, killed John Lennon to be freed from his obsession—thought of it.

At the end of August, the B-52s set out on a six-week US tour opening for Talking Heads in theaters around the US. Keith Bennett was now in charge of tuning and stringing (and re-stringing) Ricky's guitars, which had become an arsenal, each one with its own unique tuning and sound. Though most guitarists use strings starting around .011 gauge, Ricky chose strings that were significantly thicker, presumably to attack them without breaking them. "The lightest string he used was .018," remembers Bennett. "He used .058, .048, super thick strings, extra heavy pick."[76]

A week into the tour, the band headlined two nights at Irving Plaza. Keith Bennett recalls the first night. "Cindy and I were throwing flowers out the window of the dressing room down on the sidewalk below. Moe [Slotin] was like, 'Look, here's the thing. There's no down time in rock and roll.'"[77] There had been plenty of down time nine months earlier, when the B-52s played the same venue as part of the Nova Convention, but the band was now becoming part of a different rock and roll world.

John Rockwell previewed the Irving Plaza shows for the *Times* in a nearly full-page feature subtitled "How the B-52's cope with the success trap." In the first paragraph, he astutely pointed out the challenges ahead of the band:

> A career in rock music can be problematic. A band gets discovered in a club, records a first album, and if it doesn't watch out, it's projected abruptly into the big time. Critics set up expectations, and suddenly the band is playing in concert halls before show-me audiences and touring so hard and so fast that its members don't have time to write new songs. Then they're thrown back into a recording studio, turn out an inferior second album and discover to their astonishment that they're already regarded as has-beens, a novelty whose time has passed.[78]

Rockwell added, "There are ways out of this trap, of course, and the B-52's may be one group smart enough to succeed." Over the course of the article, he vacillates between optimism and skepticism as Kate worries about the band's inability to write new songs. "We just haven't had any stable place to work. In Georgia, we all had jobs, and since then we've been living in hotels, on the move." She said the band had decided to move into a house together in upstate New York where they would be able to resume writing and rehearsing. "I'm really looking forward to that house," Kate said wistfully.[79]

It would be three months before they got there. The night after the Irving Plaza shows they were in Nashville, then the next night in Atlanta (without Talking Heads this night, supported by The Brains and Pylon). New Orleans, back with Talking Heads. A night off. Houston. A night off. Two nights in Dallas. Two nights in Austin. An entire day's driving. Two nights in San Francisco. A night in Palo Alto. A night in Berkeley. Two nights in Los Angeles. On and on along the west coast through September and into October.

According to Bennett, the job was turning out to be harder than anyone had expected:

> Traveling and playing every day is hard work .... Even if you're sick, you've gotta sell it. What was amazing to me was to see them in every place, especially on those early tours when you'd play some club, the local opening act would come in and look at their gear, and just be disparaging. "Why is he setting his drum up that way? Look at these toys. Where's the bass rig?" And then they'd come out and just rock the house.[80]

There were glamorous moments, though. Bennett recalls seeing billboards on the Sunset Strip of B-52s and Talking Heads album covers, but there were also moments when everyone was in genuine danger:

> There was a death threat called in at a club. "When the B-52s hit the stage," the caller said, "two of them are dead." Doors had already been open a while, so the police had to evacuate everybody, including the staff, out into the cold while they searched the place with dogs. And then they searched everybody going back in. There were a few other similar, though not as ominous, threats along the way that tour. All in the Midwest.[81]

It's possible the differences that made the band so appealing to NYC audiences presented a danger in the less enlightened parts of America. In this light, the band's on-stage appearance can be seen as a form of protection. A *Trouser Press* feature the following year saw the writer note that Kate and Cindy wanted to be photographed with their wigs on "lest they become too easy to spot offstage." Fred added that he had grown a mustache for the same reason. "You just grow one and people don't recognize you. None of us are out to be seen or chased."[82]

A two-page feature about the band appeared in *Rolling Stone.* They weren't on the cover yet—this week it was Jimmy Buffett. A couple of pages before the B-52s article, a story about the demise of Macon's Capricorn Records, home of southern rock bands like the Allman Brothers and the Marshall Tucker Band, signaled a changing of the guard in Georgia music. Scott Isler met the band in New York, where they were temporarily living at Carmelita's Reception House on 14th Street.[83]

Sitting in a Warner Bros. office, Ricky "picks at his salad," while he and Keith tell stories about growing up in Athens. "I had bricks thrown at me," shares Keith. When asked about their sudden success, Fred says, "Our parents are more excited than we are." Isler concluded the feature by asking the band what they would do "if the dream suddenly ended." The weariness in their answers suggested the hard work was starting to catch up with them:

> Cindy would go back to waitressing; Rick [*sic*] to his job selling tickets at a bus station; Kate to raising goats; and Fred "would have a farmhouse somewhere and say, 'See ya'—or I'd be at the bottom of the Oconee River."[84]

Thankfully, the band had most of the next month off, with the time broken up by shows around the eastern seaboard.

By November, the B-52s were back in Europe again. The album had already sold 40,000 copies in the UK, and the 2000 tickets for their London shows sold out immediately.[85] Then they headed to Japan, where the band worried how their name would translate. In an effort to help, Warner Brothers preemptively distributed promotional postcards featuring two pictures: on the left was a bouffant with "THIS" clearly written underneath it, while on the right was a bomber with "NOT THIS" underneath. It wasn't a problem. Kate laughed when she saw that a Japanese fan had "taken the [album] cover and put 'B-52's Attack Japan,' and had an airplane dropping from the sky! They completely got it and played on the pun."[86] Confronted with a more reserved audience than they were used to, Fred learned the Japanese phrase for "Stand up and dance!" A few people did as he asked, but Kate later noticed an elderly man sleeping in the front row.[87] As for Keith and Ricky, they combed the shops looking for a new portable cassette player made by Sony called a Walkman.[88]

After a December 4th show in Honolulu, the band finally moved into their new house—an hour's drive north of NYC in a small town called Mahopac (pop. 8000). The band chose the remote location at Gary Kurfirst's urging, and because they had been told NYC was out of their price range.[89] This raises an obvious question: If NYC was affordable for so many musicians and artists—most of whom weren't bankrolled by a multinational corporation and selling hundreds of thousands of records—why wasn't the city affordable for the B-52s?

Keith Bennett joined the band in Mahopac, along with old friend, Robert Waldrop, who served as caretaker while the band was away. Waldrop also became the band's driver when they were in town, as Mahopac was so isolated it wasn't on either commuter rail line into the city. The only vehicle they had was the blue van Ricky and Cindy's father had lent them, which the band purchased outright when the move up north became final. Kate and Brian were now divorced, though the relationship had begun to deteriorate around the time the band formed.[90]

Cindy recalled moving in. "Ricky was especially excited to have Lake Mahopac just behind the house; he'd have a place to dock his new sailboat."[91] But it would be a couple more years before Ricky got his sailboat. There wasn't much time for sailing—or writing songs. *The B-52's* left the *Billboard* 200 just before Christmas after four months on the chart, and label and management wanted another album as soon as possible. But even when the band did nothing, things still kept happening. Rock Lobster was now climbing the charts in other countries, and the band got asked to appear on *Saturday Night Live*. They were quickly becoming one of the hottest and most talked about new bands in the world. As 1979 came to a close, the B-52s were on fire; they were positively neon.

Notes

1. Scrudato, "BlackBook Interview."
2. Williams, "Glenn O'Brien," A23.
3. Hager, *Art after Midnight*, 63.
4. Ibid.
5. Keith Bennett in conversation with authors, November 8, 2019.
6. Stein, *Siren Song*, 155.

7. Brown, *Party*, 93.
8. Goldman, "Gary Kurfirst."
9. You know what I mean.
10. Carson, *New York Rocker*, July 1979, 4.
11. Brown, *Party*, 93.
12. Ibid.
13. maureenmc2000, "Remembering Lester." This book's authors, one of whom is from Lester's hometown of El Cajon, California, believe Bangs was referring to a cosmic sense of justice rather than any kind of critical rebuke. To the best of our knowledge, he never wrote about the band before his death in 1982.
14. Carson, *New York Rocker*.
15. Ibid.
16. Redbullmusicacademy.com, "Tom Tom Club."
17. Garykurfirst.com, "Gary Kurfirst." Stories like this do little to counter accusations that Blackwell was a colonialist exploiter of Jamaican music, or as reggae pioneer and sonic genius Lee Perry called him, a vampire.
18. 1300elmwood.buffalostate.edu, "Steve Rabolvsky."
19. Eldredge, "Dancing on the Tables." The quote is from a series of reminiscences by people from the late 70s scene in Athens and Atlanta that Maureen McLaughlin guest-edited.
20. Sigerson, "B52s on Target," 5.
21. "Tom Tom Club," lecture.
22. Rambali, "The B-52s."
23. Sexton, *The B-52's Universe*, 50.
24. Uncredited Author, *The Mojo Collection*, 423.
25. Ibid.
26. Harris, "Kate Pierson."
27. Ibid.
28. Rambali, "The B-52s."
29. Ibid.
30. Ibid.
31. Pennock, "The Making of …."
32. Ibid.
33. Sexton, *The B-52's Universe*, 45. It's safe to assume that neither Robert Croker nor Jim Herbert was teaching the class.
34. George Dubose works, "The B-52's."
35. Lawrence, *Life and Death*, 24.
36. Reynolds, *Rip It Up*, 264.
37. Hager, *Art After Midnight*, 72.
38. Magnuson and Scharf, "Club 57."
39. George Dubose works, "Klaus Nomi."

40. Michael Lachowski in conversation with authors, May 16, 2019.
41. Fletcher, *Remarks*, 15.
42. Vanessa Briscoe Hay in conversation with authors, 4/25/19.
43. Brown, *Party*, 111.
44. Ibid.
45. Bill Paul in conversation with authors, May 19, 2019.
46. Chris Rasmussen in conversation with authors, July 29, 2019.
47. John Rockwell, "The Pop Life," *New York Times*, C15, July 13, 1979.
48. Holden, "The B-52s," 60. Holden admitted he hadn't seen the band in person, so he may not have realized the band didn't have a traditional rhythm section (i.e. there's no bass player). Or it may be that Kate's keyboard bass parts were so convincing that it didn't matter to him.
49. Ibid.
50. Ibid.
51. Tom Pennock, "The Making of …."
52. Simels, "The B-52's," 43.
53. Altman, "Hep Cats," 52.
54. Cateforis, *New Wave?* 107.
55. Lott, "The B-52s."
56. Cateforis, *New Wave?* 107.
57. Holden, "American Graffiti," 60.
58. Rockwell, "The Pop Life," C15.
59. Altman, "Hep Cats," 52.
60. GLAD, "Cases and Advocacy."
61. Nurse, "Ursula K. Le Guin."
62. Ibid.
63. Popoff, *The Clash*, 82. Stevens said this after the band had just finished recording Brand New Cadillac, which the band wanted to redo because each verse had gotten progressively faster and faster. Stevens insisted they use that version. In the opinion of this book's authors, the ever-increasing tempo is the best thing about the song, coupled with Strummer's out-of-control, frothing-at-the-mouth vocal take, though one could argue the latter is being inspired by the former.
64. Janovitz, *The Rolling Stones' Exile*, 45. Examples abound, but "Honky Tonk Women" and "Sympathy For the Devil" clearly demonstrate the band's ability to subtly change tempos as a unit. We would also urge readers to listen closely to John Bonham of Led Zeppelin and Stewart Copeland of the Police. Both drummers notoriously sped up, and they each appear regularly in any list of Top Ten Rock Drummers.
65. Brinklow, "Rock Lobster secrets," 429.
66. Hammond and Hughes, *Upon the Pun*, 47.
67. Turner, *The Ritual Process*, 81.

68. Turner, "Betwixt and Between," 98. Turner's entire essay is fascinating to read as a companion piece to Rock Lobster, given how much of the B-52s' story involves these kinds of in-between states.
69. Chase, "Getting Warmer?" 150.
70. Sexton, *The B-52's Universe*, 153.
71. Kent, "The B-52s, Fashiøn."
72. Ibid.
73. Savage, "*B-52s* (Island)."
74. Birch, "Dance Parties," 17.
75. Cott, "John Lennon."
76. Keith Bennett in conversation with authors, November 8, 2019.
77. Ibid.
78. Rockwell, "Pop Life."
79. Ibid.
80. Keith Bennett in conversation with authors, November 8, 2019.
81. Keith Bennett's text message to authors, November 9, 2019.
82. Isler, "The Devil Went Down to Georgia," 26.
83. Isler, "The B-52's," 16.
84. Ibid.
85. Sexton, *The B-52's Universe*, 46.
86. Sexton, *The B-52's Universe*, 47.
87. Ibid.
88. Ibid.
89. Ibid.
90. Email correspondence with Keith Bennett, August 2022.
91. Sexton, *The B-52's Universe*, 47.

CHAPTER 6

Wild Planet

This is the weird thing about success. You work hard to achieve it, but it's when you become successful that you really work hard. It becomes this thing that you have to maintain and there is this feeling that you can't stop.[1]

—Cindy

On January 26, 1980, the B-52s made their US television debut on *Saturday Night Live* (*SNL*). They played Rock Lobster and Dance This Mess Around. It's hard to overstate how big *Saturday Night Live* was at the time. Tom Hanks recalled the show's early years as "the cultural phenomenon of the age. It was truly as big as the Beatles."[2]

Five years into its existence though, an air of exhaustion hung over the show. Creator Lorne Michaels said of this period, "I had been truly drained, just spent. I was just burnt out and emotionally very vulnerable."[3] The sketches from that season reflect Michaels' state. Most of them are tediously unfunny and seem to go on forever. The person booking musical guests was still on their game though. Three weeks before the B-52s appeared, Klaus Nomi and Joey Arias performed on the show with David Bowie. Other musical guests that season included cutting-edge acts like Blondie, Gary Numan, and The Specials (along with significantly less cutting-edge acts like Anne Murray and Chicago).

S. Creney, B. A. Herron, *The Story of the B-52s*,
https://doi.org/10.1007/978-3-031-22570-3_6

The band was so nervous it affected their performance. "We looked really animatronic because we were scared," said Kate, "but it came off as being this alien sort of attitude, which served us well, because people were like, 'Whoa, this is so weird.' But we were just shy and terrified."[4] Fred added, "[It] was nerve-racking. I was so sick to my stomach, but it went really well."[5] With their wild outfits and personalities, combined with their unusual music, the B-52s were like a bomb going off. In the normally subdued *SNL* audience, someone lets out an audible shout after Cindy screams *Why won't you dance with me!* the first time in Dance This Mess Around.

The performance made a big impression on a couple of pre-teens sitting at home. Both Kurt Cobain and Dave Grohl cited seeing the B-52s on *SNL* as a pivotal moment in their musical lives. The 12-year-old Cobain even drew a checkerboard pattern on his sneakers afterward to look more "new wave."[6] Eleven years later, those two kids, now in Nirvana with their friend Krist Novoselic, would appear on the show and stage their own insurrection against social and sexual norms when Grohl and Novoselic french-kissed during the closing credits.

The B-52s' appearance sent their album shooting back up the charts. Fred said, "Just that one appearance changed everything."[7] Artists like Sting, and even the curmudgeonly Frank Zappa, began raving about the band. "I saw the B-52's playing in New York several times and I really liked them," said the latter.[8] Chic's bass player Bernard Edwards also told an interviewer, "I love the B-52's."[9]

Wild

Less than three months after their *SNL* performance, the band returned to Compass Point in April to record their next album. Their time off hadn't been much of a vacation. While in Compass Point, the Rock Lobster single began climbing the charts in Australia and Canada, where it would eventually reach #3 and #1, respectively. Once they finished recording the album in May, they would be heading to both countries in June and July to capitalize on its success. Then, after the album came out in August, they would be on tour until the end of the year. It was a punishing schedule, and the resulting album, *Wild Planet*, reflects the energy around the band at this time. No wonder their working title was *Urgentisimo*.[10]

Despite the constant touring, the band had found time to write three new songs: Party Out of Bounds, Dirty Back Road, and Give Me Back My Man. Quiche Lorraine pre-dated the band's existence, originating from a Fred and Keith Bridge Mix collaboration back in Athens. The rest of the songs on what would become *Wild Planet* had been left over from the debut.

Co-produced by Brian Eno collaborator and Roxy Music producer, Rhett Davies, *Wild Planet* is the B-52s album that benefits the most from listening on headphones. Whereas the first album saw Chris Blackwell adhere as closely as possible to the band's natural sound, *Wild Planet* features more studio-based experimentation. "I'd always be experimenting with delays," Davies said of his production style, "just to create something more than the plain thing that was there."[11] The band was also credited as co-producer, something that wouldn't happen again until 2008s *Funplex*, suggesting they had greater involvement this time.

Give Me Back My Man is the clearest example of this difference. A processed swooshing guitar swells up at the beginning of each verse, and the mix is littered with electronic popping sounds. The unnatural compression on Keith's drums and the layers of Cindy's voice over the outro conspire to create an otherworldly ambience. This production style—both minimal and complex, natural and artificial—creates an ambiguous tension that allows for a deeper listening experience than the first album provided.

After a year of constant touring, the band's playing is more aggressive than it was on *The B-52's*. Kate's keyboard bass is relentless, pumping out 8th-notes so quickly it sounds like they're being fed through a sequencer. But live recordings from this period confirm Kate was actually able to play that fast. Her basslines are also more inventive and complicated, with Quiche Lorraine being an intricate and funky example.

Keith's drumming is a revelation. On Private Idaho, he breaks out a series of rolls and fills that would have been unimaginable a year earlier. Cindy's bongos, best heard on Party Out of Bounds, are high-velocity and highly precise. Fred even trades in his toy piano for a glockenspiel solo on Give Me Back My Man that is heavenly. Ultimately though, the album is a testament to the incomparable guitar-playing genius of Ricky Wilson. *Wild Planet* is their tightest, most musically accomplished album. It is also the last album to feature all five members playing together as a unit.

Planet

If *The B-52's* is a conceptual triumph, the band's second album is a musical one. It introduces an angrier, more serious side to the band. Maybe that red cover was more symbolic than people noticed at the time. The band's playful spirit still surfaces, but *Wild Planet* is a long way from camp. Moving away from the B-52s' retro-futurist stance, the feelings of disorientation and loneliness on *Wild Planet* are now more grounded in real-life situations. Even the sex is different. Where *The B-52's* sounded playful and flirty, *Wild Planet* sounds carnal and fueled by lust. *Wild Planet* is the B-52s at the height of their powers.

The album possesses a kind of mysterious alchemy. It has song after song about being in motion, and examines the idea from multiple perspectives. It has songs about the futility of travel, about searching, about yearning. About driving. It has so many songs about driving. Reckless driving. Going 90 miles an hour. Running around. The devil is in my car, and we're tearing tar.

The album opens with a nearly 15-second drone on Kate's keyboard bass accompanied by No Wave/Gang of Four atonal bursts from Ricky's guitar. If the B-52s are, as they claim, The World's Greatest Party band, then Party Out of Bounds is The World's Greatest Party Band's greatest party song. It captures the moment between transcendence and disaster, and Fred's opening shout of "SURPRISE!" puts us right in the middle of the scene. The band acts as both disruptor and conscience. Questions are asked (*Where's your icebox? What can you do to save a party?*), but no answers are given. Alternatives are suggested (*a spur of the moment scavenger hunt, be tactful when making the rounds*), possible ways to maybe calm the party down and put Dionysus back in his box, but nobody seems to be listening.

Of all their party songs, Party Out of Bounds is the one that best supports the multiple meanings of party—a political group, a celebration, a collection of individuals bound under a legal contract. The political subtext is acutely felt, 1980 being the year Ronald Reagan pulled the Republican Party even further to the right, creating a coalition of billionaires and Baptists that has affected the direction of the country ever since. Party Out of Bounds, in its sublimated terror and its hyperventilated warnings, sounds completely of its time.

After the delirium of Party Out of Bounds, Dirty Back Road takes its time. Mysterious and hypnotic, the song feels almost Can-like in its use of repetition and deliberate pace. Unlike his drumming on *The B-52's*, Keith resists the urge to speed up the tempo, using steadiness and restraint to heighten the tension. It also evokes the South, as detailed by LSU professor Michael B. Bibler:

> The rural back road, the expression of uncontrollable desire, and the Dukes-of-Hazzard-style reckless driving evoke the landscape of what is now sometimes called the Dirty South. Furthermore, the song's association of riding the back road with sex, and more specifically anal sex, anchors it in the history of queer sexualities in the region.[12]

Kate and Cindy sing the same set of lyrics twice, but they switch their harmonies each time, exchanging positions of top and bottom in a way that reinforces the song's explicit ideas about sexuality and flux, a fluidity again neatly described by Bibler:

> Active and passive roles circulate rapidly, making it unclear precisely who is the sports car and who is the road, whose foot is on the pedal and whose feet are in the air .... This roving orientation thus queers sex and gender even further, for the male-authored but female-voiced speaker with "sand in my hair" moves (back?) from feminine to masculine as s/he moves behind the implicitly male "you" to penetrate him.[13]

The fade-out suggests the song could keep going forever. The rising sound of cicadas at the end, a staple sound of the South, represents the way nature always rises up to have the last word—in our desire, and in our death.

Runnin' Around is another song about travel. This time the pace is frantic. Fred sings a line, *chasing rainbows in the mud*, that gracefully articulates the band's beauty-out-of-trash aesthetic. The line is even more evocative interpreted through the lens of the Rainbow flag. Designed for a San Francisco Gay Pride parade in 1978, the image was already on its way to becoming an iconic symbol of LGBTQ+ identity. Heard this way, Fred's frantic search for his "baby" takes on a more radical tone.

Give Me Back My Man hits even harder than Dance This Mess Around, its "heartbroken Cindy" counterpart from the previous album. Instead of limburger, the food images here are fish and candy. Cindy remembers how the song came together:

> Down in the Bahamas, in Nassau, Ricky and I kept going over the melody and rehearsing it and figuring out the lyrics. It was amazing how it slowly came together .... Fred wrote the lyrics and I came up with the vocal melody and added my style to it. Ricky and Keith put it together.

There is a jarring line about throwing divinity on the sand, which could refer to the Southern confection as well as a higher power. The double meaning created by merging godliness and sweetness is one more example of the deeper poetry happening on *Wild Planet*.

Private Idaho was another song with political undertones. Fred described it as being about "people going into themselves, going into their shells, not communicating ... going into your private self and not relating."[14] The radium clock in the song had sinister real-life meaning, according to Fred:

> In Athens, there was one of these factories where they would make radio dials, glow-in-the-dark clocks. Women would dip their paint brushes into the radium based paint, to paint the dials on the clocks. The women eventually got cancer from the paint and they had to discontinue making them.[15]

The factory, called Luminous Processes, Inc., operated from 1952 to 1978. It was located just off the main stretch of the Atlanta Highway. The company abandoned the site in 1980, and due to financial problems, never decontaminated the property. The EPA got involved in 1981 and decontaminated the site by removing more than 2400 drums of chemicals and tons of contaminated soil.[16] A McDonald's now occupies the area closest to the former contamination site.

The dangers on *Wild Planet* are more real, more truly dangerous, than they were on the first album. The piranhas in Rock Lobster are just products of Fred's hyperactive imagination, but the radium clocks in Private Idaho had real-world implications.

Side one of the album opened with Fred shouting *Surprise!* but side two opens with him shouting for help, and Fred doesn't sound like he is kidding. Devil In My Car was inspired by hearing evangelists on the radio. It's hard not to consider that some of those sermons may have been about the sinfulness of homosexuality, or being an intellectual, or being a feminist—all issues that would have implicated the B-52s. In the South, the specter of the devil is omnipresent. There were (and still are) a lot of people out there who would have believed the devil actually was in Fred's car, and that Fred would, quite literally, be going to hell. Rather than being silly, the song becomes a rebellious declaration of intent, a refusal to change one's perceived immorality no matter the consequences.

Quiche Lorraine's camp subject matter—and it doesn't get any campier, or more stereotypically late 70s gay, than a man out for a walk with his flamboyantly dressed poodle—is delivered in a style that's deadly serious. Fred pushes past the camp surface of the song's subject matter until his hysterical cries of abandonment become rooted in genuine feeling. Peter Singer's landmark animal rights book *Animal Liberation* was less than two years old when Fred wrote the Quiche Lorraine, which he has said is about animal liberation. But the song also touches on ideas about power, control, grief, and betrayal in any kind of relationship. When Quiche runs off with a bigger and stronger Great Dane at the end of the song, the protagonist sounds genuinely anguished, and the feeling of loss is palpable.

Strobe Light is so fast and almost-but-not-quite-out-of-control that it's nearly impossible to sit still when you hear it. The rushing freight-train rhythm only adds to the song's physicality. It's also fun and funny, and freaky and sexy. Fred's use of language like *let me* and *I wanna* emphasizes that the sex, in typical B-52s fashion, is consensual. Strobe Light also features one of Ricky's all-time great guitar solos, which lasts for 30 seconds as he constantly finds new patterns and rhythms.

Wild Planet ends with 53 Miles West of Venus, an understated track with a slow-burning loneliness reflected in its metaphor of space travel—the first time on the album we've left the earth. The lyrics—nothing more than the title repeated over and over—function as a mantra, a kind of trance induction. The music sounds like the chaos of the universe condensed to a single endless vibrating hum. Kraftwerk had a song called Europe Endless, but you can imagine 53 Miles West of Venus being titled Universe Endless. The song is also a group composition that they finished writing at Compass Point. Hearing what the B-52s were capable of when they functioned as a true collaborative group makes the ensuing years of fracture, and the unnecessary delegation of musical tasks, all the more heartbreaking.

53 is exactly one digit higher than the number in the band's name, and it sounds like something you might sing to yourself while trying to sleep on a bus somewhere between Wisconsin and Nebraska. In an odd coincidence, 53 miles is also the height, determined by engineer and physicist Theodore von Kármán, at which earth vehicles are considered to have entered outer space. For legal and political reasons, anything below the Kármán line is considered an aircraft, and anything above it is a spacecraft. As such, 53 Miles West of Venus finds the B-52s once again navigating a liminal boundary, this time between the atmosphere and the cosmos.

Australia; Heatwave; Central Park; Athens

After completing *Wild Planet*, the B-52s headed to Australia, where Rock Lobster had gone all the way to #3. The tour gave them their first real taste of pop stardom. "It was incredible," said Fred. "All red carpets and limos."[17] Cindy's dress fell off during a show. "It wasn't really that bad," quipped Keith, "nothing to see."[18] Which is exactly the kind of bad joke you'd make about someone you've known since they were 12 years old. The next month took the band to Canada, where Rock Lobster had reached #1. After a quick show in Montreal, they appeared at the Heatwave Festival outside of Toronto. Billed as the "New Wave Woodstock," the festival included Elvis Costello, The Pretenders, and Talking Heads.

The show featured the debut of the Talking Heads expanded nine-piece lineup. Since the previous year's *Fear of Music* tour ended, they had been holed up with Brian Eno crafting *Remain in Light*, generally acknowledged as the band's masterpiece. The festival was a real coup for Gary Kurfirst, as critics raved about both Talking Heads and the B-52s. The writer for *Creem* was especially ecstatic:

> The B-52's were the afternoon delight of the Heatwave Festival; looking nothing like the awkward people we'd seen in Detroit last spring, Cindy and Fred and Kate and Ricky and Keith got some 70,000 drunk, stoned kids on their feet and dancing. Cindy and Fred didn't stop moving, frugging or

> ponying, whatever the song called for—and all Kate had to do was jump out from behind her organ to dance, wearing a bright red miniskirt, to bring up the day's first roar from the crowd.[19]

Reported attendance ranged from 60,000 all the way up to 100,000, by far the largest audience any of the acts had played to, though Kate wasn't nervous this time. "I thought maybe everyone was on acid … you know, because it's a festival."[20]

Two days later, the band played Central Park at the Wollman Rink as part of the Dr. Pepper Festival. When Japanese New Wave band the Plastics had trouble getting through customs, the B-52s called Pylon and asked if they could open the show, which was starting in 36 hours. "We jumped in the van and drove straight to New York," recalls Vanessa Briscoe Hay. "We literally got there just in time to do the show. There was no way to communicate with anybody, so we just drove up to Central Park."[21] Bassist Michael Lachowski drove the van, and he picks up the story:

> We were driving around in Central Park, and we have no clue how to find this entrance to load out. And we were really getting late, and we were frazzled and terrified and excited and everything. We could see it. We just couldn't figure out where the right road was. The way I remember it is, I said, "I'm just going to go cross country." And we just jumped the curb and ran towards it.[22]

The band got there, set up, and had about 20 minutes before they went on. Vanessa was resting in a room filled with Ricky's guitars when he came in. "He sits down," says Hay, "picks up a guitar, and starts noodling around a little bit. I looked over at him and said, 'What's going on Ricky?' He said, 'there's too much hairspray in the other room.'"[23]

It was the biggest audience Pylon ever played to. Lachowski recalls, "It was in the big, giant realm, like 40,000 to 80,000."[24] *NME* journalist Vivien Goldman attended the show, and described "teenage girls weeping with emotion," during the B-52s' set, and people "crushed up against the rail."[25]

The B-52s' success had affected their hometown in other ways. Bill Paul noticed the influx of tourists suddenly coming to Athens trying to find their own way to turn trash into treasure:

> We used to go to the Potter's house and one or two junk places on Park Street to get art supplies. And then suddenly we couldn't go there anymore because art students were going there, and people from all over Europe and Japan, Asia, were coming with their guidebooks, stopping people on College Ave. and asking, "Where is the Potter's House?" They wanted to go to the Potter's House to get clothes to be chic and smart.[26]

By June 1980, the University decided it had seen enough of Bill Paul's antics at GMOA. "Virginia Trotter called me one day," says Paul. "She said, 'The Board of Regent's manual said the director of the art museum serves at my pleasure, and I am not pleased.'"[27] There had been warning signs. Besides conflicts with Lamar Dodd, the Carter Exhibition had prompted a phone call from UGA President Fred Davison, who angrily asked Paul, "What the hell is going on over there, boy?"[28] The Pistoletto situation hadn't helped either. "The [county] commissioners were condemning him," says Paul. "And I guess I got fired as a part of that. Lamar thought we were just going over the edge, and maybe we were. But it was important."[29] Paul still had his tenure to fall back on, and began teaching at the art school, where he would continue to make an impact.

Reception

Wild Planet was released on August 27, 1980, one day after the Central Park show. Critics were positive, but most failed to notice the differences between *The B-52's* and *Wild Planet*. Instead, most people compared it to the first album, and saw *Wild Planet* as an inferior copy. A *Village Voice* reviewer argued the albums were even similarly sequenced: both begin with a fade-in, the third song is a Cindy showcase, side one ends with a rocker, and so on.[30] The comparison falls apart from there, and the writer abandons the idea halfway through the review, but it shows how *Wild Planet* would be judged against the debut rather than considered as its own statement. The perception still exists today. Allmusic's review of the album says, "While *Wild Planet* is not the rarefied wonder their first platter is, it's still darn good."[31]

Because critics already knew half the songs on *Wild Planet* from the band's live set, it helped fuel the narrative that these songs were leftovers, outtakes from the first album that hadn't been good enough to make the cut. Their first album had been such a shock, something so totally new and unexpected, that the B-52s were punished for not being able to repeat the trick. Instead of being a reinvention, *Wild Planet* was a natural, organic evolution, but for most critics, that wasn't good enough.

The reaction seemed to rattle the band, as it introduced a new self-consciousness into the B-52s' creative process. Seeing themselves described as formulaic made them want to break that formula, but seeing their audience continue to grow also made them want to conform to those fans' expectations. It seems strange, and traditionally showbiz, for the B-52s to imagine their audience—who at that time were as radically free-spirited as any in the rock world—being so closed-minded. But having stumbled into commercial success beyond anything they ever dreamed of, the band's main concern now seemed to be that it might go away. This created a tension between their business and their art that they have never been able to fully resolve, and has continued to affect the band's business and creative decisions ever since.

US Tour

NME sent Vivien Goldman to New York to hang out with the band. She opened the feature by imagining herself at an Athens party with Kate and Cindy, complete with a British person's attempt to write in the Southern vernacular:

> Getting on for one a.m., and things are just too quiet, man, I mean it's D—U—L—L. Hey, Cindy, pass me some more punch. Wade mean, there's none left? Jeez, this town sucks. One lousy bowl of lousy punch, call this a party? Where else is there to go? Shit, I know there were more parties than this tonight, there has to be, it's Saturday isn't it? Well, isn't it?[32]

Goldman then depicts Kate and Cindy assaulting a skeezy guy at the party, with Kate as "the ringleader." It was unheard of for a UK music journalist to write fan fiction about the band they were covering, and it speaks volumes about how the B-52s inspired so much fascination and mythology about their Athens roots.

Back in the real world, Goldman spent time hanging around the Essex House Hotel with Cindy and Kate, watching soap operas. "The B-52's are not stupid people," observed Goldman, as Kate talked to her about parties:

> I don't think parties are an escape to make you ignore everything else … the more intense things get, the more intense the parties get. It's an outlet, especially if you're powerless, which a lot of people feel they are, politically.[33]

But the most noteworthy thing in the feature is Gary Kurfirst throwing "several screaming blue fits" at Goldman after he finds out that Cindy and Kate agreed to be photographed in their everyday clothes without wigs. This prompted Goldman to wonder whether Kurfirst truly believed in the band's music. "Does he doubt that it's what's in the grooves that count?"[34]

When *Wild Planet* was released in September 1980, the band's first album was still on the *Billboard* album charts after 49 weeks. *Wild Planet* debuted at #89, and both albums began climbing up the charts.[35]

On September 11, 1980, the B-52s kicked off three straight months of touring, supported by the Plastics. This time they would be headlining many of the same venues where, the year before, they had been opening for Talking Heads. The band were now selling t-shirts courtesy of old friend Chris Rasmussen, who says, "They called me up and said, 'Chris, do you want to do some shirts for our tour? Because the manager says we can't make any money [on them], he's not interested in dealing with it.'" Keith Bennett designed the artwork, and Rasmussen, who had been doing silk-screening in high school, leapt at the chance to travel with the band and sell the shirts. "They were in the center of [the new wave/punk thing]," says Rasmussen, "and every show they played was sold out, packed, people going berserk. The intensity and energy was just amazing."[36]

With two albums in the charts simultaneously, the B-52s were now attracting the attention of mainstream America. Iconic feminist magazine *Ms.* included them in a feature on women in rock. In addition to praising the lyrics as "a sexism-free stark-raving-sane combination of off-the-wall and right on," the article also featured a wonderful, feminist interpretation of Kate and Cindy's singing style:

> Vocals range from growly to very, very shrill, and on the way from one extreme to the other, they never manage to hit "mellow," "rich," "full," or any of the other conventional definitions of a "good voice." But like Bob Dylan, their nonsingerly voices express a lot of raw emotion. And I for one am relieved and pleased to finally hear nonexquisite *female* voices selling records.[37]

October saw the release of Pylon's first album, *Gyrate*, on DB Records. *Village Voice* and *New York Rocker* couldn't help comparing them to the B-52s, and in both cases, the writers preferred Pylon. As *Wild Planet* entered, the top 20, the B-52s weren't the coolest underground band in New York City anymore.

One Trick Pony

October also saw the release of *One Trick Pony*, a film written by and starring Paul Simon that featured the B-52s in a cameo role. Simon plays Jonah Levin, a boring washed-up 60s musician making bland 70s pop. Simon provided a soundtrack of bland 70s pop for the film, which was released under his own name, even though it's Jonah Levin who performs the songs in the movie.

It sounds like a vanity project, but it's hard to think of any vanity project that was less flattering to its star. And while the film's blurring of the line between fiction and reality causes all kinds of giddy meta-thrills for those in the know, *One Trick Pony* turned out to be the biggest commercial and critical failure of Paul Simon's career.[38]

At a small club, Levin's band opens for the B-52s. The band are seen hanging out backstage for a few seconds before they walk out to perform the first 20 seconds of an incendiary version of Rock Lobster while Levin watches sadly from the dressing room. The next day, Levin's band take turns reading a review of the show that talks about how terrible Levin's band is compared to the B-52s. Whether Simon intended it or not, in real life the B-52s (here performing under their own name) do the same thing in real life to Paul Simon that they do to Jonah Levin in the film.

The Touring Never Stops

The band played an October 8th show at the 4700 capacity Greek Theatre in Los Angeles with a *Rolling Stone* writer along for the ride. James Henke was working on a story about the band, and everyone involved—Henke, the B-52s, and Gary Kurfirst—expected it to be a cover feature in December. Henke's article would open with a description of the crowd that night:

> The crowd … looks like it'd be more at home at some bizarre, early-Sixties fashion show than at a rock & roll concert. Take, for example, the three girls sitting a couple of rows in front of me. They couldn't be more than about fourteen years old; they're so young, in fact, that one of their fathers is along as a chaperone. Each girl is wearing a brightly colored miniskirt—one's fire-engine red, another's fluorescent orange, the other's indigo blue—and their faces are piled with scads of makeup to match. Then there are their hairdos: One has little pigtails sticking straight out each side of her head like TV antennas, another has a braided ponytail hanging down to the middle of her back, and the other has her hair puffed up bouffant style.[39]

Whether it's the Beatles, Madonna, or the Sex Pistols, no pop culture phenomenon is complete until it inspires imitators. After years of creating their own unique sense of fashion and fun back in Athens, the B-52s were now playing to audiences who wanted to look just like them. Henke describes the band's entrance in vivid detail:

> Already, as Talking Heads' new album, *Remain in Light*, blasts from the PA, several fans are up out of their seats and dancing. When the houselights finally go down, the crowd goes gaga. The response—the cheering, the yelling, the clapping—is so manic, one could easily be led to believe the Beatles had re-formed and were about to walk onstage. Instead, the five musicians who do take the stage—to the wacky accompaniment of a taped African tribal trumpet solo that sounds like the incessant honking of twenty Toyotas in a Tokyo traffic jam—are the B-52's.[40]

The show is a frenzy of dancing from both the band and its audience, the latter of which "greet *every* number as if it were an anthem," says Henke.

A few days later, he and the group head up the coast to Santa Barbara to hang out and conduct interviews before the next show. Kate and Henke go thrift-store shopping, where Kate buys a long chiffon dress for Cindy. Ricky is reflective. "It really hasn't sunk in yet, this success. I sort of don't believe it." He thinks for a few seconds. "I guess you would call it success, though." The band trade tick jokes back and forth ("What do you call the first tick on the moon? A lunatic.").[41]

At the Santa Barbara show that night, Henke, despite his obvious enthusiasm for the band, expresses some concerns that were starting to sound familiar:

> But this show—my fourth in six days—makes me realize that as much fun as the group's live set is, there are also a few problems. For one thing, the band has played *exactly* the same set every night—the same twelve songs, the same encores—and they've *said* virtually the same lines between songs and used the very same moves.[42]

Henke later wonders "if they will be able to exhibit any growth as a musical unit." Ricky and Keith, who Henke calls "the group's musical directors," also share his concern. "I really do feel trapped," says Ricky. "Gary [Kurfirst] was talking about our next album, and I mentioned that it might not be a dance record, and he was so shocked by that idea."[43]

Ricky seemed all too aware of the expectations, both artistic and commercial, that now surrounded the band. His use of the word "might" suggested he still wasn't sure which direction he wanted to go.

A month later, they were still on the road. A *Melody Maker* journalist showed up for their November 3rd show at the Malibu Club in Long Island, only to initially be rebuffed. The band's publicist explained that it was because "they've been interviewed by so many jerks."[44] It's possible the band had a beef with the paper, who had savaged *Wild Planet* in a review three months earlier, writing, "The joke is wearing so thin it's close to snapping point."[45]

Eventually, Keith agrees to come out and do the interview, just as the writer is launching into a tirade at the publicist:

> "What's wrong with these ego-maniacs anyway?" I tell her. "Don't they realise they're dealing with the British Press? Anyway the B52's aren't such a big deal at all over in London you know."
>
> The person standing in the shadows directly behind Gloria shudders involuntarily. "Oh," says Gloria, "by the way, this is Keith."[46]

Keith brings her backstage, where once again a writer is shocked the band isn't living up to their festive reputation. "*This* party sure isn't out of bounds," she says, "just a few warm beers on stand-by and a depressed tray of sandwiches."[47] Despite all their songs about space travel, the B-52s do actually live on the same planet as the rest of us. This scene was pretty standard for any group of traveling musicians, especially a group whose set now lasted over an hour.

The writer then asks Keith about the new album, who tells her "Most of our songs are about catastrophes."[48] During the show, however, the band is a mass of energy. Floorboards are once again strained by the ferocity of the audience's dancing, as the writer finally finds the party they were looking for. "Ricky is hunched over doing a duck walk with his guitar while Cindy's earrings are a go go, getting there fast."[49]

The next night they played the Tower Theatre in Upper Darby, Pennsylvania as America elected a new president. "They had this TV set on the side of the stage," recalled Kate, "and just before we went on … we were all watching along with the theatre crew. By the time we went on we knew what was happening and it was real depressing."[50] Ronald Reagan's election represented a clear rebuttal to the social and sexual freedoms of the 1970s, and the band knew it. Fred had spent the year dedicating Party Out of Bounds to the Republican Party as a form of protest. In an *NME* profile in early January 1981, the former meal delivery coordinator for the Athens Council on Aging ranted at length about the President-elect:

> People just convinced themselves Reagan would pull some magic strings and unveil a beautiful new nation. And he's just for the bankers and the wealthy, not the elderly or the poor. He doesn't care about human rights—so it's not gonna be a good day for civil rights! The things he said in the '60s … "If the students want a bloodbath then we'll give 'em one"—all that. It's unreal.[51]

Three days later, the B-52s played the Capitol Theatre in Passaic, New Jersey. Video footage from the show is easily found on the internet, and even though it's in black and white, it radiates a fierce kinetic energy. It provides evidence that, on Nov. 7, 1980, the B-52s were one of the best bands in the history of rock music to ever get up on a stage.

Cindy's singing and dancing on Give Me Back My Man has to be heard (and seen) to be believed. Ricky throws all kinds of sexy heroic shapes on the guitar. Kate shares her keyboard with Cindy for a solo on Strobe Light, with Cindy bending the pitch wheel while Kate plays. It sounds for all the world like Booker T. possessed by the spirit of Sun Ra, or Brian Eno manipulating the sound of Phil Manzanera's guitar back in Roxy Music.

The band is also funny. During the litany of fish in Rock Lobster, Cindy responds to Fred's *there goes a piranha* with a deadpan reply of *oh shit*.

Regardless of how exhausted they might have been, they were still having fun onstage. During the encore of Downtown, Cindy leans down over the front of the stage and invites audience members to shout the song's title into her microphone. At one point, she even runs her fingers through a guy's hair and pulls another guy's baseball cap down over his head.

The band finished up their US touring commitments with two nights at Beacon Plaza in NYC. Two weeks later they were off to Europe, where they headlined two nights at London's Hammersmith Palais. Finally, after nearly four months of touring, they played their last show of the year on December 10th in Vorst, Belgium with Talking Heads. After yet another year of triumph and hard work, the B-52s headed back to Mahopac to write their next album. If all went according to plan, it would be out in late 1981 and would consolidate everything they had accomplished so far. It would be both an artistic breakthrough and a runaway commercial success. It wouldn't be easy. *NME* writer Cynthia Rose nailed the challenge in her January 3, 1981 feature:

> Success brings pressure with a capital P: pressure to find some place in rock for maverick individuality that is more than mere caricature; pressure to keep the music fresh and funny and double-edged but this side of camp or kitsch; pressure to placate a manager and record company already eager for that THIRD ALBUM when the best of Wild Planet hailed from the early Athens days and there are no new songs in the works at present.[52]

In that same article, Kate says, "I think there's gonna be a big swing in the 80s towards everyone being in couples and away from communal living and socialising." Whether she knew it or not, the B-52s were about to fulfill that prediction, splintering off into dysfunction. During this period, Fred told an interviewer, "Right now we're letting music dominate our lives. Sometimes I really resent it."[53]

On December 11, 1980, the day after the show in Belgium, and three days after the assassination of John Lennon, the B-52s' big feature finally appeared in *Rolling Stone*. The James Henke article ran over five pages and featured beautiful photographs of the band taken by Lynn Goldsmith that would become iconic. But the B-52s weren't on the cover. The magazine had chosen to put Dolly Parton, dressed in a resplendent Santa Claus outfit, on there instead.

Bowling in Athens, GA, 1978 by Keith Bennett

B-52s in Athens 1978, by Ann States

B-52s in Athens 1978 by Curtis Knapp

Photo booth Hamburg, Germany, 1974. (Courtesy of the personal collection of Keith Strickland)

Ricky and Keith Downtown Athens, 1976. (Courtesy of Cindy Wilson)

Jeremy Ayers through the Looking Glass by Dana Downs

Kate playing guitar at the Last Resort, 1978, by Wingate Downs

Ricky on guitar, 1978, by Terry Allen

Thursday, May 3, 1979 The Athens Observer

'Walking art' show is held

Michelangelo and Maria Pistoletto hosted a three-day "walking art workshop" at the Lyndon House Art Center April 19-21. The purpose of the workshop was to provide an opportunity for artistic exchange and collaboration among the artists exhibiting in the Lyndon House Sixth Annual Art Show, their families, and friends.

Approximately 20 participants gathered at the Lyndon House to join the Pistolettos in the designing, constructing, and painting of "walking art pieces." The workshop ended on April 21 at 4 p.m., with a march through downtown Athens. The pieces were then exhibited in the front of the Lyndon House Art Center during the opening of the Lyndon House Sixth Annual Exhibition.

Walking art was a celebration of visual art presented here recently with the cooperation of visiting artist Michelangelo Pistoletto. (Photo by Barbara McKenzie)

Getting works ready for the art walk here were (L-R) Mrs. Michelangelo Pistoletto, Pistoletto, and Anastasia Kontos. (Photo by Barbara McKenzie)

Athens Trash Parade, with Michelangelo Pistoletto, 1979. (Courtesy of Lyndon House Arts Center Archives, photo by Barbara McKenzie)

Fred at the Last Resort, 1978 (left), by Wingate Downs

B-52s 1978 (right)—by Ann States

Outside their Morton Theatre practice space 1978 by Keith Bennett

Cindy and Kate at CBGB's by Keith Bennett

The B-52s (left) by Curtis Knapp

Keith Strickland in Dallas, 1979 (right), by Keith Bennett

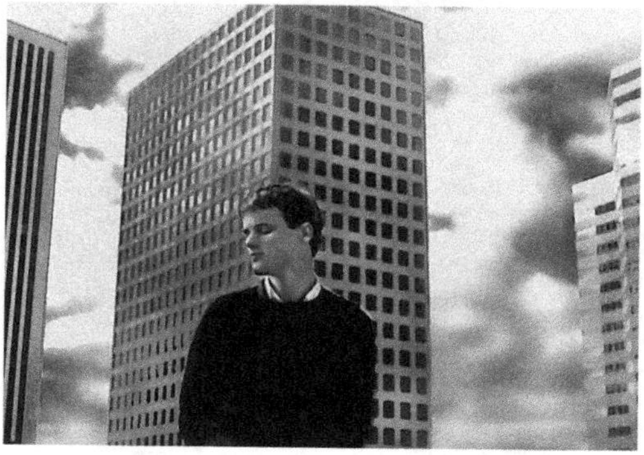

B-52s in 1982 by Terry Allen

The B-52s in Athens *With the Wild Crowd!* 2011 (above); Fred—then and now (below) by Wingate Downs

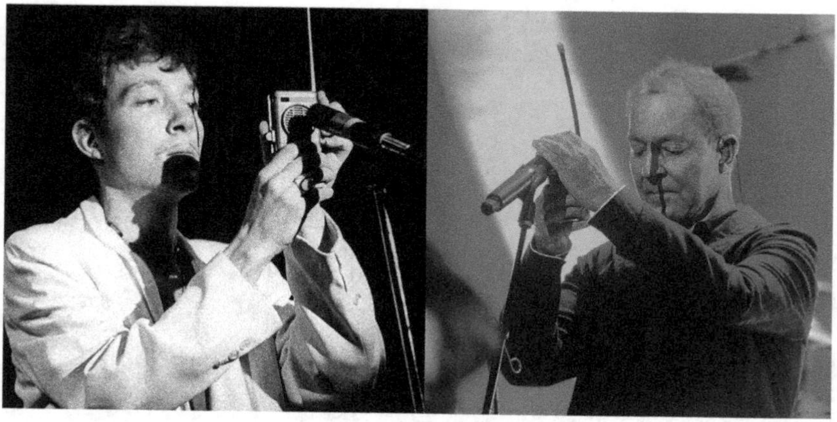

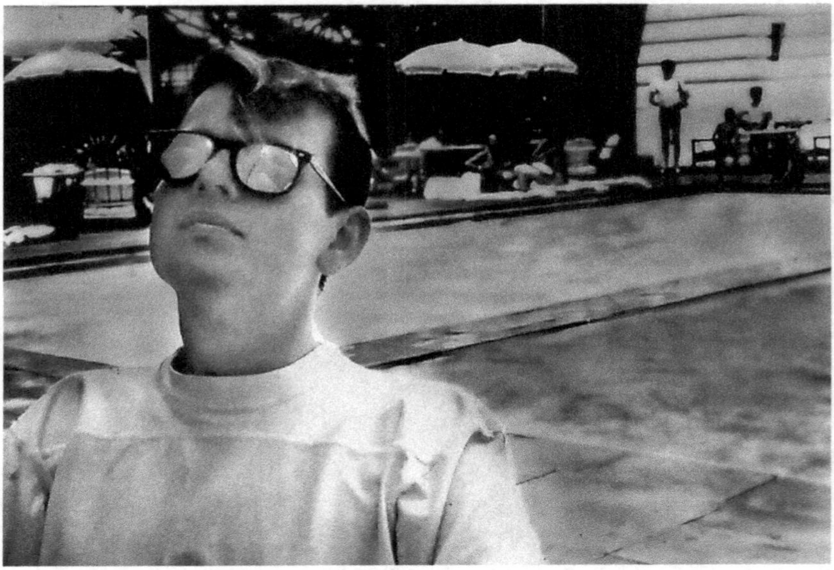

Ricky in Rio, 1985 (above); Ricky in the Bahamas, 1979 (below), by Keith Bennett

Alternate photo from DB Records Rock Lobster Shoot, 1978, by Ann States

Notes

1. Rachel, "Cindy Wilson."
2. Miller and Shales, *Live From New York*, 101.
3. Miller and Shales, *Live From New York*, 183.
4. Grow, "Love Shacks."
5. Ibid.
6. Azerrad, *Come as You Are*, 23.
7. Rose, "The B-52's."
8. Swenson, "Frank Zappa."

9. Katz, "Chic."
10. Sexton, *The B-52's Universe*, 50. The title is Italian for "very urgent."
11. Inglis, "Recording & Remixing."
12. Bibler, "Water Skis," 11.
13. Bibler, "Water Skis," 12.
14. Sexton, *The B-52's Universe*, 160.
15. Ibid.
16. EPA, "Luminous Processes, Inc." When one of this book's authors began working last year at a retail store near the site, they were told on the first day to never drink the water that came out of the sink.
17. Scrudato, "BlackBook Interview."
18. Reines, "Wild Dolls," 12.
19. Whitall, "Heatwave Festival."
20. Swanson, "Toronto Heatwave Festival."
21. Vanessa Briscoe Hay in conversation with authors, April 25, 2019.
22. Michael Lachowski in conversation with authors, May 16, 2019.
23. Vanessa Briscoe Hay in conversation with authors, April 25, 2019.
24. Michael Lachowski in conversation with authors, May 16, 2019. A prominent book about post-punk music says Paul Simon headlined this Central Park show, but Hay and Lachowski each separately confirmed he didn't.
25. Goldman, "Wild! Wacky! B-52's!"
26. Bill Paul in conversation with authors, May 19, 2019.
27. Paul expounded on the story in an email exchanged with authors, June 21, 2020. "We were about to leave for Valdosta where Sarah (oldest daughter) was to be enrolled in the Governor's Honors Program when Trotter called for me to come to her office. I thought we were going to talk about some aspect of funding for the proposed new building to house the museum. Instead, I was asked to resign as director of the museum (in the presence of Ralph Beard, dean of the law school) and, if I didn't, she'd fire me. I asked her why she had made this decision. She said the issue was a personnel matter and she couldn't discuss it. Then, she quoted the text you already have. I said that I'd done nothing wrong, and, consequently, she'd have to fire me. I was given a six month leave of absence. But, afterwards, job offers (ready for signature) vanished in thin air."
28. Bill Paul in conversation with authors, May 19, 2019. Paul had reached out to Davison three weeks earlier, but the President's secretary informed him, "He doesn't deal with small matters like that," and refused to put him on the line.
29. Ibid.
30. Gosse, "The B-52's Attack," 95.
31. Cleary, "The B-52s Wild Planet."

32. Goldman, "Wild! Wacky! B-52's!" Before writing for various UK music papers, Goldman worked for Island Records doing publicity for Bob Marley. The year after this feature, she put out a fantastic EP on 99 Records with songs produced by John Lydon and Adrian Sherwood. Her song "Launderette" is a particular highlight.
33. Ibid.
34. Ibid. It's possible, given how the wigs helped Kate and Cindy remain more anonymous offstage, that Kurfrist was simply trying to protect his artists.
35. *Billboard*, "Billboard 200" week of September 20, 1980. The highest charting debut that week was Molly Hatchet's *Beating the Odds*, two spots above *WP* at #87.
36. Chris Rasmussen in conversation with authors, July 29, 2019.
37. Brandt, "New Woman Sound," 97.
38. There's a great scene where Rip Torn—best known for his role as Artie on The Larry Sanders Show, and for trying to beat Norman Mailer to death with a hammer—plays a lying record company guy who conspires with a producer, played by Lou Reed, to further bland out Simon/Levin's already bland song against Levin's wishes. Watching the guy who made *Metal Machine Music* add syrupy soft-rock strings to a Paul Simon song while Simon, we mean Jonah Levin, wails in protest is a delight.
39. Henke, "Interview."
40. Ibid.
41. Ibid.
42. Ibid.
43. Ibid.
44. Reines, "Party," 12.
45. Barber, "Wild Planet," 27.
46. Reines, "Party." 12.
47. Ibid.
48. Ibid.
49. Ibid.
50. Rose, "The B-52's."
51. Ibid.
52. Ibid.
53. Isler, "The Devil Went Down to Georgia," 27.

CHAPTER 7

Mesopotamia

Well that's just the way life is. Everything's one big smile until you realize it's just fallen apart completely.[1]

—Fred

And so the B-52s found themselves back in rural upstate New York, again—expected to write another album, again. For the first time, they weren't sure what to do next. Their audience remained as enthusiastic as ever, but critics were starting to see the band's style as mere schtick, music that was more affected than affecting. The band felt they needed to do more than just write an album's worth of songs, they needed to find a new sound, possibly even a new style. Kate recalled this period as "a crisis point where we became pretty self-conscious."[2] Keith called it "an identity crisis."[3] The band looked back on this period in 1999, and Kate remembered, "The spark of fun was just …." Fred completed her thought. "It was gone."[4]

Bands are strange. The vast amount of time you spend together makes it more intense than any normal working relationship. Factor in the pressure that comes with success, the time spent in interviews talking about yourselves, the constant traveling, and even the closest friendships are going to be tested.

Life in the B-52s wasn't as carefree as it had been back in 1978. Whatever ambitions they may have had individually when the band started,

S. Creney, B. A. Herron, *The Story of the B-52s*,
https://doi.org/10.1007/978-3-031-22570-3_7

the B-52s had initially been about having fun. Most of the B-52s' success had been the product of timing and luck, more than any kind of Machiavellian plan. Now that the fun was gone, the only thing left was work, with nothing to look forward to except more touring, and more albums, the cycle repeating itself indefinitely. Was this what they wanted? This kind of drudgery seemed antithetical to being in the B-52s. They had two choices: push through the discomfort and hope the situation got better, or take a much-needed break until they felt inspired to make another album. Unable to agree on a course of action, they passively flailed around. They acted like passengers on a rocket ship. They had helped build the ship, but they had no idea how to steer it.

It turned out there were plenty of people around the band who were happy to try and steer it for them, people like Gary Kurfirst and Chris Blackwell, who had a financial stake in the band's success. Their advice and guidance had less to do with artistic growth, or what was best for the band as people, and instead focused on record sales. The problem with that approach was that music business people generally believe the best way to have a hit is to take as few risks as possible. At a time when the B-52s needed to take control of their career and their art, they were giving it away instead.

For the sake of comparison, consider how the Beatles worked. The Beatles had endless ambition. They wanted to be bigger than Elvis, and after they were bigger than Elvis, they wanted to stay there. Before they recorded a new album, John and Paul would get together to work on each other's songs. During these writing sessions, they would go back and listen to their own previous material. Then they would listen to the records of their contemporaries, looking to see how they fit into what was happening, and looking to see where they were in danger of being overtaken by their rivals. In the summer of 1965, the band heard the anger in the Rolling Stones' Satisfaction and the Who's My Generation, and the complex songcraft of the Supremes' Stop! In the Name of Love, and realized they needed to do better if they were going to stay relevant. Paul McCartney told a story about hearing Bob Dylan's Like a Rolling Stone at John Lennon's house. "It was just beautiful. He showed all of us that it was possible to go a little further."[5] The Beatles responded with *Rubber Soul*, a deeper and more substantial work than anything they had done up to that point. A year later they followed that album with *Revolver*, a record fueled by studio experimentation with several songs about death, both physical and spiritual.

Lacking this kind of clear-eyed ambition, the B-52s were either unwilling or unable to take the kinds of risks necessary to grow artistically as a band. As 1981 turned into 1982, they would find themselves unable to even complete an album.

Mahopac

While the band tried to rev up their creative engines, the mood at Mahopac was, according to Cindy, "ominous."[6] She elaborated two years later in *NME*:

> We'd come right off the road after all that touring and there we were, just plopped down to write a whole new album. And it was winter. And we weren't at home. I mean, we were home, but we weren't at home, if you know what I mean.[7]

Fred described the living situation as "more like a low-security institution with five inmates."[8] He soon got an apartment in NYC, only staying at Mahopac when working on songs. Kate noticed the paralyzing effect the attention was having on their ability to create music. "The first two albums were real unconscious," she noted in 1983. "We never even separated who did what; we just jammed and juxtaposed ideas. And I never felt like there was any sort of judge of who was making what."[9] That started to change now, as the leaderless band began to push and pull in different directions.

The problem wasn't the band's musical taste. A *New York Rocker* article in November of 1980 saw Keith cite PiL, Sun Ra, and Suburban Lawns as favorites, while Kate added Young Marble Giants and Psychedelic Furs.[10] A B-52s album inspired by those artists would have been remarkable, but none of those influences made it onto *Mesopotamia*, suggesting the band members were better at shooting down each other's ideas rather than working to integrate them into the collective. Ricky's response in that article speaks volumes. "Right now I'm at a low point," he said. "I don't like anybody too much."[11]

The band only had fun when they turned their attention away from music. "Most of our jams turn into TV shows—with commercials," said Fred. "If we can't think of an idea for a song, we just do a TV show. We did, let me see … The Mary Shirley Morning Show. We did the Hell To Holler Show where Ricky was host."[12] As entertaining as these shows probably were, and one hopes the tapes will eventually surface, they were ultimately an act of procrastination and avoidance.

NYC

Not only did the close quarters in Mahopac exacerbate tensions within the B-52s, but it put them an hour's drive, or two hours via train, from NYC's Lower East Side. While band members, particularly Fred and Kate, visited the city often, they missed out on the incredible musical developments taking place.

In early 1981, while the B-52s were struggling to write their next album, NYC saw an explosion of hip-hop culture as the scene migrated from its South Bronx origins to Manhattan. The ensuing cross-fertilization would spark revolutions in music, art, fashion, and language that still reverberate today. The visual side of hip-hop culture—street art defined by tagging and graffiti—impacted the art world, as Jean-Michel Basquiat and Keith Haring incorporated it into their work and found stardom.

That January, Blondie released the single, Rapture. It became their fourth #1 hit, and the first song with a hip-hop influence to top the charts. The middle of April saw a Mudd Club exhibition, coordinated by hip-hop pioneer Fred (Fab 5 Freddy) Brathwaite, who had been name-checked in Rapture after meeting Blondie guitarist Chris Stein on Glenn O'Brien's *TV Party*. A 23-year-old from the Bronx named Afrika Bambaataa (born Lance Taylor) DJ'd the opening night of the festival. Bambaataa combined his love of traditional funk like James Brown with the futuristic electronic music being made by Kraftwerk and Gary Numan, and filtered this through the new hip-hop turntable styles developed by Kool Herc and Brathwaite. Bambaataa's sets were wildly eclectic, incorporating songs from Prince, ESG, Yellow Magic Orchestra, and Hall & Oates. Bambaataa also played B-52s songs regularly. Like the band, his aesthetic had been shaped by 60s pop culture and a love of science fiction. Perhaps attracted by the song's interplanetary lyrics and its hypnotic groove, one of his favorites was Planet Claire. Bambaataa and Fab 5 Freddy also both did guest DJ spots at Club 57, the latter introduced to the club through Keith Haring.[13]

Tom Tom Club

In 1981, Gary Kurfirst's other band, Talking Heads, were in even worse shape than the B-52s. After narrowly averting a public break-up the previous year, the band were now on hiatus and working separately. "All the unspoken shit that had been building up inside that dressing room," recalled Sire's Seymour Stein, "started to hit the fan on my desk."[14] First, David Byrne decided to write a Broadway musical, and he wanted Sire to release the soundtrack. Then Jerry Harrison wanted Sire to put out his solo album. Desperate to keep Talking Heads from dissolving in bad feelings and resentment, Kurfirst encouraged Chris Frantz and Tina Weymouth to make an album of their own, and wanted Sire to release that as well.[15] "All this was turning into a mess," said Stein,[16] and the exasperated executive decided to low-ball them with his offer. That was when, according to Stein, Chris Blackwell got involved:

> Gary was an old friend of Blackwell's, and when it came to dub, Island was a logical fit for whatever rhythmic experiment Chris and Tina had in mind. So, I just concluded, "Yeah, whatever," thinking this was a classic case of a band getting lost up their own asses.[17]

Down at Compass Point, Frantz and Weymouth led a group of musicians through a series of unstructured jams, supervised by producer Steven Stanley. In February 1981, Island released the first single from the group that Chris and Tina had decided to call Tom Tom Club. Wordy Rappinghood had a bouncy danceable day-glo brightness that was a million miles away from Talking Heads, and Tina's vocal approach was clearly rap-influenced. The single not only got rave reviews and charted in Europe, but was embraced by the burgeoning hip-hop community in NYC, including kids in the South Bronx who heard the funk-infused song on the radio and could dance to it.

That summer, Tom Tom Club released their second single, the 12-inch Genius of Love. The song was an immediate smash. It was so ubiquitous in NYC that summer—in the clubs, on the radio, as well as the streets—that Seymour Stein was humbled. "I was officially King Dumbo," he said, "standing there with his dick in his hand."[18] Kurfirst offered Stein the album for a lot more money than it would have cost him six months earlier. Released in the fall of 1981, *Tom Tom Club* combined the playful musicality of the Compass Point house band with a New York sensibility, creating what one writer called "electro-funk-art-fusion."[19] The album reached a level of commercial and cultural influence that had escaped Talking Heads. When Tom Tom Club met hip-hop pioneer Grandmaster Flash for a *New York Rocker* feature, Flash complimented Frantz on Genius of Love, telling him, "You know, this is a very cool beat. You're going to be hearing a lot of this!" The song would go on to become one of the most sampled in history, appearing most notably on Mariah Carey's 1995 #1 hit Fantasy.

The Tom Tom Club album went gold that year, selling twice as many copies as any Talking Heads album up to that point.[20] When Byrne's solo album came out the next year, *The Catherine Wheel* only sold 10,000 copies, and received lukewarm reviews. Although Byrne had held all the power in the band a year earlier, Tom Tom Club made Chris and Tina equal partners, and Talking Heads decided to continue. Stein credited Gary Kurfirst for deftly managing "a messy situation … [he] earned everyone's respect, mine included."[21]

Living just across the river from Manhattan, Frantz and Weymouth had been able to keep abreast of NYC trends in a way that was harder for the B-52s. Mark Kamins, who regularly DJ'd at the couple's loft, recorded a demo in 1982 for a singer named Madonna, who was completely plugged into the NYC scene. She was friends with Keith Haring, dated Jean-Michel Basquiat, and was out every night at Danceteria. "I wanted my records to sound like what I wanted to dance to," she said of that period. "I was influenced by Debbie Harry, Talking Heads, The B-52's."[22]

Seymour Stein heard her demo, met the artist, and—no "King Dumbo" on this one—immediately signed Madonna to Sire Records, where she would go on to sell more records than Tom Tom Club, B-52s, Talking Heads, and Blondie combined.

Planet Claire Becomes Planet Rock

In a December 1980 *Creem* feature, the B-52s discussed their love for German electronic band Kraftwerk. After collectively enthusing about the new Captain Beefheart album *Doc at the Radar Station*, Kate said "We play Kraftwerk while we're traveling," with Cindy adding, "It's the *best* traveling music." The writer then asks them to name their favorite Kraftwerk album, and after some discussion, the band agree on *Trans-Europe Express*.[23] The story is heartbreaking because while the B-52s were up in Mahopac trying to figure out what to do next, some other Kraftwerk fans—and fans of the B-52s—were about to change the future of music.

In 1982, Afrika Bambaataa hooked up with fellow DJ Arthur Baker to make a song called Planet Rock. Utilizing a new drum machine from Japan called the Roland T-808, the song featured rapping from Soulsonic Force, and borrowed heavily from Kraftwerk. "I always was into Trans Europe Express," said Bambaataa, "and after Kraftwerk put 'Numbers' out, I said, 'I wonder if I can combine the two to make something real funky with a hard bass and beat.'"[24] The result birthed a genre of dance music called electro-funk, or electro, but Planet Rock's synthesis of electronic music and human voices—the way it intermingled technology and soul, the synthetic and the real—laid the template for what pop music would become. Critic Paul Morley wrote how, via Planet Rock, Kraftwerk "opened up a whole new untouched universe of sound and rhythmical opportunities."[25]

Yet it's almost impossible to hear the influence of Kraftwerk, or Planet Rock, or hip-hop, in the music of the B-52s. Which is a shame, because hip-hop's minimalist aesthetics, DIY musicianship, and spoken-sung vocals—to say nothing of its sci-fi retrofuturist aesthetics—were already present in the B-52s' music. Of all their peers, the B-52s were best suited to incorporate this new sound into their music, yet they did the least with it. Even when the B-52s eventually embraced drum machines and synthesizers on 1983's *Whammy!* the result betrayed no influence from electro.

Party Mix

As the B-52s headed into summer with still no album in sight, Daniel Coulombe, Harold Dorsett, and Steven Stanley were brought in to make an album of remixes to get a record into the stores. The result—*Party Mix!*—took three songs each from *The B-52's* and *Wild Planet*. Lynn Goldsmith photographed the band for the cover in Mahopac, using all the band's own clothes and household items in the shoot.[26]

Party Mix! turned out to be a concept ahead of its time. The next year, Soft Cell and the Human League released their own remix albums with *Non Stop Ecstatic Dancing* and *Love and Dancing*, respectively. Madonna made the excellent *You Can Dance* in 1986, and Pet Shop Boys put out *Disco* in 1987. Even extended 12-inch singles were still unusual in 1981, existing on the margins of NYC dance culture and Jamaican dub. But the format would explode as the decade progressed, with the 12-inch becoming a staple of both dance and rock culture. In 1992, a critic called the B-52s "early pioneers in the art of the club remix" because of the record.[27] It may have been the product of pragmatic necessity, but with *Party Mix!* the B-52s were able to once again made something cool and influential.

To Fred, the album also marked a personal turning point for the band. "Up until Party Mix!" he recalled, "it was so much fun for us .... As we became part of this huge thing called the music business, we started to lose the youthful enthusiasm we started with.[28]

Mesopotamia

By the fall of 1981, the B-52s still hadn't finished writing the songs for their third album, but they decided to head into the studio to record it anyway. Instead of going back to Compass Point, they chose to do it in NYC with David Byrne, though none of this was entirely their decision. "Gary [Kurfirst] had suggested working with David Byrne, but we hadn't written all the songs out," Kate said. "He kind of forced us."[29]

Gary Kurfirst loved it when his artists worked together. They regularly appeared on each other's records, and often toured together. Because he was David Byrne's manager, Kurfirst would earn a commission if Byrne produced the album, as opposed to someone like Brian Eno, or say, Afrika Bambaataa and Arthur Baker. Going back to the days of Island Artists, Kurfirst never seemed bothered by conflicts of interest. In fact, he seemed to actively seek them out. In 1991, MCA would give Kurfirst his own label to run, Radioactive Records, and his first signing was the Ramones, a band he was managing at the time. In his book about the Ramones, famed critic Everett True was dumbfounded by the arrangement:

> Usually, record labels are directly opposed to management, and vice-versa (one is always trying to screw the other). Was it a wise career move, to have both management and label as one and the same? ... The Ramones clearly thought so.[30]

Worryingly, this was Byrne's first time producing a record on his own, and he would also be working on *The Catherine Wheel* at the same time, doing his record during the day and the B-52s' record at night. Still, Byrne was excited by the prospect of working with the B-52s, and saw their unfinished songs as a plus. "They haven't had a chance yet to work things out in front of an audience," said Byrne, "to know when to shorten a verse or broaden a bridge." He continued:

> Now they have to do that in a studio, and it gives me a chance to play around with the song to try to contain them. But in some ways this is harder. It is not a group coming in to play their (finished) material.[31]

Take an underprepared band lacking confidence and combine it with an overworked producer looking to "play around," and you have a recipe for disaster. And while *Mesopotamia* wasn't a complete disaster, it turned out to be one hell of a mess.

Also, Byrne was using cocaine during this time to keep up the frantic pace. Adrian Belew, guitarist in Talking Heads during their 1980–1981 period, remembered the band before their performance at Heatwave "snorting lines of coke from the backs of guitars."[32] Byrne acknowledged the drug in a 2009 biography of Talking Heads, stating, "It was good for someone like me who wasn't a very social person."[33] Regardless of the positive effects it had on Byrne's social life, cocaine isn't known for its ability to inspire great art—not without wasting lots of time and money in the process. Bands like Fleetwood Mac and the Eagles went through the mid/late 70s spending, and snorting, millions of dollars over the course of a year just to produce a 40-minute album. Neither the B-52s, nor David Byrne for that matter, had sold enough records for anyone to give them that amount of time in the studio. Perhaps, given another nine months, *Mesopotamia* could have been the *Hotel California* or *Rumours* of the NYC new wave scene. Instead, what emerged was closer to the fragmented feel of Fleetwood Mac's *Tusk*, if the label had kicked the band out of the studio after a month and just pieced together whatever they could salvage. And if you listen closely to *Mesopotamia* and turn on your imagination, you can hear the potentially great album that never got finished.

In addition to the six songs that were released, there are four songs from this period that didn't make the record. Queen of Las Vegas would be completely reworked for 1983's *Whammy!* album, but the version recorded during the *Mesopotamia* sessions has a drama and tension that's missing in the *Whammy!* version. The melody is sharper, and Ricky's minimal, hypnotic guitar part is more memorable than what he would play a year later. It's so much better than most of what made it onto *Mesopotamia* that it underscores how bad the band's decision-making process became around this time.

Another *Mesopotamia* outtake is Adios Desconocida, a Latin-flavored ballad led by Fred, which is lovely with its lyrics about two ships literally passing in the night. A couple of months after the sessions were abandoned, the band went back into the studio and recorded two more songs, Big Bird and Butterbean. If we imagine these four songs being added to the album, and the band being given more time to keep working, we start to hear what a finished *Mesopotamia* might have sounded like.

That didn't happen, but as with other famous unfinished and unreleased albums, like the Beach Boys' *Smile*, or The Who's *Lifehouse*, the incompleteness of *Mesopotamia* invites listeners to imagine the album that might have been. There is no definitive version of *Mesopotamia*, not even the physical record itself. Without the band's prior knowledge, Island released a version in the UK with extended mixes of the songs. And for the 1991 CD release, the B-52s had all the songs remixed to remove all of David Byrne's contributions. With three different versions of *Mesopotamia* in the world, you can't tell someone you listened to it without being asked "which one?"

For the purposes of this book, we'll talk about the version issued by Warner Brothers in 1982. With only six songs, *Mesopotamia* was released as a "mini-album." Unlike *Party Mix!* this marketing strategy failed to catch on. Cindy said that "Mesopotamia didn't have the spirit it needed."[34] Or the music. Of the six songs on *Mesopotamia*, two were, by the band's admission, still unfinished. Nearly all of the songs lack anything resembling a clear chorus. There are no guitar riffs as immediately recognizable or exciting as Rock Lobster or Private Idaho, and the curious lack of dynamics suggests the band never fully worked out the arrangements.

Every song on *Mesopotamia* has an occasional great moment, but they're often fleeting, and subsumed by long periods of aimless meandering. Album opener Loveland is a perfect example. It lasts for five minutes, and barely exists as a song. The vocals sound like improvisations from Cindy that still need to be worked out into a coherent structure with clear lyrics and melodies. Sections of the song appear and disappear with no real logic, particularly the *I will show you all the shortcuts to Loveland*. The most distinctive section is the chord change when Cindy sings *Love lake can get rough*. It's beautiful, and makes the whole song lift up and float. But it only happens once, and then we're back into directionless playing and singing.

The lyrics were frothier than ever. Loveland is about sailing to a land of love across a lake of love while thinking of love. On Cake, Cindy and Kate push the sexual innuendo so far (*If you want a better batter, better beat it harder*) that it is no longer innuendo. None of this would matter if the melodies were stronger. ABBA's Dancing Queen is one of the greatest singles ever made, despite having lyrics that are, on paper, ridiculously goofy. But nothing on *Mesopotamia* has the craft or operatic emotion to elevate sentiments like *I can't wait to put the icing on the cake / 250 strokes to beat it, I just can't wait to eat it.*

Cake hits its high point at the beginning of the chorus when Cindy first sings what sounds like *I am watching it drop down the sides.* Unfortunately, she never sings it that way again, and the rest of the chorus finds Kate and Cindy searching for a catchy melody without ever coming back to the one they had. "Cake wasn't really finished," admitted Kate. "Deep Sleep, I just kind of stuck that lyric on in the studio in one take."[35]

For all his talk about helping the band structure their songs, it's hard to see how David Byrne helped in that department. Which is strange, given that even the most esoteric Talking Heads songs have a songwriting discipline lacking on *Mesopotamia.* This may not have been entirely Byrne's fault. The sessions were marked by a tense atmosphere, with the band plagued by dissension and splintering into factions. Even something as mundane as Kate working on Deep Sleep by herself with Byrne could create tension in the studio. There's also a distinct lack of Fred on *Mesopotamia.* He only appears on two of the six songs. As Keith admitted years later, "David got a bad rap for that album, but he didn't put this big stamp on it. It was us, our fault it didn't work."[36]

As it turns out, the mini-album's title track is the one moment where everything comes together. Mesopotamia's confident rhythm, its angular rigidity and jigsaw syncopation, is a revelation. It's as breakdance-worthy as Planet Rock or Genius of Love, and still sounds contemporary today in a way that those songs don't. On Mesopotamia, the song, you can hear the B-52s incorporate Kraftwerk and the latent electro-funk movement into their music and take the step forward they were so desperately trying to make.

Chris Blackwell hated it. "He thought the song was weak," according to Kate. "I don't know why. He just thought it wasn't strong enough."[37] Blackwell didn't even want to include it on the record. However, a DJ in Detroit, The Electrifying Mojo, played the song constantly on a Black radio station, where it became a local hit. Kate recalled, "We got a great crossover audience and a big following in Detroit through that song. We still get a big cheer whenever we play Mesopotamia there."[38] The

Electrifying Mojo, born Charles Johnson, played a role in the emerging Detroit techno scene, as did the B-52s. In Mike Sicko's history of the genre, *Techno Rebels*, Hassan Nurullah, a Detroit high school student, recalled seeing the first B-52s album at the mall:

> I remember Mike Bonner and I were at Northland [Mall] when the B-52's first album came out. We saw this bright-ass yellow record and weird-looking people singing weirder songs. "There's a moon in the sky and it's called the moon." "What is this weird crap?" we laughed. But soon we were out buying Hawaiian shirts, bright yellow cargo pants, wild sunglasses … the brightest, most obnoxious stuff.[39]

Detroit DJ and producer Rick Wilhite said, "the roller-skating rink was dominated by B-52s records …. You'd be surprised how many people in Detroit know the words to their music."[40]

The group played a role in the development of house music in Chicago as well. Jesse Saunders has called the B-52s, "one of my favorite groups actually." Talking of *Mesopotamia*, he said, "I used to play that to death! I mean, I would play that two or three times a night, 'cause I loved it so much."[41]

House and techno would both shape the future of electronic dance music. But as with the development of hip-hop in NYC, the B-52s again missed an opportunity to connect themselves to emerging new music scenes, even when they were populated by fans of the band.

Mesopotamia had been a perfect storm of bad decisions. Living in Mahopac didn't help. David Byrne didn't help. Having a record label and management more interested in commercial success than artistic growth didn't help either. Already confused and uncertain about their music, it had to be devastating for the B-52s to hear their best song called their worst by someone who had once understood them completely.

Critical Reception

Mesopotamia was released to puzzled reviews and lackluster sales. Compared to cutting edge trends in dance, pop, rock, punk, and the new genre of hip-hop, the B-52s were no longer considered cool. In his comprehensive history of NYC dance music in the early 80s, *Life and Death on the New York Dance Floor 1980–1983*, Tim Lawrence includes playlists from influential DJs during that period. As the book progresses, the B-52s go from appearing in nearly every DJ's set to, by 1983, appearing in none of them.[42]

The B-52s would go on to make great music, but after *Mesopotamia* their critical reputation began to slide. The same *Melody Maker* writer who had praised *Party Mix!* called *Mesopotamia* "the sound of a band chasing its own reputation round and round in ever-decreasing circles." He concluded "It's not all—not exactly ever—really bad. It's just that for all the fussing and busy bodying about, what finally surfaces is a band … desperately in search of just one decent tune."[43]

Meso-America Tour

However underwhelming *Mesopotamia* might have been, it didn't matter to the B-52s' core audience. 1982 saw the band head out on the Meso-American Tour to promote their mini-album, and the band brought saxophonist Ralph Carney and trumpeter David Buck along to flesh out the sound. Known unofficially as "The Horny Horns," Carney recalled the tour as fun, even if "there wasn't an exceptional amount of music for [me] to play."[44]

They also had a new tour manager. Matthew Murphy had been his brother Elliott's tour manager back in the 70s, and Moe Slotin had worked backline for him. Moe called Matthew and set up a meeting with Kate at a health food restaurant. Murphy got the job and met the band in New Orleans on February 22nd to start the tour. The date coincided with a famous local holiday. "We were at some place on Canal Street," recalls Murphy, "and the Mardi Gras parade went by. It was fantastic."[45]

Despite the lackluster response to *Mesopotamia*, the band was rapturously received by audiences. The first two albums were still selling, and the band packed venues averaging between 2500 and 5000 people. They played a former Piggly Wiggly in San Antonio called The Rock Saloon, then headed to Austin to play the 6000 capacity Austin City Coliseum. "The crowd was just going wild," recalls Murphy. "They were just killing it on stage. It was a gigantic party."[46]

Even to a road veteran like Matthew Murphy, the B-52s were an impressive rock band:

> When they took the stage, Ricky on guitar and everything, it was electric …. His method of playing, and how he moved on stage was very dynamic, and

> a big thing. And then Keith on drums, smacking that snare drum. Keith was a fantastic drummer back then. Man, he smacked that snare drum.[47]

The attack of Keith's drumming posed the biggest challenge to the people doing sound. Murphy says, "They weren't quiet on stage." They made their way west for seven shows in California, including four in the L.A. area.

During a two-week break, the band made time to appear on the long-running CBS soap opera *Guiding Light*, performing as themselves at the show's fictional club. The whole thing is surreal to watch—and to think deeply about—but the band were excited to see their names in *TV Guide*.[48]

When the B-52s headed back out on the road in April, they enlisted Hoboken-based group the Bongos to open most of the dates. The band had a lot of NYC buzz at the time on the strength of a handful of excellent avant-pop independent singles. The Bongos felt a kinship with what was happening in Athens and found inspiration in an early B-52s show. Band frontman and guitarist Richard Barone tells the story:

> It was on that ride home, in fact just a few blocks from CBGB's, maybe like a block away, that Frank, the drummer said, "How about the Bongos?" And it was because of Cindy. We thought she was a really cool musician. She was slapping the bongos, and we loved that. And so, we named our group after her playing the Bongos.[49]

The B-52s were as generous to the Bongos as they had been to Pylon, having their crew unload and set up the opening band's gear. The two bands hung out regularly, hitting the thrift stores during the day and buying records. Barone remains in awe of Ricky's guitar playing. "It's just very uniquely him," says Barone. "It has a lot of fun, a lot of energy, just the way he did. The spirit of true rock and roll is in that."[50]

Even though the Bongos were being heavily courted by major labels at the time, the two groups never discussed business. They were too busy having fun. The bands attended a house party one night after a show. The B-52s arrived first, and then the Bongos pulled up in the mobile home they were touring in. Richard Barone recalls that night:

> Cindy would crawl into our mobile home all the time. They would somehow end up in our mobile home. Ricky came outside to greet us with our drinks as we were arriving. That's what kind of host he was.[51]

According to Barone, Ricky called the drinks "donkey dicks," a strong cocktail with vodka and rum.[52] The tour ended May 16th in Richard Barone's hometown of Tampa, Florida at the Jai Alai Fronton. The Bongos, along with the road crew, decided to surprise the B-52s by covering the stage with a bunch of large, inflatable beach toys, and dressing up in flippers, swim caps, and masks. According to Barone, the band was "shocked." Someone told him later the B-52s had all been tripping on LSD that night. "My parents were there and came backstage after the concert to meet everyone," says Barone. "Champagne bottles were popping. My folks loved the show, but my mom whispered to me 'Honey, your friends are strange.'"[53]

Stuck Inside of Mahopac with the Athens Blues Again

The B-52s and The Bongos returned to Mahopac to throw an end-of-tour party. Richard Barone recalls:

> We had a wild party up there. Let me just say that it was like a wild party. The Bongos were there, and the B-52s, and some very intimate friends. Many of us got naked and jumped into the lake. They were magic. I know Captain Beefheart had his Magic Band, but the B-52s were my magic band.[54]

Relations between the B-52s and their neighbors were becoming strained, as the band found themselves sued in local court for trying to build a rehearsal studio in their garage. "If it were the New York Philharmonic," said one plaintiff, "it would be very nice to be able to sip a cocktail and listen. But a rock band will drive you crazy."[55] The band had already spent money to renovate and soundproof the garage, but it made no difference. An incredulous Keith Bennett told the local paper, "All we do is eat, sleep and watch M*A*S*H."[56]

After three years in upstate New York, the band began to look for another place to live. But first they had a festival to play.

US Festival

Conceived by Apple co-founder Steve Wozniak, the US Festival (US as in "you and me," not the United States) was an 80s attempt to recreate the magic of Woodstock, only this time in San Bernardino. Like its 60s predecessor, the US festival drew nearly half a million people and lost millions of dollars. On September 3, 1982, the B-52s flew in on helicopters, and went on during the day, between Oingo Boingo and Talking Heads. Quite simply, the band were incredible. The Police headlined that night, and drummer Stewart Copeland said, "It has to be said that the B-52s owned that day of the US Festival."[57] *Rolling Stone* agreed:

> Their nonstop dance numbers turned the area in front of the stage into a man-made dust storm; by the time the band finished "Hot Lava," the white spotlight aimed at Fred Schneider looked for all the world like a car headlight cutting through heavy fog.[58]

The band referred to it as "The Dust Festival" for many years. It was so hot backstage that Kate took off all her clothes and poured a cooler of water over her head.[59] Whatever problems existed within the band, they still possessed the alchemy that made them such a great live band. At the US Festival, the B-52s laid down the law.

Afterward, the band moved to Manhattan. Cindy, Ricky, and Keith—the three Athens natives—purchased a building on 13th Street. Kate and Fred got their own apartments elsewhere in the city.[60] It helped ease some of the band tension, though a 1990 profile would note that despite the move, "internal and external pressures were creating divisions within the band."[61]

The band played three shows that November, including a festival in Jamaica. Two days after that show, they played the Citrus Bowl in Orlando, Florida, opening for the Who. It did not go well. The Who attracted a rough crowd, including a rowdy group of biker gangs in the front. A B-52s fan drove down from Atlanta for the show and recalled getting heckled with shouts of "You must be here to see the B-52s, you faggot."[62] Joan Jett was first on the bill. When she got booed and pelted with garbage, the B-52s knew what was coming for them. "Cindy and I had big hair that day," recalled Kate, "and we were dressed in our usual retro space-age cool. I guess the bikers didn't appreciate that look."[63] They sure didn't. They started chanting for the Who before the band played a note, and it only got worse when the music began. Fred and Kate had to dodge Coke cans and plastic cups. Cindy got hit in the stomach with an apple. According to the fan who had been heckled, a "big biker mama" pulled a dildo out of her purse and threw it at Kate's face.[64] Kate said in 2010, "This was actually the first and only time in the band's 31-year touring history that we got a bad reaction."[65] They played a few more songs and split before things could get really ugly. The Who apologized backstage, but that didn't change anything.

The band headed home and tried to catch their breath. In a couple of weeks, they would be heading back to Compass Point. It was time to try and record another album. This time Steven Stanley would produce. He had worked wonders for Tom Tom Club, and maybe he could help the B-52s get to wherever it was they were trying to go.

Notes

1. Ellen, "B-52's," 32.
2. Richardson, "B-52's Regain Their Stride."
3. Lepidus, "B52's Born," 24.
4. Groome, "The B-52's: Still Crashing," 39.
5. Levy, "How Bob Dylan Made."
6. Rose, "The B-52's."
7. Ibid.
8. Schoemer, "Beehives & Ballyhoo," 44.
9. Rose, "The B-52's."
10. Ellen, "B-52's," 35. Anyone who loves the B-52s and has never heard Suburban Lawns should go listen to the song Janitor immediately.
11. Ibid.
12. Wilkinson, "wig wam bam!" 28.
13. Johnson, "Club 57" Liner notes *The World of Keith Haring*.
14. Stein, *Siren Song*, 189.
15. Connelly, "Byrne."
16. Stein, *Siren Song*, 190.
17. Ibid.
18. Stein, *Siren Song*, 197.
19. Chin, "Disco File," 18.
20. Connelly, "Byrne."
21. Stein, *Siren Song*, 198.
22. Doyle, "Madonna Interview: MOJO."
23. Norton, "Surpriiiise," 45.
24. Mizek, History of Electro.
25. Morley, *Words and Music*, 137.
26. Sexton, *The B-52's Universe*, 163.
27. Blashill, "52 Pickup," 124.

28. Wilde, "B-52's," 9.
29. Harris, "Kate Pierson."
30. True, *Hey ho let's go*, 271. In addition to his writing career, True is also a well-respected gardener and chef.
31. Kozak, "Rock'n'Rolling," 73.
32. Elephant Blog, "Anecdote #606."
33. Gittins, *Talking Heads*, 59.
34. Sexton, *The B-52's Universe*, 59.
35. Harris, "Kate Pierson."
36. Snow, "The B-52s."
37. Ibid.
38. Ibid.
39. Sicko, *Techno Rebels*, 15.
40. Arnold, "The B-52s."
41. Ibid.
42. Lawrence, *Life and Death.*
43. Sutherland, "Garbage Beat."
44. Sexton, *The B-52's Universe*, 61.
45. Matthew Murphy in conversation with authors, May 28, 2019.
46. Ibid.
47. Ibid.
48. Sexton, *The B-52's Universe*, 61.
49. Richard Barone in conversation with authors, May 9, 2019.
50. Ibid.
51. Ibid.
52. Ibid.
53. Richard Barone, email message to authors, May 10, 2019.
54. Richard Barone in conversation with authors, May 9, 2019.
55. Battaglio, "Mahopac neighbors," 3.
56. Ibid.
57. YouTube, "B52s Kate Pierson."
58. Pond, "Backstage."
59. YouTube, "B52s Kate Pierson."
60. Sexton, *The B-52's Universe*, 61. Sexton's book says the building was purchased by Cindy and Keith Bennett, but KB insists otherwise.
61. Schoemer, "Beehives & Ballyhoo," 44.
62. Watching the Wheels, "Jukebox Hero 1."
63. Kandel, "The B-52s' Arcade."
64. Watching the Wheels, "Jukebox Hero 1." The fan also says Joan Jett went on after the B-52s. Kate has said it was the other way around.
65. Kandel, "The B-52s."

CHAPTER 8

Whammy

We've made mistakes and we realize that.[1]

—Fred

Only 24 at the time he produced *Whammy!*[2] Steven Stanley was considered something of a whiz kid. Raised in Kingston, Jamaica, he began working in local studios at 17 before being tapped by Chris Blackwell to come to Compass Point, where he quickly became a fixture at the studio.[3] Working as an engineer on Talking Heads' *Remain in Light*, Stanley impressed Chris Frantz and Tina Weymouth so much that they asked him to work on their Tom Tom Club album. He took a hands-on approach, even playing keyboard on Genius of Love.

Stanley was already familiar with the B-52s' music—having worked on *Party Mix!*—and tried to emphasize the fun parts of making a record. "I make sure the human element stays on top and the rest is underneath," said Stanley. "Except when it's necessary to get freaky, then I go wild."[4] According to Kate, he was also a great dancer. "He'll just spin around and punch all these buttons and the drums will come up real loud," she said.

> Then he'll hold onto the board, putting his legs up behind him. We'd be singing in the studio and we'd see his head just going back and forth with this big smile on his face. But he is exacting; he never lets you off with, oh, that's good enough.[5]

S. Creney, B. A. Herron, *The Story of the B-52s*,
https://doi.org/10.1007/978-3-031-22570-3_8

The band had started using an Oberheim DMX drum machine during their jamming and songwriting sessions in Mahopac, but felt conflicted about using it for the album. Keith particularly had mixed feelings. "They're nice to a certain extent," he said, "but I think they do get kinda cold. They're so precise they don't vary the tempo enough, really."[6] According to Fred, Steven Stanley ultimately cast the deciding vote. "When Steven said, keep it in, we did … and that definitely changed the tone."[7]

According to Stanley, this time the band was well-prepared, with all the songs written in advance. They also seemed to be getting along better in Compass Point. On breaks from recording, the band swam and snorkeled. Kate nearly got stung by a stingray, and Ricky "fought off an army of crabs on his front porch,"[8] which sounds like a Fred Schneider lyric, but isn't.

That didn't mean everything in the band was running smoothly. The self-consciousness that had set in during the writing of *Mesopotamia* hadn't gone away, and that record's failure seemed to have shaken the B-52s' confidence—in the band, in themselves, and in each other. Keith had already openly expressed his concerns about the band's "identity," worrying, "We were really in danger of becoming a parody of ourselves."[9]

It had to be hard for Keith, and to a lesser extent Ricky. When most critics talked about the B-52s, they talked about the band's outlandish costumes and over-the-top personalities, but Ricky and Keith dressed more conservatively and tended to be quieter than their bandmates. No one in the band has ever discussed any specific conversations that took place, but in interviews that year, Kate and Fred each emphasized the importance of involving Keith and Ricky more. Fred said, "Keith and Ricky have never sung. We like to promote all five of us …. Be sure attention is paid equally to everyone this time round."[10]

On *Whammy!* Ricky and Keith would play all the instruments, as well as make their first vocal appearances on Song For a Future Generation. This new arrangement meant a reduced role for the rest of the band, particularly Kate, and it says a lot about the depth of the band's friendships that Fred, Cindy, and Kate accepted this new working situation so generously. Still, in the same interview where he talked about the importance of expanding Ricky and Keith's role, Fred also talked about his plans for various solo projects. And Kate worried that Keith stepping out from behind the drums and relying on the drum machine would cause the band's live show to suffer.[11]

Whammy! may have been more egalitarian, but it was an equality achieved by clearly defining, and limiting, certain roles within the band. As a result, its harmony feels more like the result of negotiations and peace treaties than the spirit of true collaboration that had been present in the band's first two albums.

Whammy!

After *Mesopotamia*, most people were just grateful the B-52s had finally made another album, even if the result had more to do with pragmatism than a band at its creative peak.

That's not to say *Whammy!* isn't a good album. Legal Tender is one of the best, and sweetest songs, the band ever created, and it's one with a rebellious, criminal heart at its center. Robert Waldrop's lyrics tell the story of a group of counterfeiters in a basement that could have been next door to Bob Dylan's basement in Subterranean Homesick Blues. Instead of mixing up the medicine, the B-52s are printing up the money, though any jubilation they might feel is undercut by the sadness of the melody. The reference to heavy equipment indicates how theft can be its own kind of work.

Legal Tender's story of turning trash into cash echoes the story of the B-52s, and examines the similarities between rock stars and outlaws more effectively than the Eagles did on *Desperado*. With its line about rising prices, Legal Tender can also be heard as a reaction to the economic recession in the US at the time. The jelly jars in the song echo Depression-era values of thrift and scarcity, and the line about *gangster presidents* suggests the protagonists know their history.

The next song isn't called Whammy, or even Whammy! It's called Whammy Kiss (not Whammy! Kiss, or Whammy! Kiss! either). The song transcends what could have just been a Devo homage (right down to its use of the word *mammy*), on the strength of its songwriting. The unorthodox D#-G#-D-G chord progression used in the chorus is the product of a higher musical intelligence.

Cindy said of Song For a Future Generation, "It was our anthem—we're all in there and we're all contributing."[12] An ode to computer dating that's only gotten more relevant in the age of online hook-up apps, Future Generation isn't just a good joke, it's also slyly subversive. The song touches on a familiar B-52s theme—finding your way through loneliness and isolation. When they mention wanting to be the captain of the

Enterprise, it evokes the interpretation of Star Trek as an idealized multicultural socialist utopia. Ultimately, the song is about wanting to create something, and needing someone else to make it happen.

Butterbean's increased velocity allows the band to untap their pent-up aggression. You can almost picture the frost on the windows up in Mahopac and the neighbors complaining, the same old shit on TV again, and the claustrophobic and homesick band stuck trying to write songs. Kate and Cindy stretch the last syllable of Butterbean into something dark and avant-garde, and the song features Ricky's greatest synth playing.

Christopher Connelly called side two a "waste" in his *Rolling Stone* review that year.[13] And while that feels a little harsh, neither Trism nor Queen of Las Vegas is as satisfying as anything on side one. Both have good ideas, but as with *Mesopotamia*, the arrangements feel haphazard and kind of flat. Trism has this wonderful drum fill that appears in the verses almost at random, and it can take years of listening before you realize that the ascending synth part where Cindy and Kate sing *Trism* is supposed to be the chorus. The song dated back to the Bridge Mix days of Keith and Fred making stuff up in Athens. As for Queen of Las Vegas, the vocals are great, but the synthesized music removes all the swagger and drama from the version left off *Mesopotamia*. The song tells a poor-girl-in-the-big-city story that's an update of Bobbie Gentry's Fancy. It's fun to imagine the song's protagonist as a drag queen assembling her identity, even though at its heart, Queen of Las Vegas is ultimately a song about watching your mother die.

Don't Worry was improvised in the studio, and it's a lot of fun, especially if you know the original version by Yoko Ono. Hers was a proto-No Wave screamer about fighting for custody of your child, but the B-52s turn it into a pop mantra. "I gave each member of the band a track apiece," said Steven Stanley, "and they just jammed all over the place .... That song was like working on a jigsaw puzzle."[14] A good cover takes something unheard in the song and foregrounds it for everyone to hear in a way that redefines both artists. The fact that the B-52s were able to hear the pop nugget in Ono's version and draw it out makes a case for the band's musical and conceptual genius.

The *Whammy!* liner notes credit "All instruments Played by Keith Strickland and Ricky Wilson except on Big Bird Saxophone Played by Ralph Carney and Trumpet Played by David Buck," but Big Bird raises some questions. The version included on *Whammy!* was recorded earlier in the year, and features bongos played in Cindy's signature style and a keyboard bass part that sounds exactly like Kate. When the band performed the song live on the ensuing tour, Kate and Cindy played those instruments, and replicated the album parts effortlessly. Which makes you wonder: If Kate and Cindy could play the song live, and it sounded incredible, why didn't they play it on the album? And if they did play on the album version, which is what it sounds like, then why weren't they credited for it?

No matter who played on it, Big Bird is one of the most powerful songs the band ever recorded. Fred says the song is about a plane, but it's hard not to hear the bird in this song as a raven, a crow, or the mythical Thunderbird described by ancient peoples of the Southwest, as some kind of harbinger of death. In NYC at this time, rumors were flying about a new disease that only seemed to affect gay men. By the time *Whammy!* came out, the disease had a name—AIDS—and the reality would turn out to be far more terrifying than the rumors.

On tour, the B-52s played Big Bird as a full band, and the May 1983 performance in Dortmund, Germany is a revelation. Cindy's bongo playing and Ralph Carney's saxophone turn the song into a Dionysian frenzy. The song burns and burns, and the B-52s sound for all the world like they're about to either take flight or rip the earth open and liberate the prisons of hell.

That version of Big Bird is so good that it underscores what's missing from *Whammy!* as a whole. The musical interplay between the members had been a major strength of the band, and without that sense of groove to fall back on, *Whammy!* relies on the strength of its songwriting. By songwriting, we mean hooks—memorable riffs, cool chord progressions, words that stick in your head or make you think. When a song on *Whammy!* has those things, as with Legal Tender, it sounds wonderful. When a song doesn't, it just sounds boring.

The album ends with Work That Skirt, a fun and bouncy instrumental. Kate said in an interview that the band "always wanted to have one instrumental on each record because Keith did a lot of the instrumentation and he didn't get the recognition."[15] On Work That Skirt, the band finally got its wish.

The decision to embrace synthesizers and drum machines was, on its surface, a good one. We argued in the last chapter how the band were in danger of being left behind by new developments in music, yet the electronics of *Whammy!* sound closer to what Yellow Magic Orchestra had done in the late 70s than any current trends. The years 1983 and 1984 were incredible years for both pop music and the underground, and the B-52s were out of step with both. They were making records that were less interesting or commercial than mainstream fare from Michael Jackson, Madonna, David Bowie, Cyndi Lauper, and Prince. Furthermore, independent bands like Husker Du, the Minutemen, and the Replacements were making music that felt more raw and vital, messier and more visceral, than what *Whammy!* had to offer.

The B-52s had made a good album, one with two or three songs that deserved to be on the radio. But while a song like Legal Tender is danceable and emotionally moving, it suffers in comparison to contemporary songs as groundbreaking as, say, Shannon's Let the Music Play, which features a drum machine that lays down a better groove than anything on *Whammy!*

The band had liked the way the songs flowed into each other on *Party Mix!* without any separation, so they wanted to do the same thing with *Whammy!* The idea wasn't completely unprecedented. Soft Cell's 1981 album, *Non-Stop Erotic Cabaret*, had utilized this approach and been a commercial success. Tainted Love, a single from the album, reached #1 in the UK and the Top 10 in the US, something the B-52s had yet to achieve. Gary Kurfirst, however, nixed the idea. "Gary told Steven we couldn't do that!" said Keith. "We always had complete control over our writing and what we do."[16] Nonetheless, the band acquiesced to Kurfirst's wishes.

Murmurs

Whammy! was released on April 7, 1983. A week later saw the release of the debut album from another Athens band. R.E.M.'s *Murmur* was a terrific piece of art-pop, and it received ecstatic reviews. *Rolling Stone* critics named it their album of the year, and the magazine's review concluded, "R.E.M. is clearly *the* important Athens band."[17]

R.E.M. had played their first show on April 5, 1980. In Athens tradition, it was at a party. The B-52s caught some of their early shows. Jeremy Ayers was an early fan of the band and took Kate to see them. Cindy also caught an early show. A friend of Peter Buck recalled the R.E.M. guitarist telling him, "I can't believe Cindy Wilson thought we were good!"[18]

"When The B-52's put out their first single on Danny Beard's label, it blew my mind!" recalled Buck. "Literally, there hadn't been anyone from Georgia to get a record contract that wasn't beer and boogie and cowboy hats, ever."[19] In Buck's enthusiastic rush to condemn the mid-70s ubiquity of southern rock, he managed to forget about Ray Charles, James Brown, Otis Redding, and so many others.

When they started out, R.E.M. were savvy enough to realize they weren't much more than a very good band playing unoriginal garage rock. It took nearly a year before a unique sound emerged, one defined by Stipe's poetic, enigmatic vocals, and Buck's chiming, arpeggiated guitar. R.E.M. waited until June 1981 before they finally played New York, though in a concession to Athens tradition, they did open for Gang of Four.

The band was also savvy in other ways, as if they had paid close attention to the B-52s' career and were determined not to repeat the same mistakes. For one, R.E.M. employed two managers with clearly delineated responsibilities. Bertis Downs focused on the legal side, and Jefferson Holt focused on the band's day-to-day activities. Importantly, both men were fans of the band, motivated more by enthusiasm than money. And what their management lacked in connections, they made up for by sharing the band's vision. After being courted by RCA—a major label that eventually signed the Bongos, to disastrous results—R.E.M. instead chose to sign with IRS, an independent label distributed by a major (A&M). There, R.E.M. would be able to make their own decisions, to be as commercial or as uncommercial as they wanted. Buck said IRS were "the only [label] who didn't say, 'Boys, if you guys cut your hair and stop wearing dirty clothes, I can turn you into the Go-Go's.'"[20]

It also helped that Bill Berry and Pete Buck brought a deep knowledge about the music business to R.E.M. Berry, a Macon native, had spent his late teens working for Capricorn Records. Buck got his education behind the counter at Wuxtry Records, the Athens record store that had usurped the now-defunct Chapter III as the coolest store in town. Buck also insisted the band split the songwriting credits (and the money that came with it) equally, as a way to prevent internal conflicts. They also chose to remain in Athens even after they began to have success, with the band members purchasing houses in town that were only a bike ride away from their practice space.

Without a manager or a label constantly pushing for big sales, R.E.M. were able to grow their career slowly. They released an album every year between 1983 and 1988, each selling slightly more than the previous one. It wouldn't be until 1987 that The One I Love, from their fifth album, *Document*, gave R.E.M. their first Top 40 hit, eventually reaching #9. When their IRS contract expired the following year, they then signed to Warner Brothers for an undisclosed amount rumored to be around $10 million. There, they were given a level of creative freedom the B-52s could only have dreamed of.

Video Tactics; Radio Static

That summer, the reunited Talking Heads had their first Top 10 hit with Burning Down the House. The resulting album, *Speaking in Tongues*, hit the Top 20. At the end of the year, they decided to film a performance from their tour to release as a film. Financed by Gary Kurfirst and directed by Jonathan Demme, *Stop Making Sense* became one of the most critically acclaimed concert films ever made. In *The New Yorker*, Pauline Kael called it "close to perfection."[21] Talking Heads would make three more albums before breaking up in 1989 when David Byrne finally left the band for good. In 2002, they were elected to the Rock and Roll Hall of Fame. During the induction ceremony, Frantz thanked Gary Kurfirst, who was there in attendance.

Burning Down the House was a success, in part, because the song had a captivating video that was played regularly on MTV. The channel began broadcasting in 1981, and by 1983, it had become a viable commercial force. With their visual flair, the B-52s seemed like a natural fit for the channel. According to Fred, the band wanted to make videos, but were discouraged by Kurfirst:

> [He] said, "What do you want to do videos for? You don't make any money from them. Look at David Byrne, he puts out videos, he doesn't make any money from them." Gary didn't get the point. I guess you wouldn't say he was a visionary in that respect.[22]

Burning Down the House must have changed Kurfirst's mind, because the band took a couple of days off while on tour that June to film videos for Legal Tender and Song For a Future Generation. The video for the latter song features candelabras, chandeliers, and columns that the band found lying around the set after a Liberace show—one more example of the B-52s' trash aesthetic. Despite the videos' bright, bubbly beauty, and all five members looking like stars, neither video got played much on MTV. The songs didn't do any better on the radio. Legal Tender only reached #81. Whammy Kiss and Future Generation didn't even make the charts.

The B-52s still had a loyal audience, but each release was selling less than the one before. This had to concern Warner Brothers, and by extension, the band. Major labels aren't known for their infinite patience. If this downward commercial trend continued, the band's career would soon be in jeopardy.

Tour

Despite the cool critical and commercial response to *Mesopotamia* and *Whammy!* the B-52s were turning into one of those bands who cultivate a love from their core audience that verges on the unconditional. The tour for *Whammy!* would put that love to the test though, as Kate's concerns about the drum machine became reality.

The band's new set-up didn't just affect the sound, it affected the show's pacing. Keith needed to switch back and forth between playing keyboards and playing live drums, and the transition made for a lot of down time during the band's set. A show on June 10th in Austin, Texas saw the band open with Future Generation, which had all five members out in front singing to a backing track. Forty-five seconds then pass as Ricky and Keith get set up to play before the band starts the next song. After three more songs—Strobe Light, Give Me Back My Man, and Planet Claire—in this configuration, they go back to the drum machine and synths to play Butterbean, Queen of Las Vegas, Whammy Kiss, and Legal Tender. This time the reconfiguration takes 40 seconds. The transition after those songs then lasts nearly a minute.

All of this can feel like an eternity when you're standing on stage, and it can suck the momentum from the show if you're in the audience. Most disturbingly, songs from the first B-52s albums are greeted with loud cheers, while the *Whammy!* songs receive a more muted response. During a July 22nd show in West Hartford, Connecticut, you can even hear the crowd talking audibly among themselves during the drum machine songs, only perking up during the full band numbers.

Every show wasn't like the one in West Hartford. The *New York Times* called their August 5th show in Forest Hills, NYC, "pure rock-and-roll jubilation."[23] The writer also noticed that when the band introduced themselves during Future Generation, Ricky got the biggest cheer.

On tour, journalists were still asking questions about *Mesopotamia*, so much so that the B-52s ended up talking about their last record as much as their new one. As the tour wound on, *Boston Rock* caught up with the band. When asked if they felt restricted by being B-52s, the writer was "greeted with a pregnant pause." Kate admitted there were restrictions, and Keith agreed, saying "In a way, we feel kind of trapped." Ever the optimist, he immediately qualified his statement. "I don't want to sound negative. It's a good trap."[24]

In another interview, Fred sounded almost resigned to their new reality. "Now we just don't care. We know our fans want us to entertain them .... Granted, we look funny, but that's what people want."[25]

In November, the band played their first show in Athens since 1978. Around 3500 fans filled the UGA Coliseum, including Ricky and Cindy's grandmother. While on tour, the band got a call from Yoko Ono's lawyers. Ono liked their version of Don't Worry, but, as the songwriter, she wanted royalties for her song. Instead, the band decided to remove the song from the album. Looking for a replacement, the B-52s faced a familiar problem—not enough songs. Instead of just writing a new one, they used an electronic update of There's a Moon in the Sky they had made at Compass. They named it Moon 83, and it would appear on all future editions of *Whammy!* The song is fine enough, but there's something profoundly strange about an artist covering a song from their first album on their third one. When asked for an explanation, Fred said, "I don't know why we chose that."[26]

The following month, Pylon decided to quit playing music. After two albums and several years of touring, they found themselves being pressured to make better business decisions, including going on tour to open for U2. "We were like, let's just quit while we're having fun," said Vanessa Briscoe Hay.[27] The band wouldn't perform again until 1989. As for the B-52s, they concluded the *Whammy!* tour with three shows in NYC at the Ritz, November 21–23.

For the sake of pop culture history, we should mention that 1983 was also the year the B-52s met an Atlanta musician named RuPaul when they saw Ru's band Wee Wee Pole perform in Atlanta.[28]

Hiatus

The band took all of 1984 off from being the B-52s. Mostly, they just rested. Fred, always the busiest member, found a way to occupy himself by releasing a solo album that year called *Fred Schneider & the Shake Society.*

John Coté played guitar on the album and wrote nearly all of the music. The backing band included P-Funk veteran Bernie Worrell on synthesizer, and the album featured a plethora of guest stars. Patti Labelle performed a duet with Fred called It's Time to Kiss. Ricky played guitar on I'm Gonna Haunt You, and Kate sang backing vocals on a few songs, including the album's best-known track, Monster. That song's video was banned by MTV, reportedly due to a claymation creature that looked a lot like a penis. Though Fred claimed innocence, lines like *There's a monster in my pants / and he does a nasty dance* did nothing to dissuade that interpretation. Kate and Tina Weymouth appeared in the video, along with old friends Keith Haring and NYC underground theater legend Ethyl Eichelberger. Fred looks super-cute, and struts through the video with the best set of dance moves he ever concocted. Sadly, the album only sold 35,000 copies.[29]

Rio

Even though the band didn't tour during 1984, they were asked to play a couple of big shows at the Rock in Rio Festival in January 1985. Based in Brazil, the festival lasted ten days, and featured AC-DC, Queen, and the Go-Go's, as well as Brazilian artists Gilberto Gil and Alceu Valença. The B-52s enlisted Chris Frantz and Tina Weymouth to play drums and bass on the *Whammy!* songs, perhaps as a reaction to the challenges on the *Whammy!* tour. The expanded group played three warm-up gigs in the northeastern US before flying to Brazil.

These would be some of the largest crowds the band ever played to, with nearly 250,000 people in attendance each night.

Neither night featured the band at their best. Maybe the time off had an effect, or maybe it was the long flight, but the group sounds sluggish and lethargic. The presence of Chris and Tina doesn't add anything to Legal Tender, and underscores how Kate and Keith formed a terrific rhythm section.

Fred keeps trying to ramp up the energy level, reminding you of how much the band relied on his confidence in the early days. But every time a song comes to life, the intensity drops again after a few bars. Ricky's playing is unusually off during both shows, and his right hand, normally a blur of precise motion, is more tentative than usual. The problems could have stemmed from many things—sleeplessness, poor sound monitors, the size of the stage—but it's hard not to wonder if he was feeling the effects of something more serious.

Tour manager Matthew Murphy accompanied the band on the trip and recalls an interaction he had with Ricky backstage. "I'll never forget, down there at Rock in Rio, he said to me, 'I've got this lump under my arm,' one of the glands there."[30]

Notes

1. Rose, "The B-52's."
2. Do we have to type the exclamation point every time we mention the name of the album? [Checks notes] Apparently, we do.
3. Trakin, "Steven Stanley."
4. Ibid.
5. Rose, "The B-52's."
6. Ibid.
7. Ibid.
8. B-52'S FAN CLUB NEWSLETTER #3, Mats Sexton B-52's memorabilia collection, Box 1, University of Georgia Libraries Special Collections.
9. Rose, "The B-52's."
10. Ibid.
11. Ibid.
12. Suwak, "Cindy Wilson."
13. Connelly, "The B-52s."
14. Trakin, "Steven Stanley."
15. Sexton, *The B-52's Universe*, 179.
16. Sexton, *The B-52's Universe*, 64.
17. Pond, "Murmur."
18. Sullivan, *R.E.M.*, 11.
19. Fletcher, *Remarks*, 14–15.
20. DeCurtis, "R.E.M.'s Brave …," 33. Originally appeared in *Rolling Stone* April 20, 1989.
21. Kael, "Three Cheers."
22. Marks and Tannenbaum, *I Want My MTV*, 92.
23. Holden, "Rock-And-Roll."
24. Lepidus, "B52's Born," 24.
25. Richardson, "B-52's Regain Their Stride."
26. Sexton, *The B-52's Universe*, 179.
27. Cohan, "Pylon's Brilliant Punk."
28. B-Hive Fall 1997 Issue #10, Mats Sexton B-52's memorabilia collection, Box 1, University of Georgia Libraries Special Collections.
29. Thomas, "Monster."
30. Matthew Murphy in conversation with authors, May 28, 2019.

CHAPTER 9

Satellites

It was really a hard, dark, dark time, and I guess it took us years to get over it. And personally, you never really get over it.[1]

—Cindy

The trajectory of the B-52s would forever be changed by the AIDS epidemic. AIDS had begun to spread in the late 1970s, as doctors saw patients coming in with unusual symptoms that were the result of extremely rare diseases. As the AIDS crisis unfolded, doctors had no idea what they were dealing with until well into the 1980s.

The fourth person to die of AIDS in the US, Rick Wellikoff was diagnosed with Kaposi's Sarcoma, an extremely rare form of skin cancer, by a doctor in NYC in September of 1979. This happened while the B-52s were playing their first west coast shows. Wellikoff's visit had been prompted by his sore and swollen lymph nodes and the strange rash developing on his skin. In January 1981, his friend Nick Rock died with infections running all through his body, strange infections with names like Toxoplasmosis and Cytomegalovirus. They found one infection in his lungs that was so rare, doctors couldn't even tell what it was.[2]

Two days after *Wild Planet* was released, on June 29, 1980, San Francisco had its annual Gay Pride Parade. Around 30,000 people marched, and the event drew over 200,000 spectators. One of them was Gaetan Dugas, a flight attendant living in Nova Scotia. While in New York

S. Creney, B. A. Herron, *The Story of the B-52s*,
https://doi.org/10.1007/978-3-031-22570-3_9

City, he had recently visited a doctor to have a purplish bump removed from his face. The doctor performed a biopsy and found that Dugas had Kaposi's Sarcoma. This extremely rare form of skin cancer was suddenly becoming more common.

On June 5, 1981, while the band was in Mahopac writing songs for *Mesopotamia*, the Centers for Disease Control and Prevention (CDC) published the first official report about AIDS, concerning five gay men who had contracted a rare lung infection. The presence of other infections in their body suggested a problem with the immune system. By the time it was published, two of the men had already died. A New York dermatologist saw the report, and immediately called the CDC to notify them about the large number of Kaposi's Sarcoma cases he was seeing. Within days, the CDC was receiving similar accounts from all over the country.

A month later, a newspaper in San Francisco published an article on "Gay Men's Pneumonia." The *New York Times* ran an article on page 20: "Rare Cancer Seen in 41 Homosexuals."[3] In September, as the B-52s began recording *Mesopotamia*, the CDC and the National Cancer Institute held the first conference to address the growing epidemic.

At the beginning of 1982, Gay Men's Health Crisis (GMHC) opened in NYC, the first community-based organization supporting people with AIDS. That February, the band began their Meso-American tour. In April, Congress held its first hearings on the disease. Dr. James Curran, head of a CDC task force on what was being called Kaposi's Sarcoma and Opportunistic Infections, testified that tens of thousands of people were likely already infected. By the time the B-52s finished their tour in May, the disease had two names, AID (Acquired Immunodeficiency Disease) or GRID (Gay-Related Immunodeficiency). The second term reinforced the false public perception that the disease exclusively affected gay men, and would soon be dropped. A month later, a gay activist group in San Francisco handed out the first pamphlet calling for "safer sex." In September, the CDC used the term AIDS, and two Democratic congressmen introduced the first bill to allocate funding for AIDS research. It would die in committee. That month, the B-52s played The US Festival.

In March 1983, Larry Kramer, writer, AIDS activist, and co-founder of Gay Men's Health Crisis, published an article in the *New York Native* entitled "1,121 and Counting." Kramer wrote:

> Our continued existence as gay men upon the face of this earth is at stake. Unless we fight for our lives, we shall die. In all the history of homosexuality

> we have never before been so close to death and extinction. Many of us are dying or already dead.[4]

He was right. In 2019, a book about the history of AIDS said of this period that “at least half of all gay men living in New York [City] and San Francisco had already contracted the virus causing AIDS, although may were unaware and asymptomatic.”[5] Kramer concluded his 5000-word article with a call for civil disobedience. In 2017, he explained what it was like to watch the crisis unfold:

> The first people who got sick were friends of mine. In the Village, you couldn’t walk down the street without running into somebody who said: “Have you heard about so and so? He just died.” Sometimes you could learn about three or four people just walking the dog. I started making a list of how many people I knew, and it was hundreds. People don’t comprehend that. People really were dying like flies.[6]

That April, the B-52s released *Whammy!* The following month, the first AIDS candlelight vigils were held in San Francisco and New York. Three days after the band appeared on German TV, Congress finally passed the first bill to fund AIDS research—for the paltry amount of $12 million.

During this time, Marcus Conant, one of the first doctors to diagnose and treat AIDS patients, met with a Reagan official in Washington DC to advocate for more funding. He and his colleagues were stunned by the callous response, “[He said that] this was a legal problem, not a medical problem,” because the victims, simply by being gay, “were breaking the law.”[7] In August, as the band was completing the first leg of their US tour in support of *Whammy! Newsweek* ran a cover story on AIDS. That same month, the B-52s lost a close friend when Klaus Nomi died from the disease, one of the earliest celebrity casualties. In September, a NYC physician was threatened with eviction from his building for treating people with the disease, and the first AIDS discrimination suit was filed as a response.

Sometime around the end of 1984, Ricky Wilson began to exhibit the symptoms of AIDS. As the disease progressed, he elected not to tell anyone about it except for Keith, who he swore to secrecy. Keith explained, “It was so early in the epidemic, and it was very difficult because Ricky really didn’t know how to deal with it, and I didn’t either.”[8] As 1985 began, Ricky's health began to visibly deteriorate, and people around him started asking questions. He blamed his weight loss on all the Mexican food he was eating, but Cindy asked him directly if anything was wrong. "I looked him straight in the eye," she said, "and he laughed and said, 'Nooooo.'"[9]

That April, Cindy and Keith Bennett got married in Athens. Ricky attended, but didn't want to appear in any pictures. Roy Bell, Ricky's old high school friend, was there, and they got to talking. Ricky told Bell he wasn't feeling well and was going to skip the reception, but asked him to come out to his parents' house that Monday so they could catch up. Bell had a wife and two kids, and had to work that Monday, so he couldn't make it. "I know that Ricky didn't tell anybody that he was sick," recalled Bell. "I'm not foolish enough to think that he was going to tell me he was sick, but I think that he was maybe going to tell me goodbye."[10]

Bouncing

After the wedding, the band spent two more months working on the songs for their next album. A sense of sadness pervades *Bouncing Off the Satellites*, but it would be oversimplifying to attribute it to Ricky's illness, or the effect AIDS was having on New York. Put simply, the B-52s were now barely functioning as a band. Fred said, "We had started to drift apart. Everybody was doing their own songs because we were finding it harder and harder to jam and agree on things."[11] The five members were only able to collaborate on four songs: Wig, Detour Thru Your Mind, Theme for a Nude Beach, and Communicate. Ricky and Keith decided that Kate and Fred should each go off and write a song while Ricky and Keith continued to work with Cindy.[12] Kate wrote Housework with NYC artist and teacher Tim Rollins, her partner from 1981 through 1996. Fred called on his Shake Society collaborator John Coté to write and play the music for the song that became Juicy Jungle. Kate recalled the band dynamics around this time as "fragmented, and I felt alienated, as I think Fred did, too."[13]

Once the songs were written, the band headed into the studio. This time, they elected to record in New York City with producer Tony Mansfield, whose resume included two hits for Naked Eyes (Always Something There to Remind Me and Promises, Promises). Mansfield's other production experience included Aztec Camera and A-ha. The latter band's album *Hunting High and Low*, had reached the US Top 20, but

both its singles (the US #1 Take On Me, and US #20 T
Shines On T.V.) were re-recorded because A-ha wasn't sat
versions they did with Mansfield. The two Aztec Camera singl
Walk Out to Winter) also found greater success after they
with somebody else. *Satellites* would prove to be Mansfiel
profile production gig.

To his credit, Mansfield was considered a master of the Fa
a synthesizer/sampler adopted early on by UK art rockers P
and Kate Bush. It's probably best known for the electronic sou
erated on hits like Power Station's Some Like It Hot, Tears
Shout, and the theme song to *Miami Vice*.

Instead of using a drum machine like they did on *Whammy!*
composed their drum parts on the Fairlight with Tony Mansfie
Keith said, "I brought in a cassette of sounds that I had Tony sa
They were from other records—I'm not gonna say which ones—but the
was this great record from the Sixties having to do with the zodiac."[14] Once they loaded the sounds into the computer, they arranged the beats using a primitive version of a sequencer. They also employed the Fairlight for other sounds, like the sitar on Wig. "The Fairlight is strange," recalled Keith. "It's so impressionistic. It always changes things and makes them hard and brittle."[15]

Keith and Ricky again handled all the music, except for Kate and Fred's solo songs. As Fred later observed, "We were still friends, but we had been falling apart a bit as a group."[16] Aside from some percussion Keith contributed to Housework, no other B-52s members played on the two songs. Kate had wanted to record Housework live with her full band, but was "disappointed" when she was overruled, and the drums were done through the Fairlight. "I really hated that thing," said Kate.[17] Ricky and Keith worked so fast that, as Kate remembered, "a lot of what they did overlapped."[18]

Noticing Ricky's condition, the band pushed Keith for more information. If anyone knew what was going on with Ricky, it would be him. But he "didn't feel at liberty to say anything, because it was Ricky's decision. I encouraged him to talk to Cindy about it and I think he intended to."[19]

They finished the album in a month and titled it *Bouncing Off the Satellites* after a line in Communicate, but when they delivered it to their record label, they weren't prepared for the reaction. "Warner Brothers was kind of shocked when they heard it," said Kate. "They thought, this doesn't sound like the B-52's."[20] Keith added, "I think they thought it ch of a departure."[21] In time-honored record company fash- nd was ordered to go back and write a hit single. They began around a song they called Creature in a Black Bikini. The title ike someone's clichéd idea of a B-52s song—retro sci-fi, beaches, —but it would never be released.

at summer of 1985, movie icon Rock Hudson was diagnosed with S. While his homosexuality was an open secret in Hollywood, he had to come out publicly. After Hudson appeared at an event looking seri- sly ill, rumors began to circulate that he had AIDS. Initially, his publi- ist denied the claim, insisting Hudson had inoperable liver cancer, but a few days later on July 25th, Hudson issued a statement admitting he had contracted AIDS. In Randy Shilts' history of the early stages of the epidemic, *And the Band Played On*, he wrote that Hudson's revelation "became a demarcation that would separate the history of America before AIDS from the history that came after."[22] At this point, Ronald Reagan still hadn't publicly acknowledged the disease, but he immediately called Hudson, who he knew from his time in the movies, to offer sympathy. Though as Shilts wrote, "By the time America paid attention to the disease, it was too late to do anything about it. The virus was already pandemic in the nation."[23]

People magazine went to Olney, Illinois, Hudson's hometown, to get people's reactions to the news. Their responses give an idea of the attitudes among heteronormative Midwesterners. Lela Scherer said, "Never would we think he would be that. He was just always such a good person."[24] Mrs. Scherer was Hudson's aunt. In the article, Joan Rivers told a story about trying to organize an AIDS benefit two years earlier and being unable to get one major star to show up. "It ended up just being me and a transvestite on stage."[25] She did get plenty of death threats and hate mail for her efforts though.

On October 2, 1985, Rock Hudson died of AIDS-related complications. A few days later, Congress approved $221 million toward developing a cure. Millions more began pouring in from private contributions.[26] On October 9th, Cindy Wilson was at home when she got a phone call from Memorial Sloan Kettering Hospital. An intern asked her if she knew she was living with someone who had AIDS. "All of a sudden everything made sense," she said later. "And a coldness came over me."[27] By the time she got to the hospital, Ricky had slipped into a coma from which he wouldn't wake. Three days later, on October 12, 1985, he died of

pneumonia-related AIDS, though the cause of death should a ude
government neglect and societal indifference.

Nearly 30 years later, an interviewer asked Cindy if she had an
Keith for keeping Ricky's illness a secret. "Not at all," she sai
Keith and Ricky were in this horrible hell. Ricky and I were living t
and he was away a lot. I thought, oh, he's sick of living with his
Keith responded, "Hearing that breaks my heart."[28]

Curtis Knapp was living in Japan at the time, working as a comm
photographer. He was getting ready to do a shoot with Yukihiro Takah
a member of pioneering synth band Yellow Magic Orchestra, and a
friend of Keith and Ricky's, when he got a phone call. "I'm not s
whether it was Vic Varney who called me—somebody did," recalls Knapp
"Yuki just burst into tears, and I had to postpone the shooting for some time."[29] Roy Bell heard the news, and 20 years later lamented, "I regret to this day that I didn't actually spend the time with him and learn why he wanted to see me and what he wanted to talk about."[30] Chris Rasmussen was leaving Ricky and Keith's apartment that October. He owned a record store in Connecticut now and was rushing to catch the last train:

> He stopped me and he said, "Chris! Hi, how are you?" and looked me in the eyes and you could tell he wanted to talk, and I said, "I'm sorry I have to go get the train." And that was the last time I saw him. Keith called me a week later and said he was gone, and I just couldn't believe it. It was just that moment where he wanted to have a moment with me that I didn't get to have.[31]

Bongos frontman Richard Barone shared his impression of Ricky 30 years later:

> He was very smart, very artistic. I mean, none of what he did on guitar, or his personality, onstage or offstage, was by accident. He was well-mannered. He was really gentle. He had all the qualities of a Southern gentleman, and the wild spirit too. He was a really joyful guy.[32]

The band was devastated. Their friendship pre-dated, and transcended, the B-52s. Fred had known Ricky since 1972. "I thought that he'd been so nervous—we were under so much pressure. He was losing weight and .... He was fine one week, and then the next week I found out he was gone."[33] For Cindy, the loss was unimaginable:

> .s more than a brother—he was a mentor. He was the coolest person . He had the greatest sense of humor and uniqueness about him. He ly had a vision about him. He was one of the strongest elements of the 52's in the beginning, the conception. He was everything.[34]

And then there was Keith. They had known each other since high school and shared so much together. Even before the B-52s, they had played music together, traveled together, and lived together. Now Keith was alone. Kate expressed the sense of loss everyone in the band felt. "It was the most shocking thing," she said. "It seemed as though we … would never get over it."[35]

Meanwhile, the B-52s still owed the record company a song. Nobody was in any shape to finish Creature in a Black Bikini, but they desperately wanted the album to come out. "Ricky worked very hard on this record," said Keith, "and in that sense we felt that we should get out and do our best to make sure that it was heard."[36] Keith Bennett visited the Warners building to deliver the album's cover art, a painting by old friend Kenny Scharf, and to advocate for the band. "I remember going up to an A&R guy," he recalls, "a bigwig up there in New York."

> I was like, "It's Ricky's dying effort, and it's really a good record." He was like, "Look," and he pulled out this chart that has Madonna, Fleetwood Mac, Prince, just on down. He goes, "These get the money." We are going to throw money at the ones that are already making money. And this [Bouncing Off the Satellites] is not going to make money. We're going to shelve it and take a tax write-off."[37]

Eventually, Warners relented. They took the tracks the B-52s had recorded and rearranged the running order to put the two singles, Summer of Love and Girl From Ipanema Goes to Greenland, at the beginning. They also brought in Shep Pettibone to do post-production work on both songs. Finally, on September 8, 1986, nearly a full year after Ricky's death, *Bouncing Off the Satellites* was released by an indifferent label. It was only the B-52s' second full album since 1980.

Warner Brothers weren't the only ones who didn't like *Bouncing Off the Satellites*. The album is the lowest charting, worst-selling album they ever released, and it's still considered the critical nadir of their career. Of their pre-*Funplex* discography, it's the only album not to sell at least 500,000 copies. It didn't help that the record was essentially sabotaged by conflicts between the band and their label. "There was a lot of pressure to go ahead and get another guitarist," said Kate.[38] The band, still shell-shocked by Ricky's death, refused, and Warners gave up on the album. Even so, a few stations put Summer of Love into heavy rotation, including KROQ in Los Angeles and WLIR in New York. Keith Strickland told a story of a Warners executive "running down the halls saying, 'this record is taking off. We have to do something,'" but nobody paid any attention to him.[39]

The band, mainly Fred and Kate, did as much press as they could. The interviews are gut-wrenching to read. Every article mentions Ricky, but the accompanying photographs only feature the four surviving band members. In an interview with a college newspaper, Fred even slips and says, "Keith and Ricky do the music," referring to Ricky in the present tense, as if he had forgotten for a moment what had happened.[40]

At the beginning of 1987, the band traveled to the UK to promote the album. They did a handful of interviews, then went back in July to appear on the ITV show "Get Fresh," where they mimed to their new UK single, Wig, and oddly, Planet Claire. Both clips are online, and they are simultaneously wonderful and heartbreaking to watch. Keith is on guitar, and he wears a blond wig in both songs. A long-haired guy whose name is lost to history is behind the drums. Wig struggled to #79 on the UK Charts. The top song that week was the epic It's a Sin by Pet Shop Boys.

Two weeks prior to the release of *Bouncing Off the Satellites*, the B-52s' *One Trick Pony* co-star Paul Simon released an album called *Graceland*. His previous album, 1983's *Hearts and Bones*, had been a flop, and along with his film's lack of success in 1980, Simon was considered hopelessly uncool. *Graceland* turned out to be a triumphant comeback both critically and commercially, as it became his best-selling album in over 15 years. "Everybody makes mistakes," said Simon, looking back on how he pulled himself out of his creative slump, "just as every career has ups and downs. If you don't give yourself the opportunity to do something extraordinary, the chances are you won't."[41] As the B-52s hit their own commercial and critical low point, it was advice worth remembering.

It's a shame *Bouncing Off the Satellites* was received so poorly. For all the complaints about the stiffness of its sound, the album emits a beautiful shimmery quality, like a thin veil between one world and the next. Even if Ricky and Keith were the only ones who knew the extent of Ricky's illness, everyone in the band knew something was wrong. The result is the most deeply emotional collection of music they had released to this point.

The album opens with Summer of Love and Girl From Ipanema Goes to Greenland, two of the most dazzling songs in the band's catalog. On the first, Cindy's waiting for the man downtown just like Lou Reed did. Lou was waiting for hard drugs, but Cindy's waiting for orange popsicles and lemonade. That's not to say there's anything innocent about the song. Its light orbits around a planet of darkness, making the declaration of the title feel more like a desperate wish. As Cindy said, "What was going on in the country was so scary, so we needed to have a place called the 'Summer Of Love.' We needed that."[42]

Girl From Ipanema Goes to Greenland takes the darkness, and the prettiness, of Summer of Love to even greater extremes. The line *Witch doctors are screaming / this girl's lost someone* sounds chilling in light of Ricky's death. Kate talked about the song a couple of months after the album came out in the halting, stumbling language of someone still trying to process a trauma:

> Looking back on it there are all sorts of references, you know, that apply but that were, I don't know whether they were just coincidence or synchronicity .... There are lots of things in the lyrics, later when I look back.[43]

The 80s production that elevates the first two songs on the album is the undoing of Housework. Whatever feminist power Kate wrote into the song ends up being undermined by stiff, late-night talk show-sounding synth stabs and slap bass. Kate understood the politics of work and recognition all too well. As someone who played two instruments at once while singing across a range of octaves and dancing, Kate had been the hardest working musician in the B-52s. Housework remains a furiously smart plea for men to help with women's unpaid labor—not just by providing emotional support, but by doing the physical and material work as well. When she sings, *someone to share dreams and wishes / someone to help me do the dishes*, Kate defines her vision for equality through recognition and shared labor.

Detour Thru Your Mind is the fourth song on the album, and it marks Fred's first appearance on the album. He had now gone from being considered the band's frontperson to disappearing from albums for long stretches. Keith plays guitar on the track, and his solo at the two-minute mark gives us a preview of his future style, all Rolling Stones riffs and bent notes. Perhaps inspired by Keith's "tasty licks," Kate and Cindy add some woo woo's straight out of Sympathy for the Devil.

It is said that a psychedelic experience can unlock repressed emotions and fears. Detour Thru Your Mind presents itself as a silly joke, but lines like *Who am I? Where have I been? Where am I going?* and *I need to leave my past behind* can be interpreted as real questions surrounding the band at the time, and Fred's life in particular.

In Wig, the band takes its campest subject matter (and worst jokes) to date and burns a hole straight through the irony. Like Butterbean on the last album, thinking back to Athens inspired the band and resulted in music with a noticeably faster tempo. It's the only song on the album that sounds free and uninhibited and totally in the moment. The *TAKE IT HIGHER* section feels rooted in something far beyond silliness. It's so convincing, and moving, it can feel like the song exists just to provide protective covering so the singers can tap into a rawness they weren't comfortable expressing directly.

In the midst of all the struggle of making *Bouncing Off the Satellites*, Theme for a Nude Beach presents a vision of utopia. It's worth noting that the two most optimistic songs on the album, this one and Wig, feature all five band members working together. Ricky plays bass on the song, and even on a different instrument, it's easy to hear his rhythmic and melodic creativity.

Nude Beach is another song about the beach as a place of freedom where boundaries dissolve. What was implied in Rock Lobster is made explicit on Nude Beach. Air mixes with land, as does the sea. Fred is a woman. Kate is a man. Even when *everything is revealed*, it still remains *so mysterious*.

The suits they throw into the sea could mean more than bathing suits. They could represent the constraints of a professional career, a reference to the very real business pressures the band were under. The act could also be a desire to escape from their identities as members of the B-52s. Were they dreaming of giving it all up? Cindy has said, "I don't know if the band would have lasted or not if Ricky had lived. I think Ricky was going to eventually sail away on his sailboat and go around the world."[44]

On the surface, Ain't It a Shame is a country-tinged song about a relationship that has run its course, with some flying saucers thrown in for B-52s sake. But with lines about a love like *a fuse that's burned out long ago*, it can also be heard as a lament for (and to) the band. If this had been the last album the B-52s made, Ain't It a Shame would be heard far differently, and more deeply. Keith and Ricky's backing vocals on the chorus only add to the poignancy. *Bouncing Off the Satellites* is a showcase for the emotional intelligence and empathy in Cindy's singing. With her uncanny ability to express the lived experiences of others, Cindy probably would have made an incredible actor.

A lot of songs on the album go on longer than they need to, especially on side two, but no song goes on more longer-than-it-needs-to than Juicy Jungle. Still, Juicy Jungle, inspired by a Kenny Scharf painting, is one more expression on the album of loss and anxiety. On the surface, the song is about preserving rainforests and the animals who live there, but it's also a shout from someone who is angry he isn't being listened to. Coupled with Fred's pleas that anyone with an "axe to grind" take it somewhere else, Juicy Jungle becomes more substantial than its rooty-toot fun factory sound might suggest.

In 1979, the AT&T phone company rolled out a series of iconic commercials with the slogan "Reach Out and Touch Someone." The ads ran into the 90s, and they seem to have made an impression on the B-52s, as the band appropriated the slogan for Communicate's chorus. On the surface the song is lyrically trite, and the most musically underdeveloped song on the album—though there's a great PiL reference in the bridge's bass line. But as an expression of the band's situation, there's a bleak and devastating irony hearing the singers extol the virtues of communication at a time when so much within the band was going unsaid. Communicate is one more song on *Bouncing Off the Satellites* that functions as a dialogue (or soliloquy) about the band itself.

She Brakes for Rainbows is the only song in the band's catalog credited solely to Ricky and Keith, and it's one of the loveliest. The lyrics are almost haiku-like in their sparse evocation of nature. They tell the story of Brenda Holiday, a character who, much like Ricky, doesn't talk much but sees everything. *She knows where the rain goes* reveals an optimism based in experience, rather than naiveté. Combined with its open, yearning melody, it's hard not to hear Rainbows as an ecstatic elegy. In 1986, the rain falling on the B-52s was torrential. Some days it must have felt like it would never stop. As the album ends, the song's power lingers in the air long after the record has stopped playing.

Bouncing Off the Satellites is filled with stories of loss. An air of finality hangs heavily over the album, previewing an emotional depth that the band would further develop on *Cosmic Thing*. Given everything going on in and around the band, *Bouncing Off the Satellites* could have been an artistic failure. But much like The Beatles' White Album, it documents a group of close friends falling apart, and the ensuing confusion, and bitterness, comes across so strongly you can hear it in the record's atmosphere.

AIDS in America

In Mats Sexton's 2002 book about the band, he wrote, "Cindy decided not to disclose the true nature of Ricky's illness."[45] The obituary in the *Athens Daily News* didn't list a cause of death, and the family asked that "contributions be made to the American Cancer Society in memory of Mr. Wilson."[46] This secrecy put the other band members in a difficult position. As Kate later explained, "We were keeping it a secret and people thought we were ashamed ... but we couldn't say anything because we wanted to protect Cindy's family."[47] Fred added, "We didn't know what to say. His family wanted it private."[48] Keith opened up about the issue in 1999:

> You have to remember ... the change of attitude in people's minds has been really enormous since then. Ricky feared how people would treat him if they knew, more than death itself. I feel I can say that because we talked about it.[49]

Keith makes an important point about the political and social climate at the time. On December 19, 1985, only two months after Ricky's death, a *Los Angeles Times* poll found that a majority of Americans thought AIDS victims should be quarantined indefinitely. 48% said they should be issued special identification, and 15% said they should be forcibly tattooed so they could be identified in public.[50]

The fear surrounding the disease led to a rise in violence against its victims. In 1987, a family in Arcadia, FL with three hemophiliac children living with AIDS had to move after their house was burned down by local residents.[51] The political implications were terrifying. As detailed in L.A. Kauffman's *Direct Action: Protest and the Reinvention of American Radicalism*. "AIDS hysteria was fueling new attacks on gay and lesbian civil rights, which had been far from secure to begin with."[52]

Between 1981 and 1987, 40,000 people died of AIDS in the US, and the numbers would grow exponentially in the coming years. By 1992, the disease was the leading cause of death in the US for men between the ages of 25 and 44.[53] Around 300,000 people had tested HIV-positive, and 100,000 had died from AIDS. By October 1996, 350,000 Americans had died, 100,000 of them in New York City.

Drugs developed in the mid-90s began to turn the tide. In 1993, 51,000 people died from AIDS, but by 1997, the number would drop to 21,000. Antiretroviral therapy (ART) was so effective that doctors called its development "the Lazarus effect" because it brought people back from the dead.[54] These breakthroughs could have happened many years earlier if people had been motivated to fund the research. It took networks of grassroots activism, in many different forms, to provide that motivation. "Being silent doesn't make the fear go away," said AIDS activist Phil Wilson. "In fact, being bold, speaking, helps us deal with the fear."[55]

One of the bravest, and angriest, groups formed in March 1987 in New York City, the AIDS Coalition to Unleash Power (ACT UP). Larry Kramer was one of the founders, and he brought his combative anger to the cause, repeatedly doing what he called a "famous shtick":

> I said, "O.K., I want this half of the room to stand up." And they did. I looked around at those kids and I said to the people standing up, "You are all going to be dead in five years. Every one of you fuckers." I was livid. I said, "How about doing something about it? Why just line up for the cattle cars? Why don't you go out and make some fucking history?"[56]

Brandishing an iconic SILENCE = DEATH logo, ACT UP would play an important role in increasing research funding, gaining cheaper access to medicine, and reversing discriminatory policies. Though they were (and are) one group among many, their willingness to put their bodies on the line is nothing short of inspiring.

1987 also saw the formation of AIDS Athens, a group of volunteers dedicated to helping people living with AIDS all over northeast Georgia. Local health officials had reported 15 regional cases to the CDC at that point, but Kris Taro, an infections control nurse who worked with AIDS Athens told a local newspaper there were certainly more cases than that. One of AIDS Athens' earliest volunteers was UGA art professor and former GMOA director, Bill Paul:

> I was the person assigned to the first client for AIDS Athens. It turned out that all of the people knew him. He was just terrible, hard to get along with …. I said, you know I made a commitment to come here twice a week and stay for at least an hour, and if you don't like it that's just tough shit. But I remember one day he actually said thank you, and I just broke down. Because he was so bad, finally, we had to take his car keys away from him. And his family wouldn't have anything to do with him.[57]

The stigma in Athens was real. On March 10, 1988, an Athens paper ran an article on a local support group for the loved ones of people with AIDS living in the area. The time and location of the meeting was kept secret in the article out of concerns for people's safety. "I would like to express that my son has a disease that is incurable," said one parent. "It would be different if he has leukemia. People would ask, 'How's he doing today?'"[58]

Bill Paul recalls a local family, who "lost both of their boys, one was 18 years old, the other 16, both from blood transfusions. They were hemophiliacs." Another patient died a couple of hours after Paul left his room:

> His mother called to ask, "How did my son die?" And I said, "Without you. Why weren't you there? My parents would have been there. If I were at death's door. They wouldn't have to call some stranger and ask how did their child die."[59]

Paul channeled his anger into his art, which would become more provocative and graphically explicit going forward. In the 90s, this work would gain its own notoriety, creating moral panics that found him on the front pages of newspapers from Seattle to Savannah.

In 1988, the B-52s took their first tentative steps toward making the private aspects of their lives public when the band appeared in an Art Against AIDS public service announcement. Featuring their song Summer of Love, the clip aired regularly on MTV. It was directed by NYC artist Tom Rubnitz, a former Club 57 cohort who also served as the videographer of Cindy's wedding. The PSA recreated the cover of Sgt. Pepper's Lonely Hearts Club Band with artists and musicians filling in the scene, including Allen Ginsburg, Keith Haring, David Byrne, Kenny Scharf, Nile Rodgers, and Joey Arias, among many others. Haring would die of AIDS in 1990, and Rubnitz in 1992. But Joey Arias, who performed with Klaus Nomi, is still alive as we write this, and married his long-time partner in 2014. The story of AIDS is a story about unspeakable tragedy, but it is also a story about courage and survival.

On May 27, 2020, while the world was in the midst of another pandemic caused by a virus no one fully understood, Larry Kramer died at age 84. The listed cause of death was pneumonia. In a 2002 *New Yorker* interview, Kramer still wasn't taking anything for granted. "These kids better learn how to scream, because being sweet won't work. That much I know. Honey doesn't get you a fucking thing."[60]

Notes

1. YouTube, "B-52s Live Part 1."
2. Bausum, *Viral*, 11–12.
3. "A Timeline of HIV and AIDS," https://www.hiv.gov/hiv-basics/overview/history/hiv-and-aids-timeline.
4. Ocamb, "Larry Kramer's Historic Essay."
5. Bausum, *Viral*, 38.
6. Leland, "Twilight of a Difficult."
7. La Ganga, "First lady who …."
8. Sexton, *The B-52's Universe*, 72.
9. Ibid.
10. Bell, "RB 24," Rabbit Box Storytelling, Mixcloud.
11. Azerrad, "The B-52's."
12. Sexton, *The B-52's Universe*, 186.
13. Hann, "Everyone."
14. Tolinski, "The B-52s," 31.
15. Ibid.
16. Darling, "B-52 Pick-Up," 14.
17. Sexton, *The B-52's Universe*, 187.
18. Darling, "B-52 Pick-Up," 14.
19. Sexton, *The B-52's Universe*, 74.
20. Darling, "B-52 Pick-Up," 14.
21. Harold De Muir, "An Interview with Fred Schneider and Keith Strickland of the B-52's," Unknown title, January 28, 1987, Mats Sexton B-52's memorabilia collection, ms 4110, Book 6, University of Georgia Libraries Special Collections.
22. Shilts, *And the Band Played*, xxi.
23. Ibid.
24. Yarbrough, "Rock Hudson."
25. Ibid.
26. People, "Rock Hudson."
27. Sexton, *The B-52's Universe*, 74.
28. Tannenbaum, "The B-52s Say Farewell" AR-14.
29. Curtis Knapp in conversation with authors, April 17, 2019.
30. Bell, "RB 24."
31. Chris Rasmussen in conversation with authors, July 29, 2019.
32. Richard Barone in conversation with authors, May 9, 2019.
33. Azerrad, "B-52's."
34. Ibid.
35. Hann, "Everyone."
36. Sexton, *The B-52's Universe*, 77.

37. Keith Bennett in conversation with authors, November 8, 2019.
38. Corcoran, "B's Wax," 125.
39. Sexton, *The B-52's Universe*, 77.
40. Haecker, "Bouncing About," 15.
41. Hilburn, *Paul Simon*, 251.
42. Suwak, "Cindy Wilson."
43. Corcoran, "B's Wax."
44. Sexton, *The B-52's Universe*, 80.
45. Sexton, *The B-52's Universe*, 74.
46. Obituary, *Athens Daily News*, 4.
47. Sexton, *The B-52's Universe*, 79.
48. Malins, "Shiny Hippy People," 35.
49. Groome, "The B-52's," 40.
50. New York Times, "Poll Indicates Majority Favor."
51. New York Times, "Family in AIDS Case."
52. Kauffman, *Direct Action*, 108.
53. Bausum, *Viral*, 87.
54. Ibid.
55. Ibid.
56. Specter, "Public Nuisance."
57. Bill Paul in conversation with authors, May 19, 2019.
58. Conoly Hester, "When Loved One Has AIDS," unidentified newspaper, March 10, 1988, Box 1, LGBT Resource Records, UA17-009 University of Georgia Libraries Special Collections.
59. Bill Paul in conversation with authors, May 19, 2019.
60. Specter, "Public."

CHAPTER 10

Cosmic Thing

We'd be sitting on this bus, watching it get bigger and bigger. It felt like we were in the center of a huge storm .... It was totally unreal.[1]

—Fred

In the wake of Ricky's death, it was impossible to imagine the B-52s continuing. "We felt that maybe that was the natural end of the band," said Kate.[2] Keith began attending Buddhist retreats to help with his grief. Cindy, in particular, was struggling:

> I was just so out of it and depressed. I couldn't function, and there was so much to do, business to take care of, like Ricky's estate, and just everything to deal with, and I was just completely gone. I couldn't deal with it. I needed a religion or some kind of belief system when Ricky died, and I had a hard time, because nothing fit. I was waiting for some kind of spiritual relief, and nothing came.[3]

Keith and Kate moved to upstate New York, near Woodstock, where they lived across a pond from each other. "For Keith and me," Kate recalled, "it was a sense of peace we found up here. Just being in this small town, it was the same as it was in Athens."[4] Keith added, "I ... rented a little cabin on a pond off Wittenberg Road that was covered with lily pads and abundant with wildlife. It was idyllic and very healing."[5]

S. Creney, B. A. Herron, *The Story of the B-52s*,
https://doi.org/10.1007/978-3-031-22570-3_10

Fred published a book of poetry, *Fred Schneider and Other Unrelated Works*. It wouldn't make anyone forget Anne Sexton, but it might help them remember Edward Lear. It came with cover art by Kenny Scharf. Fred and Kate made an appearance at People for the Ethical Treatment of Animals' (PETA) first Washington D.C. rally.

With no clear future as a recording band, and no way of touring, there wasn't much money coming in. "We really had to tighten our belts," said Fred. "We were just barely staying afloat."[6] Luckily, the band's first two albums continued to sell. *The B-52's* and *Wild Planet* were on their way to becoming classics. "We were basically living on the royalties from those records," said Fred in 1991. "Every time there's a new generation of college students, they discover the first two records and go wild."[7]

Whatever the B-52s felt about their future, the band's label and management were sure the band was finished. Fred said, "People just wouldn't look at us or talk to us .... The way we were being treated was pretty abysmal."[8]

Gary Kurfirst no longer returned the band's phone calls, but when the B-52s decided to look for new management, they found that Kurfirst wasn't going to make it easy for them. The band ended up taking him to court to get out of their contract, where the judge ruled that, due to a sunset clause, their now-former manager would be entitled to a percentage of all future album royalties as long as the B-52s stayed together as a group.[9] This also included their publishing royalties, as Kurfirst had been receiving one-sixth of all their songwriting money.[10] Despite all the negotiating leverage the B-52s had back in 1978, and despite their fears about being ripped off, they still ended up signing a bad contract, and they still ended up getting cheated.

Having no other options, the band accepted their fate and jettisoned Kurfirst. Despite seven years of hard work, selling approximately a million albums, and constant touring, the band found themselves practically broke. The bank was going to foreclose on the property Cindy, Keith, and Ricky had purchased, so they sold it. "The accountants were not very good," recalls Keith Bennett, of the people Kurfirst hired to manage the band's finances. "We owed the government all this money."[11]

In the process of putting their lives back together, the band began to reconnect as people and as friends. Keith recalled, "We spent a lot of time just talking, and we needed that."[12] Keith continued to make music "just for my sake, not for the B's at the time."[13] Though Keith had played guitar and keyboards on previous records, and co-written some of the music, working without Ricky was hard. Cindy said, "It took a lot of gumption and a lot of strength to do what Keith did. It's amazing. I think it was really scary for him."[14]

One day, when Cindy and Kate came to visit, he played them some songs he had been working on. One of these, an instrumental called There Is a River, caught their attention. The music stirred up memories, and they began to sing *We're the deadbeat club*. At first, they sang the words in an exaggerated Morrissey parody, but then "they started thinking it was nice," remembered Keith.[15] The three then called up Fred, who found Keith's music "brilliant and inspiring." Although the band had some "trepidation" about making a record, Fred added that "once we … got to jamming, everything fell into place really quickly."[16]

As 1988 began, the B-52s took definitive steps toward becoming a band again. They got a rehearsal space in New York City on Murray Street and dedicated themselves to writing new songs. Working four days a week, with nothing left to lose, the B-52s held nothing back. Maybe it was the desperate situation they found themselves in, or the perspective they had gained, but Fred recalled, "There was a harmony and a togetherness in it that were lacking in the last few albums. It made us realize how far we had drifted apart as writers."[17] Even Kate, who had been shut out of the musical decision-making in recent years, acknowledged there was now "a very collaborative, collective attitude. That's a very female principle. We try to nurture that aspect of the band."[18]

Something began happening that ran deeper than just making an album. Keith said, "Working together was sort of like our religion and way of dealing with and coming to terms with Ricky's loss and getting on with our lives."[19]

The band had always been at their best when everyone worked together, each contributing to the best of their abilities for the greater good of the band. As Fred pointed out, "I had to learn to work closely with Keith for the first time in a way. It was the same for all the group. Everyone always had a big contribution to make but, on this album, it was much more focused."[20] Cindy concurred:

> We really did have to work a lot harder. We had to take other parts and do other jobs in the band. We all sat and arranged together instead of just leaving it to one or two people. We had to pull extra things out of ourselves.[21]

Robert Waldrop contributed lyrics for the song Roam. Even he noticed the new spirit of cooperation, saying, "I think they just really wanted to get it right this time."[22] He also observed, "Everybody relied on Ricky to make a lot of decisions. Once he was gone, they … started making those decisions themselves. Something broke and they got together and mended it."[23]

Not that it was always a smooth ride. It wasn't until they had their first complete song, Junebug, that Keith knew they were capable of writing together. Cindy had a copper heart engraved with the song's title to commemorate the occasion.[24] Even when problems surfaced, they continued to support one another. Cindy was in deep mourning during the sessions, and admitted she was "probably pretty difficult." She added, "I was having these emotional flare-ups. I wasn't that easy to get along with sometimes. But they were great—and very patient."[25]

Another friend from their earliest days of touring, Moe Slotin, helped them assemble a backing band that featured Pat Irwin to play keyboards and guitar. A veteran of the No Wave scene, their relationship went back to the B-52s' early NYC days when Irwin lent the band an amp for a 1978 gig at the Mudd Club. He signed up for a three-week tour, and would end up spending 18 years with the band. Slotin also suggested English bassist Sara Lee, who had played with Gang of Four. Zachary Alford signed on as the drummer, and the B-52s were a full-fledged band again, with the addition of a formidable rhythm section.

They also hired new managers, Direct Management, a younger company based in LA who were more modern and forward thinking. Most importantly, they encouraged the B-52s to just be who they were.[26] The band also found a new label in Reprise, a smaller label under the Warners umbrella that specialized in alternative bands.

When they were ready to record the album, Kate brought a list of producers to a psychic, who told her "The spirit gods really love Nile."[27] It wasn't just the spirit gods—everybody loves Nile Rodgers. After topping the charts as a guitarist and co-songwriter in Chic, Rodgers became one of the most successful producers in the 80s, working with Diana Ross, David Bowie, Madonna, and Duran Duran, among others. As Keith said, "Nile's great. He was very familiar with us—he's known what we've been doing for a long time."[28]

The first song they worked on together was Shake That Cosmic Thing, for the *Earth Girls Are Easy* soundtrack. The film came out in September 1988, and the song's title would gain parentheses when it was released on the *Cosmic Thing* album the following year. Because Rodgers' schedule was filled for the next several months, Fred suggested they record some songs with Don Was. Fred was a fan of the producer's most recent album with his band Was (Not Was). He was an inspired choice. Was had been a fan of the band for years, having heard them back in Detroit on The Electrifying Mojo's show. They convened near Woodstock at Dreamland studio to work on three songs: Junebug, Channel Z, and Bushfire. Was proved to be a perfect mix of laid back and detail oriented. 30 years later, he still remembered the experience fondly:

> It was lovely, man. I don't remember any stress. I recall driving one night we saw the Northern Lights at a Zen monastery on a mountain. I remember it as a very moving and warm experience up there.[29]

Keith said, "This album, we worked real hard at getting a live performance in the studio. It was set up so that Fred, Kate, and Cindy would be in the booth all singing."[30] The band only booked seven days in the studio, but things went so quickly they still had time remaining at the end of the session. Was said the band then decided to show him this other song they were working on, but warned him, "It's 12 minutes long and we don't know what to make of it."[31]

The song had started with an idea Fred had about a real place they used to go to just outside of Athens called the Hawaiian Ha-Le. Fred said, "It was an African-American club that had a lot of good shows. It looked like a shack, and when you opened the door, it was a wild band playing." Cindy added that the building had a rusted, tin roof, and the dancers would do Soul Train-style dance lines.[32]

During the writing, Kate had argued that a section needed to repeat: *The love shack is a little old place / where we can get together.* Don Was agreed with Kate, and urged them to turn that part into the chorus.[33] The band weren't certain they had a hit, but they knew they liked it. Engineer Dave Cook recalled Cindy "being pretty down for a lot of the process. I would look at her, thinking, 'Wow, this must be really tough on her.'" Don Was added, "You can hear it in that 'Tin roof—rusted' thing. Cindy got very emotional. It was like in 12 seconds she went from extreme glee to really depressed about that roof rusting. The intensity of what she did was startling."[34]

That fall, Kate's brother Kenneth died of lung cancer. At times, it had to feel like the band was cursed, but they still trudged on. It was time to record the rest of the album with Nile Rodgers in NYC. He worked on Deadbeat Club, Roam, Dry County, Follow Your Bliss, and Topaz, adding his distinctive guitar playing to the latter. *Cosmic Thing* continued to run smoothly, but Nile Rodgers expected the band to work harder than they had in the past. "I had them do things on that album that they'd never done before," said Rodgers. This included getting Kate and Cindy to stack their harmonies on top of each other by recording multiple takes. The result was some of the most beautiful singing the B-52s ever recorded. "I remember, when I finished," said Rodgers, "calling the record company and saying, 'I hope you do the right thing here, because you've got a smash on your hands.'"[35]

Though a series of session drummers played in the studio, Sara Lee played bass on all the tracks, even adding vocals and keyboards to Follow Your Bliss. Her bass playing is the perfect mix of melody and groove—the ascending run into the chorus of Deadbeat Club, her Stax-like breakdown on Love Shack, and the entirety of Roam, are all high points. Kate and Fred also played on the album, contributing keyboards and percussion respectively. The B-52s were collaborating in ways they hadn't in years. Still, the night before the album was due to be mastered, Keith decided they needed to change the running order:

> I was sitting in my hotel room in New York and I went, "We can't do it this way." The album to me had this natural sequence so I just made this other alternate sequence and we just cut it that way. Hardly anyone else heard it that way—I called up Fred and Kate and Cindy and called up Nile and I said, "Look, I've got this other idea, I think we should really do it this way.[36]

Though the original running order is unknown, it turned out to be the right choice. It was a brave move to open with the title track and Dry County, holding back the more commercial songs until later in the album. Now, the B-52s were making decisions for artistic reasons instead of trying to second-guess the market. Ironically, the result would be the most commercially successful album of their career.

Cosmic

On *Bouncing Off the Satellites*, the B-52s had explored deep sadness, but on *Cosmic Thing* they manage to transcend it. It's the most emotionally moving album in their discography. Part of that is because we know the band's backstory, but plenty of artists have made music in a state of emotional devastation without reaching the heights of *Cosmic Thing*. The album works because the band were open to the process, and able to put everything around them and everything they were experiencing into their art. The songs obliterate the line between sadness and joy to the point where the two ideas become indistinguishable from each other. As Kate later explained, "Life and death are part of the same thing. It's kind of liberating, in a strange sort of way."[37]

Where previous B-52s albums began with a long instrumental section or a fade in, *Cosmic Thing*'s title track comes roaring out of the gate, pulsating with impatient energy like an amped-up version of You Can't Hurry Love. After a quick drum fill, Fred jumps in, ordering us to gyrate. The shouts of "Cosmic" from Kate and Cindy, followed by their "whoooooo"-ing in unison, come straight from the Little Richard playbook, and the song's velocity never lets up.

Despite its otherworldly title, *Cosmic Thing* is firmly set on earth. The political side of the B-52s became more overt on the album, from the title track's plea, *don't let it rest on the president's desk*, to Channel Z's barrage of environmental and governmental disasters. Channel Z is the rare political song that manages to be funny, hopeful, and angry, sometimes all at once. Fred's *politicrits pushing dope* line refers to the US State Department giving money to drug dealers in Nicaragua. With its stories about secret wars and lying good old boys, not to mention the subject of our imperiled ecosystem, and how the onslaught of useless information impedes our ability to think clearly, Channel Z is still relevant. After the song's litany of impending disasters, the final four slams that end Channel Z achieve an exasperated catharsis.

On *Cosmic Thing*, the band learned how to tell a good story. They wrote with a new level of detail, immersing their songs in concrete imagery and direct emotions. The lyrics of Deadbeat Club are almost cinematic. We can see the torn sheets. We can hear the jukebox. We can feel the caffeine buzz. These elements combine to create a sense of place that brings the listener into the story.

The lyrics are supported by the music, where melody after glorious melody unfolds, capped by a stunningly minimalist guitar solo from Keith. Deadbeat Club is a song about memory that seems straightforward on its surface (remember all those good times we used to have?) but contains unfathomable depths. The song switches verb tenses almost compulsively, from past to present to future, as if to remain fixed in one spot for too long would break the spell. The memories in the song were real, according to Kate:

> It's about things that really happened. We had a going-away party for our friend Robert Waldrop: a silent party. We met in this garden and it was silent. It was raining, and we had sheets and blankets around us, and we were naked except for the sheets. We ran around him and swooped around him. Very art school-y, but we thought we were the first people to ever do that.[38]

Three years after *Cosmic Thing*, R.E.M. would release their own song about Athens memories, right down to the skinny-dipping. Like the B-52s' song, Nightswimming changes verb tense and functions as both a celebration and an elegy. Both songs struggle to reconcile their younger innocence with the realities of the present. Unasked questions hover throughout Deadbeat Club, just off to the side. *Will we ever feel that alive again? Was our joy only possible because we were young? How can we ever feel that way again, knowing what we know now?* All of this is communicated through Cindy and Kate's singing, which is so subtly evocative as they slide gracefully up and down the melody that it recalls Dionne Warwick, especially the way Kate and Cindy sing *And the jukebox plays real loud / 96 tears.* Deadbeat Club's present-tense ending is ambiguous. Are they back in the past, or have they achieved some kind of resolution and are now charging forward as better versions of their younger selves?

Where thoughts of Athens sped up the tempos of Butterbean and Wig on the previous two albums, it has the opposite effect on *Cosmic Thing.* It's almost like they want things to slow down so they can savor the memories. Thinking of Athens also meant thinking of the South, and more than any other album in their catalog, *Cosmic Thing* abounds with Southern imagery. From Dry County through Junebug, the band sings of porches and tin roofs, water moccasins and red mud.

The imagery also could have been inspired by the music Keith brought them. His guitar style echoes the double stops of Steve Cropper and the chicken scratch style of James Brown guitarist Jimmy Nolen. Love Shack has become so ubiquitous that it can be hard to hear it for what it is—a barnburner that draws on a long history of Southern music. The song often gets compared to Motown, but it's closer to Memphis-based Stax, with a structure that draws on gospel.

Southern music is inescapably entwined with the church. A cousin visiting from New Orleans introduced the young Keith Strickland to rock and roll by bringing him records by Little Richard, Elvis, and James Brown—all Southern, all soulful, and all influenced by church music.[39] Little Richard's music and style had clear antecedents in gospel music. His ecstatic scream, that distinctive orgasmic squeal, was inspired by gospel singer Marion Williams, an influence he openly acknowledged.[40] Williams sang for a time with the Clara Ward Singers, a group who "had their hair stacked into beehive wraps and sang with divine abandonment."[41]

In *Good Booty*, her 2017 examination of eroticism in popular music, critic Ann Powers discussed Little Richard's "strategic outrageousness," in a way that could just as easily describe the B-52s. Powers writes of Richard "bursting every seam apparently for the hell of it, but really as a way of sharing subterranean secrets of two centuries' worth of … sexual nonconformists."[42]

Richard's penchant for using flamboyance to mask the incendiary content of his music was a deliberate choice. "We decided that my image should be crazy and way out so the adults would think I was harmless," said Richard. "I'd appear in one show dressed as the Queen of England and the next dressed as the Pope."[43] It appears the B-52s were not only inheritors of Little Richard's musical freedom, but his fashion sense and sexual subversiveness as well.

Love Shack is the B-52s' most gospel-influenced performance. As the band shouts their lines, you can hear a congregation responding with whoops of encouragement. Ethnomusicologist Glenn Hinson's description of gospel dynamics, as cited in Powers' book, applies equally well to Love Shack's breakdown:

> Start low; rise high; return to low …. Turn up the fire; let it sizzle; then turn it down. But never turn it down all the way. Never fully return to the last point of rest. Instead, keep raising the bottom, ever boosting the ambient energy, ever bringing the sustaining lows closer to the fiery peaks.[44]

The *bang-bang on the door* section utilizes gospel's call-and-response. It also employs a spiritual/secular double entendre—in this case, the door could refer to heaven, or something more carnal—while slowly building its way to a passionate release. Cindy's near Pentecostal exclamation of *Tin roof! / rusted* baffled listeners and critics for years. An urban legend developed that it referred to an unintended pregnancy, but eventually, Cindy set the record straight, explaining it was simply an image she had of the shack's roof—both the remembered image of a literal place and an imagined place deeply rooted in Southern iconography. Regardless of her intent, the delivery is so ecstatic and uninhibited that it echoes Little Richard, as well as his gospel antecedents. It's Cindy's version of *a-wop-bop-a-loo-bop-a-lop-bam-boom*.

Love Shack's musical backing also brought out one of Fred's finest singing performances. He gets to try out his Elvis when he sings *love shack ba-a-by*. And the way he snaps the consonants of *funky little shack* and hits the prepositions in *folks lining up outside just to get down*, is a masterclass in soul singing. By the time he gets to screaming *on the door*, he sounds like a man possessed. Fred has cited in numerous interviews how Martha & the Vandellas changed his life. On Love Shack, he repays the debt.

Keith's re-sequencing allowed the album to flow more like a story. The songs on side one look back, either into their collective memories, or to Athens, or to both. On side two the songs open out into the world and leave the past behind, beginning with Roam, a celebration of all the possibilities of life. The B-52s knew all about the inherent chaos of the universe, its capacity for destruction and sadness, as well as its capacity for beauty. Kate and Cindy sing about finding joy and freedom in that uncertainty. The song's message—that the messiness of life can be an adventure if we have someone to share it with—is embodied in their singing, with Kate taking the first verse, Cindy the second, and both singing together on the third.

You can also hear the South in Kate and Cindy's harmonies throughout the album. Kate has described how they blended their voices intuitively, and how they were "doing calls, weird sounds, and wailing and then these harmonies just happened naturally, in a sort of Appalachian style."[45] The result on *Cosmic Thing* at times sounds closer to traditional Sacred Harp singing than anything tied to the pop/rock tradition. The way they sing *up the road* on Dry County is a clear example, where they bend the last note to introduce a discordant chord lament in the midst of joy. Cindy and Kate also switch high and low parts with abandon, turning Topaz into perhaps the most stunning performance of their career. The result there is breathtaking, so much so that the music fades out early so the listener can just revel in the beauty of their voices.

The album's closer, Follow Your Bliss, doesn't have any words, just voices. It functions as a healing mantra and radiates the pure joy of its title.

Post-Album Work

With *Cosmic Thing*, the B-52s had proven they were still a band, that they could still write songs, that they could enjoy making music, and that they could make a great record. Now they had to convince the rest of the world. Cindy said, "We had to prove ourselves to the record company. It seemed like a lot of people thought we were a joke."[46] Even Fred was unsure what would happen. "If it took off, we would continue. If it didn't, then the possibilities of our carrying on were *dim*."[47]

It helped that the folks at Reprise loved the new album. The only problem the record company had this time was deciding which songs to release as singles, with different executives arguing vehemently for certain songs. In the end, it was decided to lead with Channel Z.

With the album completed, and a band assembled, the B-52s were ready to return to the stage. They played two warm-up shows at the small NYC club Under ACME. Unfortunately, the shows were marred by yet more tragedy when some of their gear got stolen after the first night. The haul included one of Ricky's most cherished guitars, as well as Cindy's bongos.

On March 24, 1989, the B-52s played their first high-profile show in over four years at Brooklyn Academy of Music. It was a benefit to save the Brazilian rainforests hosted by Madonna and Kenny Scharf called "Don't Bungle the Jungle." The audience of 2000 was subdued most of the night, but according to *USA Today*, the B-52s "brought the crowd to its feet."[48] Fred would later say, "It was really gratifying … we didn't know what to expect."[49] Ann Magnuson also performed, dressed as a Chinese student protester carrying a red flag with a McDonald's logo, and "did an abstract dance to the music from the NBC Nightly News."[50] The next day, the band headed to CBGB's to film the video for Channel Z, then went to upstate New York to film some more footage.

Back in Athens, the B-52s weren't the only Athenians applying their party sensibilities to political causes. That spring saw a group of locals hold a fundraiser that would become an institution. The first Boybutante Ball was held to raise money for AIDS Athens and a local shelter for women experiencing domestic violence. Described as a mix of Halloween and Mardi Gras, the event centered around a drag ball and became an annual Athens tradition. The Boybutante organization evolved into a non-profit that, since 1989, has raised over $900,000 to support people with HIV/AIDS in northeast Georgia. Coretta Scott Queen, one of the original performers, looked back on that first show. "I remember sitting on someone's living room floor with a cocktail in hand, listening to someone say: 'Let's throw a ball!' And what a ball it has been."[51]

Album and Tour(s)

On June 27th, *Cosmic Thing* was released into the world to favorable reviews. Even the *New York Times* noticed "the substance beneath the kitsch."[52] A month later, the band appeared on *Late Night with David Letterman* to perform Love Shack, with Kate singing the *tin roof rusted* line because Cindy was sick. Then they headed out on the road for their first real tour since 1983, with no idea what to expect. "I had to learn Ricky's parts," said Keith, "but I never wanted to imitate him, because I couldn't. It was a good 10 years before I was comfortable playing guitar onstage. The whole tour I was hanging by a thread."[53]

The five-week tour focused on coastal cities where the B-52s were likeliest to draw a large audience. During the band's hiatus, there had been a rise in what were called "modern rock" stations in places like Los Angeles, NYC, Boston, and San Diego that played bands like R.E.M., the Smiths, and Depeche Mode in heavy rotation. To these stations, the B-52s were a legacy band, and they played their music—going all the way back to the first album—the way classic rock stations play Led Zeppelin and the Eagles.[54] They were also regularly playing Channel Z, and this airplay led to the band's initial shows being met with packed venues and enthusiastic audiences.

Still, critics were skeptical. Writer Mick LaSalle expressed the general attitude in his live review for the *San Francisco Chronicle*. "I'd come to think of the B-52s as a band that had passed its peak. And then in 1985 Ricky Wilson, the lead guitarist, died of AIDS. Could they maintain their wackiness and spontaneity after a tragedy like that?" LaSalle attended all three shows at the Fillmore and came away stunned. "It was easily the best rock concert I've been to in several years," he wrote, before concluding the show was "nothing less than a compensation for mortality."[55]

The band took a side trip before their Phoenix, Arizona show, heading up the highway to new-age hotspot Sedona. When they saw people performing rituals in the positive-energy vortexes on Bell Rock, they decided to perform a ritual of their own. "We held hands, the whole band," recalled Cindy. "We put out the energy that the world would be a happier place, and also that this would be a successful album."[56] That same day, Channel

Z reached #1 on *Billboard*'s Modern Rock chart, where it would reside for three weeks.

With a month off before their next tour, the band went to Plattekill, New York, about an hour south of Woodstock, to film their next video, Love Shack. The band invited a bunch of friends to the shoot, including RuPaul, who helped organize the dancing. "It wasn't going right." said RuPaul. "So I had to step in and say, 'OK, listen. This is how you do a Soul Train line.' It's like two wheels that are sort of smashing pasta out; it's like a pasta machine."[57]

Despite their success to this point, the band still wasn't getting played on Top 40 radio. For Love Shack, Fred took matters into his own hands. "I had to go with our A&R person, bless her heart, and beg radio stations to play it—they thought it was too weird."[58] On September 2nd, Love Shack, already #1 on the alternative chart, entered the US Top 100, their first single to do so since Legal Tender. The band headed to Europe for a month of shows, and by the time they returned to start the next leg of their American tour, Love Shack had become the first B-52s song to crack the US Top 40. MTV was now playing the video on what seemed like an hourly basis. This tour wasn't going to be like the others.

B-52s Mania

The first show was in Athens, then they headed to Florida for a series of shows there. A critic was stunned by the bedlam the B-52s inspired:

> With the B-52's messages of peace, it's nearly impossible to understand how violent some of their audiences have gotten. In Pensacola and Gainesville, the show ended before the final encores, the first night because Pierson got cut over her eye by an object thrown from the audience and the second night because the crowd was pushing so hard, the barrier in front of the stage nearly collapsed."[59]

The B-52s were becoming rock stars. This wasn't a kitschy, campy devotion the B's inspired among their fans, more like a surging energy teetering on the edge of violence and destruction. The tour wound on for nearly three months. As the band continued to play for larger and more frenetic audiences, Love Shack continued to climb the charts. On November 4th, during a day off between shows in South Carolina and D.C., the song entered the Top 10. Two weeks later it peaked at #3. Ten days after that, the band decided to share their new success with their hometown.

On November 28th, AIDS Athens became a non-profit, and the B-52s donated $37,000 to the group. This gift allowed the organization to hire their first paid staff member and move into an office. AIDS Athens also began printing informational brochures to distribute in the area. Around this time, Bill Thompson, one of the group's chairmen, estimated that northeast Georgia had "as many as 50 [cases] if you go back to the early 80s."[60] On January 28th of the following year, AIDS Athens and UGA Health Services would hold an all-day seminar on campus. Among the speakers were Ric Crawford and David Maddox, two Athenians living with AIDS. Maddox said, "My friends and I thought AIDS could always be a concern of ours, but we thought that's for New York and San Francisco, not for us." Crawford spoke candidly about his anger and depression, then concluded, "Death doesn't bother me as much as it used to …. We're *all* going to die. There hasn't been anybody who beat that."[61] Within the year, the University of Georgia health center began offering free AIDS tests, and a campus group formed called UGAIDS.

By December, the band was playing arenas. Karen Schoemer, a writer at *Spin*, attended a December 29th show the band played to 9000 people at San Francisco's Civic Auditorium:

> A wide circle clears in front of the stage for slamdancing skinheads. Nearby, a fist fight breaks out between two surfer dudes. As the music builds, one throws his fist, staggers with the force of the follow-through and contorts his body wildly in time to the music as his lips, in perfect synch with Fred Schneider's voice, form the words "Planet Claire.[62]

Schoemer marveled at the audience's reaction to the band's older songs, calling the scene "beyond bacchanalia. These songs from the band's first two albums … have carried over to an entirely new generation."[63]

By January, the band were playing arenas in smaller markets like Salt Lake City and Cedar Rapids. As Love Shack left the Top 40, Roam quickly took its place, entering the chart on January 20th. Six days later, *Rolling Stone* writer Michael Azerrad attended a show in Minneapolis and found an audience dancing so hard they were causing parts of the building to collapse. "Folks we have a dilemma here," announced Fred to the audience, "because we're tearing down the house—literally. The plaster's falling off the balcony. So people in the balcony, if you would, don't dance."[64]

The band had come full circle. They had gone from playing house parties in Athens where people thought the floor was going to break, to playing arenas in Minnesota where it actually was; from playing small venues in New York where they had to ask people to dance, to playing huge venues in middle America where they had to ask them to stop. Azerrad wrote the balcony was "bouncing a good twelve inches up and down," and the promoter had to send someone backstage to tell the band, for safety concerns, not to play Rock Lobster. They played Planet Claire instead, as Kate urged everyone to "dance in your minds."[65]

The B-52s had become one of the biggest bands in America. On February 6th and 7th, they filled Radio City Music Hall for two nights. That same week, they attended the Grammy Awards, having received their first nomination (Best Pop Vocal Performance by a Duo or Group—they lost to Linda Ronstadt and Aaron Neville). Then the band finally got a three-month break. While they rested, Roam continued to climb the charts. It reached #3 in March, giving the band their second Top 3 hit in less than four months. *Cosmic Thing* was now selling 200,000 copies a week.[66] They appeared on the cover of *Spin*, and that same month, the B-52s finally made the cover of *Rolling Stone*. Azerrad wrote in his article, "A year ago the scene at the University of Minnesota would have been unimaginable .... But in the past six months the B-52's have staged a stunning comeback."[67]

Next, the band returned to Athens to film a video for Deadbeat Club, a sepia-toned affair that saw the band surrounded by old friends, including Jeremy Ayers. On April 21st, they played Channel Z and Cosmic Thing on *Saturday Night Live*, nearly ten years to the day after their previous appearance. The next day they played an Earth Day celebration in Central Park alongside Hall & Oates and Edie Brickell and the New Bohemians that drew 500,000 people.[68]

That June, with Deadbeat Club in the Top 40, the band headed back out on the road. This time they were headlining arenas in middle American suburbs like Burgettstown (outside Pittsburgh), Nobelsville (outside Indianapolis), and Bonner Springs (outside Kansas City). It doesn't get more mainstream than playing to 15,000 people at The Met Center in Bloomington, Minnesota (outside Minneapolis). In August, the band played four nights at the iconic Red Rocks Amphitheatre in Morrison, Colorado (outside Denver).

Coincidentally, the summer of 1990 also saw the "Escape From New York Tour," a package tour of artists still managed by Gary Kurfirst:

the Ramones, Debbie Harry, and Tom Tom Club. During the June 28th show, the Ramones actually dedicated a song to Kurfirst. None of the participants had managed a hit in years, and the tour was met with critical and commercial indifference. "We're going back to touring clubs after this," said Tina Weymouth in an interview.[69]

Still, all was not well with the B-52s either. It had been over a year since that first David Letterman appearance, and they were still touring. For all the excitement and vindication of *Cosmic Thing*, the success had brought more work, just like it always did. "We've never thought of ourselves as professionals," said Keith. "We're still saying, 'Are we?' Now we're realizing that we are."[70]

It seemed like nothing could stop the band. No matter what happened—exhaustion, creative blockages, even Ricky's death—the machine kept going. Success just meant you had to continue showing up. There were always more buses, more sound checks, more press, and the label was already asking about another album, the sooner the better. Back in 1987, when everything was broken, the B-52s had wanted to start working again. Now that it was 1990 and they were experiencing unimaginable success, it felt like the work would never stop. It seemed no matter what anyone did, this thing called the B-52s—a name that had come to Keith one night in a dream and had defined them for ten years—would control their lives forever.

In the middle of a tour, Cindy took a couple of days to reflect. When she next saw the band, she informed them she would commit to one more year of touring, but after that she was quitting. Everyone hoped she would change her mind. Nevertheless, the tour rolled on.

Despite feeling burnt out, Cindy was still grateful for everything that was happening. "The success has helped me tremendously," she said in the *Rolling Stone* article. "It's like Ricky's having some kind of effect on our whole success. It's like he's up there seeing to it."[71] Still, it must have been difficult to sing songs soaked in memories of the past every single night. In some performances from around this time, Cindy's eyes are uncharacteristically closed as she sings. She taps a tambourine. Occasionally, she remembers to dance.

A week after playing an old football stadium on the campus of San Diego State University, they began a tour of Australia and New Zealand where they played a dozen shows, including three nights in Sydney. Then mercifully, nearly 15 months after *Cosmic Thing* had been released, the B-52s were finally able to rest. During that time, they had gone from barely existing as a band to becoming one of the biggest bands in the world. It was one of the greatest, most unexpected comebacks in music history, made possible by one of the best albums they would ever make.

Now they needed to make another one. Only this time, they would have to do it without Cindy. The band had gone from five to four and managed to survive. If they wanted to keep going, they would have to survive going from four to three.

Notes

1. Wilde, "B-52's," 8.
2. Sexton, *The B-52's Universe*, 77.
3. Azerrad, "Mission Accomplished."
4. Hart, "B-52's."
5. Ibid.
6. Azerrad, "Mission Accomplished."
7. Matthews, "Fred Schneider," 15.
8. Wilde, "Refused to Die," 8.
9. Sexton, *The B-52's Universe*, 78.
10. Keith Bennett in conversation with authors, November 8, 2019. This meant Kurfirst got paid more in songwriting royalties for Rock Lobster than Kate did.
11. Ibid.
12. Grow, "Love Shacks."
13. Sexton, *The B-52's Universe*, 79.
14. Azerrad, "Mission Accomplished."
15. Ibid.
16. Hart, "Cosmic Thing."
17. Wilde, "Refused to Die," 9.
18. Azerrad, "Mission Accomplished."
19. Sexton, *The B-52's Universe*, 80.
20. Wilde, "Refused to Die," 9.
21. Kass, "B-52's Whirlwind."
22. Schoemer, "Beehives & Ballyhoo."
23. Azerrad, "Mission Accomplished."
24. Keith Bennett in conversation with authors, November 8, 2019.
25. Azerrad, "Mission Accomplished."
26. Email correspondence with Keith Bennett, August 2022.
27. Ibid.
28. Felder, "B-52's Organic," 29.
29. Hart, "Cosmic Thing."

30. Felder, "B-52's Organic," 29.
31. Schultz, "Classic Tracks," 17.
32. Grow, "Love Shacks."
33. Harris, "Kate Pierson."
34. Schultz, "Classic Tracks," 17.
35. Spitz, "Return," AR24.
36. Issue #12, *The B's Connection*, July 1993, Mats Sexton B-52's memorabilia collection, Box 1, University of Georgia Libraries Special Collections.
37. Schoemer, "Beehives & Ballyhoo," 44.
38. Hann, "Everyone Is Welcome."
39. Sexton, *The B-52's Universe*, 28.
40. Boyer and Yearwood, *How Sweet the Sound*, 192, as cited in Powers, *Good Booty*.
41. Carpenter, *Uncloudy Days*, 430.
42. Powers, *Good Booty*, 128.
43. White, *Little Richard*, 23–25.
44. Hinson, *Fire in My Bones*, 130.
45. Sandall, "Love Shack Shakes Again."
46. Azerrad, "Mission Accomplished."
47. Wilde, "Refused to Die."
48. Ayers, "Madonna Struts."
49. Sexton, *The B-52's Universe*, 83.
50. Hochswender, "Jungle Is Given," B-3.
51. Ellis, "Boybutante."
52. Schoemer, "Recordings: At Home."
53. Tannenbaum, "The B-52s Say Farewell," AR-14.
54. One of this book's authors grew up near San Diego in the mid-late 1980s and remembers hearing the B-52s catalogue regularly on alternative station 91X long before *Cosmic Thing* came out.
55. LaSalle, "B-52s Airborne Again."
56. Horn, "B-52s' Cindy Wilson."
57. Parker, "B-52's' Fred Schneider."
58. Greenblatt, "The B-52s: Stories Behind."
59. Bordowitz, "B-52's," 29.
60. Conoly Hester, "Are AIDS Cases Under-Reported in NE Georgia?" Box 1, LGBT Resource Records, UA17-009 University of Georgia Libraries Special Collections.
61. Kim Henderson, "I Never Thought AIDS Could Touch Me," January 28, 1990, Box 1, LGBT Resource Records, UA17-009 University of Georgia Libraries Special Collections.
62. Schoemer, "Beehives & Ballyhoo," 41.
63. Ibid.

64. Azerrad, "Mission Accomplished."
65. Ibid.
66. Ibid.
67. Ibid.
68. Sexton, *The B-52's Universe*, 91. Brickell was dating Paul Simon at the time, and they would soon marry. We promise this will be the last time he is mentioned in this book about a band that is not Paul Simon.
69. Reinolds, "Escape From New York."
70. Azerrad, "Mission Accomplished."
71. Ibid.

CHAPTER 11

Good Stuff

We had not had that kind of success before, and everything changed. For me it got too heavy. It just had to stop.[1]

—Keith

Popular music is probably the only art form where dying young is considered part of the medium. There is no "27 Club" among film directors, or even actors. But then, music is more physically demanding than any other art form. The challenge of performing every night in front of an audience, the rush of adrenaline, the grind of traveling, the dancing, the singing, the sheer physicality of playing an instrument night after night, is something that writers and painters don't have to experience. As such, popular music is an art form with a body count.

Part of this is because everyone around you—managers, labels, agents, crew—encourages you to keep going, especially when you're selling a lot of records. They only make money if you make money. And aside from the road crew, none of those people experience the same pressure and strain that the musicians do.

As 1991 began, Cindy reminded the band's management that she was leaving, as her one year's notice was up. It seemed that no one had really believed her. "They were very surprised that I really was going to do it," she said.[2] On January 20th, the B-52s got together to attend the Grammy

S. Creney, B. A. Herron, *The Story of the B-52s*,
https://doi.org/10.1007/978-3-031-22570-3_11

Awards. Gathered in her hotel room, Cindy told the band she was truly leaving. Tears were shed, but she gave them her blessing to continue without her. Kate said, "We were coming off this really big album and definitely wanted to continue, but it was weird for us."[3]

Like the plant in Little Shop of Horrors, a band is an animal that needs constant feeding. And the bigger it gets, the more rapacious its hunger. *Cosmic Thing* had sold nearly two million copies. While that produced a lot of income for the band, it had generated even more money for their label. If Cindy refused to keep the machine going, the machine would have to keep on without her. Too many people needed it, including her three bandmates, who were too practical and too ambitious to stop.

While Cindy was retreating from the spotlight, Kate's profile was expanding, as her activities outside the band saw her become the best-known B-52. Iggy Pop was recording a solo album with Don Was, and when Iggy needed a second vocalist on the song Candy, the producer suggested Kate. "I went into the studio," she recalled, "and [Iggy] gave me pretty much carte blanche to reinterpret the lyrics, so I changed a few minor bits in the talking part."[4] The song gave Iggy his only Top 40 hit and put Kate back on the radio.

Around the time Candy came out, R.E.M. asked Kate to contribute background vocals to their album *Out of Time*. One of the songs she sang on, Shiny Happy People, reached the Top 10, and in April 1991, Kate appeared on *Saturday Night Live* again, this time alongside R.E.M. Kate and Michael Stipe also made cameo appearances on the wonderful Nickelodeon TV show *The Adventures of Pete & Pete* (other guest stars on the series included B-52s' friends Ann Magnuson, Debbie Harry, and Iggy Pop). Warners decided to cash in on the B-52s' success by having Reprise reissue Fred's *Shake Society* record, changing the name of the album to *Fred Schneider* and having Monster remixed to sound more contemporary. Fred did some press to promote the album, and people liked it a little better this time. It reached #85.

Keith stayed home making music. Once summer arrived, the three band members convened in upstate New York to start writing the next album. Kate said, "Some days we'd do nothing, and other days we'd write a song."[5] Things didn't always run smoothly. Keith said, "It was difficult. We had to find a new balance, and we weren't sure .... It was more thought out this time around—it wasn't something that just occurred."[6] Kate described the conundrum they faced missing Cindy, saying, "When Cindy left it was like a puzzle. How is the energy going to happen with the three of us?"[7]

To their credit, they put in enough time and work to complete ten songs, and toward the end of 1991, the band were ready to start recording. They decided to repeat the formula that had worked so well on *Cosmic Thing* by splitting the work between Don Was in Bearsville and Nile Rodgers in NYC.

Keyboardist Pat Irwin played on the sessions, and recalled it wasn't easy trying to repeat the success of *Cosmic Thing*. "We were exhausted from being on the road for 18 months straight."[8] The Bearsville sessions featured "blood-curdling" ping pong matches between Pat and Fred. Everyone played Tetris. Don Was recalled laughing through all six takes of Hot Pants Explosion. "It's constant levity!" he said. "I think the craziness of their music is something that is therapeutic for them."[9] While there, they completed five songs: Is That You Mo-Dean? Hot Pants, Bad News, Breezin', and Good Stuff, all of which aspired toward the constant levity Was had been talking about. The band then headed to New York to work on the rest with Nile Rodgers.

Looking back, Rodgers observed that the band "wasn't ready for the bigness of *Cosmic Thing*," and that by 1992 "the group was floundering."[10] Considering Nile's substance abuse had gotten so bad that he was pronounced dead at an NYC hospital in 1990,[11] the group must have been having serious trouble. After years of battling his addictions and his demons, Nile got sober in 1994.[12] And in 2013, he co-wrote and played guitar on Get Lucky, a Daft Punk song that was one of that year's biggest singles.

If *Cosmic Thing* had been the product of humility, *Good Stuff* was turning out to be the product of arrogance, though one more rooted in naiveté than swagger. The B-52s were now reaping the benefits of the big time. Years later, Keith looked back on this period, and said, "I think at that point we were a little overwhelmed at the success we were having with Cosmic and with Cindy leaving and not being that grounded."[13] They even brought in some Hare Krishnas to sing on the seven-and-a-half-minute epic, Dreamland. "Somebody in the studio's cousin was in the Hare Krishna temple in Brooklyn," said Fred. "And so one phone call and boom."[14]

Keith later said the recording got "flattened by technology .... I think we knew what was happening in production," he said, "but didn't really take the reins and say, 'Hey wait a minute!'"[15] Keith also blamed outside pressures to finish the album and get back on the road. It was like it was 1982 all over again:

> I felt like we rushed it. I would have liked to have spent more time on it. About midway through I realized—we had already decided on a deadline, so kind of all the machinery had gone into motion and about midway through I was having the feeling that I wanted to spend more time on this.[16]

Listening to the album, it's hard to hear how more time would have helped. If anything, *Good Stuff* has too many ideas. Whereas *Mesopotamia* sounds unfinished, *Good Stuff* sounds *over*-finished. It's crammed with overdubs to the point where it becomes hard to hear any one instrument clearly. The effect is like when you mix all your paint colors together and the result is brown. Ultimately though, the production doesn't matter. If ABBA, Daniel Johnston, Britney Spears, Tall Dwarfs, and the Carter Family have taught us anything, it's that a truly great song will come through no matter how it's recorded. The truth is the songwriting on *Good Stuff* wasn't up to par. There isn't a single song as emotionally resonant as Deadbeat Club, or as much fun as Love Shack.

Close listening raises so many questions. For example, if you got abducted by aliens, why would you need to take a bus and a plane before boarding the UFO? Why are all the songs so slow? And so long? What is the line *the pearl melts before I drink it up* supposed to mean? Also, did they think nobody would notice they already used the Sympathy for the Devil woo-woo's two albums ago?

The lyrics are also a weak spot. They contain some of the worst puns the band ever sang. Phrases like *Untamed melody* or *break out of the mold before the mold sets in* are a long way from the attack and subversion found on Rock Lobster or Channel Z.

It turned out that, with only two lyricists, the songs became more of a dialogue between Kate and Fred. As a result, they direct a lot of sexy talk toward each other with lines like *studball hunky baby rock me* and *I wanna wallow in your hollow* that feel more juvenile than erotic. Not juvenile as in adolescent, but juvenile as in childish, a third-graders' idea of sexiness.

They try so hard to be over the top that all you can hear is the effort. There's no fun on *Good Stuff*, just people working hard to make something happen—the world's greatest party band throwing a bummer of a party. The result is an album of forced smiles that keeps asking, "Are we having fun yet?" For all but the most devoted B-52s fan, the answer was no.

The best song on *Good Stuff*, by some distance, is the title track. It's got a chorus so catchy that the lines about toe-nibbling and growing love-honey don't matter. The only problem is it takes an eternity (nearly two entire minutes on the album version) to get there. The song spends more time asking if we're ready for the chorus than it spends actually singing it.

This happens a lot on the album, where a good idea surfaces, only to be quickly abandoned. Fred's singing on the verse of Dreamland is beautiful, but the song goes off the rails when it hits the chorus, and gets even worse when it reaches the bridge. Too much of the music on *Good Stuff* feels uninspired. Keith's favorite move is to hold one chord for a long time during the verse, then at the end of the line throw in some blues chord changes that are closer to Eric Clapton than Ricky Wilson.[17] The problem wasn't just Keith. Pat Irwin and Don Was added guitars to Bad Influence, but it sounds like jam night at the House of Blues. How did three innovative guitarists—Irwin played with Lydia Lunch in 8 Eyed Spy—end up churning out generic 80s-sounding mainstream rock in 1992?

The whole project reeks of excess, of too much time spent in the studio. Only a successful band could have made an album like *Good Stuff*, as everyone around you says your ideas are great and no expense is spared. With its cluttered sound, slow tempos, and profit-fueled hubris, *Good Stuff* resembles Oasis' *Be Here Now* to such a degree you might think Noel Gallagher was directly inspired by it.[18]

There are many great songs with the word Revolution in the title—songs by Spacemen 3, T. Rex, Tracy Chapman, Nina Simone, Neil Young, and Beat Happening all come to mind—but Revolution Earth is not one of them. It is, however, possibly the only song with Revolution in its title that is literally about the earth revolving around the sun. It's one of many songs on *Good Stuff* to feature images of nature and earth, which is ironic because the album itself doesn't sound natural at all. Instead, it sounds tightly controlled and antiseptic. This distance between content and form is so vast that it undermines the group's message. As the reviewer in *Spin* noted, "the words 'movement' and 'vision' pop up so many times you begin to wonder whom to make out the checks to."[19]

It's never a good sign when an album cover is more interesting than the music inside, but *Good Stuff*'s cover is fascinating. There is so much symbolism, it almost invites over-interpretation, like a renaissance painting. Each band member holds an object—Kate a large ring, Keith a cat's cradle, and Fred a pyramid that looks eerily similar to Ricky's grave marker. Also, their reflections in the water beneath them are distorted, suggesting a disconnect between who they are and what they appear to be. The back cover features only their distorted images accompanied by the song titles. It's far and away the most thought-provoking moment on *Good Stuff*.

"Here It 'Tis"

In March 1992, three months before the release of *Good Stuff*, the band played their first show without Cindy Wilson. It was a benefit for Democratic presidential candidate Jerry Brown. Don Was played bass, Nile Rodgers played some guitar, and Athens native (and Hollywood actress) Kim Basinger filled in for Cindy. Kim did fine, but she wasn't about to abandon her acting career. So the band recruited Julee Cruise, who was best known for singing the theme to David Lynch's *Twin Peaks*—although her song Mysteries of Love from *Blue Velvet* is up there with the Cocteau Twins and This Mortal Coil for transcendent gothic bliss. Julee said getting asked to join the band was like "getting asked to join the Beatles."[20]

Good Stuff came out on June 23rd. Despite their attempt to replicate the success of *Cosmic Thing*, the experience would turn out to be very different this time. The music world had changed a lot in the three years since that album, as Nirvana had spearheaded a pop culture revolution—one that placed an emphasis on raw anger and visceral emotion.

Buoyed by the B-52s' status as a legacy band, *Good Stuff*'s title track managed to reach #1 on alternative radio. It stayed there for three weeks, but other songs on the chart included edgier fare like Sonic Youth's 100% and L7's Pretend We're Dead. Even a song like Catherine Wheel's Black Metallic leapt out of the radio with an angry desperation that wasn't present on Good Stuff. In an era of noisy sincerity, the B-52s sounded lightweight and complacent by comparison. Though the B-52s had helped birth the alternative movement, they no longer had anything in common with edgier acts like PJ Harvey and Ministry, whose songs Sheela-Na-Gig and N.W.O. entered the alternative charts the week Good Stuff left.

The band had chosen to play it safe at a time when artists were being rewarded for taking risks. Like so many record executives and managers before them, the band thought a conservative approach was the smart move. As a result, *Good Stuff* saw the B-52s amplify the goofy, party band image they had worked so hard to dismantle.

The band now belonged to the moms and dads, appearing on *The Tonight Show* as Branford Marsalis adding a horn solo to Good Stuff. The single would only reach #28 on the pop charts. The #1 song that week was Baby's Got Back by Sir Mix-A-Lot, a song that, with its juvenile parade of bad puns and PG sexuality, must have made Fred furious he hadn't thought of it first.

Good Stuff also had the bad luck of being released during an economic recession. The country was in no mood to party. Consider three songs that sat higher on the charts when Good Stuff peaked at #28: Arrested Development's Tennessee, Red Hot Chili Peppers' Under the Bridge, and En Vogue's My Lovin. The first song struggles with a family member's death and references lynching. The second is about alienation and scoring drugs, and the last song is a sassy kiss-off female empowerment anthem. All went deeper than anything the B-52s were bringing to the table. In trying to appeal to everybody, *Good Stuff* ended up appealing to hardly anybody.

Whatever its faults, *Good Stuff* is valuable for the way it reveals how Cindy and Kate's different styles works to the bands' advantage. Hearing the B-52s without Cindy is like hearing the Beatles without John, since Cindy serves the same role in her band that Lennon did in his—she's the band's soulful emotional anchor. You don't feel any distance between what she's feeling and what she's singing. In that same vein, you can make a case that Kate is the Paul in the group, the supportive, technically perfect virtuoso craftsman who makes everything work. This is oversimplifying, just as it is when people talk about the individual Beatles, but it's a useful tool for analyzing how the band works. And just like that other B- band, it makes for deeper listening and fun conversations. The fact the B-52s had a third singer, Fred, who wrote the bulk of the lyrics on their first two albums, and who wrote and sang in his own unique voice, shows what a distinctive mix of talent and personality make up the B-52s.

Tour

The possibility had always existed, given their precarious balance between sincerity and humor, that the band's live show could tip into Vegas-style schlock. Maybe it was Cindy's absence, or maybe it was the large venues, but on the *Good Stuff* tour, the band finally succumbed to rock-star cliché excess. Even the name of the tour, "Interdimensional Tourgasm," was ridiculous. There were now more people onstage who weren't technically in the B-52s than actual band members. The dance moves looked coordinated and synchronized, with arms out airplane-style during Mo-Dean when they sang the part about a plane. The bulk of the tour ran from August through November, then picked back up again in January for another two months.

Interviews meant endless questions about Cindy, making every day an exercise in diplomacy. The band's core group of fans still loved them, but to the rest of the world, the B-52s had become hopelessly uncool, and now they weren't popular either. An *NME* writer called their music "sad pseudo-mainstream pap" in her live review.[21] An October show at the San Diego Sports Arena found the venue only half filled, with the reviewer wondering, "Does anyone else get the feeling that the B-52's is a band of bright and talented people trapped in a clown suit?"[22] A profile in *Details* found the writer hanging out with the band for a few days and coming away dejected. "The B-52's are so hard to get to know," wrote Pat Blashill. "In person, Fred and Kate and Keith are sincere, but cautious, even when they're protected by a cordon of P.R. people." Blashill was, and is, a fan of the band, but the scene he depicted was of an "inhibited" band that wasn't having any fun. "Schneider is the king of the stale one-liners," he observed, "but I only hear him laugh out loud once."[23]

In September, *Good Stuff*'s second single Tell It Like It T-I-Is struggled to reach #13 on the alternative charts, below Pearl Jam, Temple of the Dog, and a slew of other artists who sounded nothing like the B-52s. The song didn't even crack the Top 100. Revolution Earth, with a video directed by old Athens friend Jim Herbert and lyrics by Robert Waldrop, followed in February. It didn't make the pop or the alternative charts. Keith told an interviewer that Reprise didn't want to release the next single, Is That You Mo-Dean? "because all the others flopped,"[24] but they put it out anyway. That one flopped too.

When the B-52s tour came through Atlanta, the band had a special guest in the audience—Cindy Wilson. She and Keith Bennett had moved to Atlanta, and the two sat toward the back watching the show. Cindy wore a large hat so she could avoid being noticed. "It was like having an out of body experience," she said. Afterward, she went backstage, and the first person she went up to was Julee Cruise because Cindy wanted to tell her what a good job she had done.[25]

Politics

The political content on *Good Stuff* was more pronounced than on *Cosmic Thing*, but the lyrics this time were almost comically non-specific. Tell It Like It T-I-Is exhorts it listeners to *See the situation* and *Open those eyes and get the real picture* because *Things are getting so bad*. What things? What situation? The band wasn't saying. Bad Influence tells us, *It's time for liberation to flow*. Whose liberation? It continues, *Let the barriers tumble down*. Which barriers? Breezin' urges us to *get it together with everyone else* with an ethos of *Give and let live / Love and be loved*. The lyrics sound more like the beginnings of half-baked manifestos, where sadly, the details are never filled in.

The band was more specific in interviews though, as Kate despaired at how US society had changed since the 70s:

> The sixties uncorked the bottle. The genie escaped and people went wild: dropping out, taking acid, exploring their bodies. What the Reagan and Bush administrations have tried to do is put that genie back into the bottle.[26]

The message that had always been implicit in the B-52s' music—personal and political freedom—was now being pushed front and center in interviews. If they had people's attention, they were going to make the most of it. Kate continued, "What we need is a new, new left that's politically aware and can dance that mess around."[27] Fred told an interviewer, "It would be pretty empty to just get up on stage and make money. How could we enjoy that when there's so much to be done?"[28] The B-52s wanted people to know they weren't doing this for the money. They were doing it for the animals, for people with AIDS, for reproductive rights, for the planet.

This was admirable on the surface, but while the B-52s were taking tentative steps toward political activism, other people were charging out ahead of them. In the wake of the AIDS epidemic, every aspect of gay life had become politicized, including people's privacy. ACT UP's slogan was SILENCE = DEATH, and to a sizable portion of the LGBTQ+ community, celebrities had an obligation to be completely public about their sexuality. This put Fred and Keith in a difficult position, trapped between a music industry still riddled with homophobia and a gay community that saw being publicly out as an important way to combat that homophobia. Furthermore, increased visibility led to more funding for AIDS research.

Two months before *Good Stuff* was released, *Rolling Stone* ran an article after Freddie Mercury's recent death from AIDS about homophobia in the music world. Mercury had remained in the closet his entire life, and the writers observed that his "reluctance to address his illness publicly is all too typical of how the rock world has dealt with AIDS. It's a world where silence is the rule."[29] Ricky's death, and the band's ensuing secrecy, was addressed in the article, with Kate observing, "There's a fear among rock artists who have so much invested in their image and have a fear of being identified with AIDS or as gay."[30] Neither Fred's nor Keith's sexuality was discussed.

In a June interview with *Queer Weekly*, a writer forced the issue with the B-52s. At first, Keith deflected the question, saying "whether you're gay or not gay, if you're happy with yourself and honest and straightforward with people, they'll accept that."[31] That didn't satisfy the interviewer, so they went for a more direct approach:

QW: Do you think that people from Whatevertown, America are aware that you two (Fred & Keith) are gay?
Keith: I don't know. I just take it on a one on one basis. If somebody asks me if I'm gay I just say yes. I would tell them.
Kate: Who wants to broadcast their sexual preference?
Keith: It just seems so unfair that because you're a public person you always have to say, "I'm gay." I understand why it's necessary in a way, because we do have a society that doesn't want to accept it.
Kate: It's not like "Oh everyone should just say what their preference is, and everything will be alright."

Coming-out is more of a process than a single event. Keith said in a 2002 feature in *The Advocate* that he considers his official coming-out to have been in 1992 during an interview with UK music magazine *Q*. "There was a war going on," Keith reflected, "and I thought, *We're doing all this stuff, but we're not talking about being gay* (italics in original)"[32] According to Keith, coming out in *Q* was "great. Nothing changed, but I felt it was important to say it."[33]

However, a year later, Keith was still uncomfortable discussing the subject, as seen in this interview with Liesl Dano for her B-52s zine:

Liesl: You guys are outspoken on a lot of issues, AIDS, the environment, pro-choice. Yet even though the B's have a large gay following, the band hasn't made any strong gay rights stands as prolific, as, say your stand on animal rights.

Keith: Umm (pause) I think we've kind of always dealt with it in a way that we most feel comfortable. I think we, the B-52's, we definitely have a gay sensibility, and I think it's kind of always been there and I've always felt it was obvious, so I felt we didn't need to really…

LD: … draw attention to it?

KS: Well, become militant about it. And I've never felt completely comfortable with being a spokesman for the gay community. There's the fear that if you start talking about it, that's all that anyone will ever think about or talk about.[34]

This was a valid fear on Keith's part. He added later in the interview that, "You don't want the media to just dwell on that part … well, now I'm a gay person, whereas before I was Keith Strickland."

Fred, who guarded his privacy more fiercely than Keith, had an even harder struggle. Lance Loud had appeared in a 1973 PBS documentary about a California family. Loud, then in his early 20s, came out publicly on the show, causing considerable controversy at the time. He then moved to New York City and became a journalist and a musician. His band, The Mumps, were regulars at Max's and CBGB's. By June 1994, Loud was a columnist for *The Advocate*, and reached out to Fred for an interview, only to be rebuffed. Loud wrote, "Why would it be so difficult to reach Schneider for an interview? Because little old me asked to speak to Schneider about his being gay." Loud explained his motivation. "Many times since my appearance on … *An American Family*, I've been approached by gays and lesbians who have said that they were comforted during their own emergence from the closet by my televised coming-out."[35]

Eventually, Loud got a response from a member of the B-52s' press team. "He doesn't want to discuss the gay thing," they said. "It might hurt him, I guess." Undaunted, Loud decided to fax his questions. The next day Fred responded. Though he ignored a question about Ricky's death, he answered, *Why do you feel so guarded about your sexual orientation?* by saying, "I'm on the same side of the fence as k.d., Elton, and Frederick the Great. I just don't like to share my personal life with the public."[36] Despite Fred's clear signals, Loud brusquely concluded, "Well Fred, thank you for sharing." Heartbreakingly, Lance Loud died in 2001 from a combination of hepatitis C and AIDS.

Meet the Flintstones

During the summer of 1993, the B-52s were approached about contributing a couple of songs to a movie soundtrack. Someone had the idea to make a big budget live-action movie of the iconic 60s cartoon *The Flintstones*. Keith didn't want to do it initially, but felt pressured by Kate, Fred, and the management. He did like the idea of being in a film with Elizabeth Taylor though. Cindy wasn't approached for the project. "I wasn't in the band at the time, and it would have been weird," she said. "There wasn't friction, but I don't think anybody in the band knew what they were doing at that point."[37]

For a band that had always bristled at being labeled a cartoon, it was a baffling decision. They ended up covering the theme song, and appeared in the film as "The BC-52's," playing a reworked song from the TV series called The Bedrock Twitch.[38]

The film came out in 1994, and had a star-studded cast featuring John Goodman as Fred, Rosie O'Donnell as Betty, Halle Berry as Fred's villainous secretary, and Kyle McLachlan as Fred's even more villainous boss. It didn't go well. *The Washington Post* critic said, "It isn't just awful. It bombs itself into the Stone Age."[39] Gene Siskel called it "movie as product," adding "It looks great but is a complete bore."[40] Neither writer does justice to the film's badness. *The Flintstones* movie may be the most bizarre, jaw-dropping thing Kyle McLachlan has ever appeared in, and he's been in three David Lynch movies, as well as *Showgirls*.

There aren't any sex scenes in *The Flintstones*, but there's unending innuendo—along with endless bad puns and jokes (the families go to see a movie called "Tar Wars," get it?). The strangest thing is you can't imagine the actors, or the writers, doing a better job with the material they had to work with. It's just that—like someone said in another Steven Spielberg-produced mid-90s dinosaur film—they were so preoccupied with whether or not they could, they didn't stop to think if they should.

Because no bad deed goes unrewarded, the band's version of the theme song reached the pop charts and went to #33. It would be the B-52s' final Top 40 hit (to date). Despite its commercial success, the song has never appeared on any of the band's greatest hits compilations. You can draw your own conclusions. In the *Melody Maker*, semi-satirical hate-spewer Mr. Agreeable lit into the band with a vicious glee:

> You pitiful, can't-afford-to-retire bunch of f***ing scumsuckers! This is the ultimate f***ing humiliation, carrying around a f***ing sandwich board for the latest mega-f***ing Hollywood disaster! Let's face it you did this for the money .... Because when it comes to a choice between dignity and artistic integrity and barrowloads of greenbacks, the ackers win every f***ing time, eh? Twats![41]

Melody Maker's Everett True put it more succinctly in that week's singles column. "When is a joke not a joke? When it's not even funny."[42] That was the entirety of the review.

After the B-52s finished working on *The Flintstones* movie, they played a series of shows in early 1994. However, Julee Cruise wasn't performing with the band anymore. She had been replaced by someone named Cindy Wilson.

Notes

1. Spitz, "Return," AR24.
2. Sexton, *The B-52's Universe*, 95.
3. Ibid.
4. Harris, "Kate Pierson."
5. Sexton, *The B-52's Universe*, 96.
6. Clarke, "Serious Fun," 37.
7. Ibid.
8. Pat Irwin Music, "B-52's—Good Stuff." Technically, it was 14 months that had a three-month break in the middle, during which time they did TV and made videos.
9. "The B-52's Only Official Correspondence Club," The B-52's Dec 191/ Jan 1992, Mats Sexton B-52's memorabilia collection, Box 1, University of Georgia Libraries Special Collections.
10. Spitz, "Return," AR24.
11. Rodgers, *Le Freak*, 262–3.
12. Ibid.
13. Keith Strickland interview, *B-Hive*, Summer 1998 Issue 13, Mats Sexton B-52's memorabilia collection, Box 1, University of Georgia Libraries Special Collections.
14. Clark, "Serious," 37.
15. Ibid.
16. *The B's Connection*, Issue #12 July 1993, 5, Mats Sexton B-52's memorabilia collection, Box 1, University of Georgia Libraries Special Collections.
17. In terms of chord theory, this means Keith favors I-III-IV or I-VII-IV progressions for his rock. When he goes pop, usually for the chorus, he

gravitates toward some combination of the I-IV-V chords. There's hardly anything on *Good Stuff* as unexpected as Love Shack's chorus, which starts in C and ends with a held G# that isn't in the song's home key but works perfectly. This is also a good place to mention how Roam subverts its rock-based E-A-D-B chord structure by walking down from D to B via a C# on the bass that adds an unexpected melodic element to the song.

18. Except Noel Gallagher doesn't listen to records with women on them.
19. Rogers, "Reviews."
20. Sexton, *The B-52's Universe*, 100. Sexton's quote concludes with an exclamation point, but it looked weird in the text. Let's just use this space to note she was super excited.
21. Morris, "B's Bomb?"
22. Reprint of review by Robert J. Hawkins of San Diego Sports Arena show (likely *San Diego Union-Tribune*), *B's Connection*, Issue #10, November/December 1992, Mats Sexton B-52's memorabilia collection, Box 1, University of Georgia Libraries Special Collections.
23. Blashill, "52 Pickup," 124.
24. *The B's Connection*, Issue #12, July 1993, 7, Mats Sexton B-52's memorabilia collection, Box 1, University of Georgia Libraries Special Collections.
25. Sexton, *The B-52's Universe*, 161.
26. Frank Owen "Flying High: The B-52's Strike Back" uncredited article, Mats Sexton B-52's memorabilia collection, ms 4110, Book 8, University of Georgia Libraries Special Collections.
27. Ibid.
28. Brown, "B-52's Testing Edge."
29. Hochman and Herczog, "AIDS and Rock."
30. Ibid.
31. *Queer Weekly*, June 21, 1992, reprinted in *B-Hive*, Spring/Summer 1997, Mats Sexton B-52's memorabilia collection, Box 1, University of Georgia Libraries Special Collections.
32. Che, "52's Still Rockin'," 62–64.
33. Ibid. Despite our best efforts, we were unable to locate this issue of *Q*.
34. *B-Hive*, Spring/Summer 1997, Mats Sexton B-52's memorabilia collection, Box 1, University of Georgia Libraries Special Collections.
35. Loud, "B-52 Bummer," 109.
36. Ibid.
37. Sexton, *The B-52's Universe*, 106.
38. Both songs appeared on the soundtrack, surrounded by contributions from other artists who make for a fun game of "Hey! Let's remember some 90s bands!": Stereo MC's, Crash Test Dummies, My Life With the Thrill Kill Cult, and Green Jelly. You can buy the CD online for a couple of bucks, but the vinyl will set you back over $100. Such are the laws of supply and demand.

39. Howe, "The Flintstones."
40. Siskel, "'Flintstones'"
41. Mr. Agreeable, *Melody Maker*, 58. Ackers is UK slang for coins, apparently.
42. True, "Singles," 29. While True is best known for being the first UK critic to write about Nirvana, and for introducing Kurt Cobain to Courtney Love, in our house he's best known for his piano playing and love of women's tennis.

CHAPTER 12

Aftershocks

It's an amazing story, really.[1]

—Cindy

After the debacle of *Good Stuff*, the B-52s would spend the next 25 years doing what they wanted to do. And for the most part, they would do it whenever they felt like it. There would be tours. There would eventually be one more album, *Funplex*, released in 2008. There would be greatest hits compilations. Solo albums. Solo projects. Projects that had nothing to do with the B-52s, even projects that had nothing to do with music.

There would be no public breakups, no public reunions. Hardly any manufactured drama to increase ticket sales. When they felt like working, they would work. When they felt like resting, they would rest. In this, they have so far managed to maintain their dignity in a way that other bands like, say, the Who, whose first farewell tour was in 1983, and have since undertaken nine additional "farewell tours," have not.

Cindy returned to the band in 1994, and they played about 20 shows that year. After *Good Stuff*, there were tentative attempts at making another album that turned out to be a series of false starts. Sometimes Fred was involved; sometimes Fred wasn't involved. When things weren't working creatively, they didn't try to force it like they had in the past. They just walked away.

S. Creney, B. A. Herron, *The Story of the B-52s*,
https://doi.org/10.1007/978-3-031-22570-3_12

The year 1995 saw the first "Party Out of Bounds" benefit. A group of B-52s fans, including fan club members Mats Sexton and Liesl Dano, threw a dance party at Athens' only gay club, Boneshakers. The event was held to raise money for AIDS Athens, now called AIDS Coalition of NE Georgia. It generated $1500 and became an annual event. The next year, Kate and Keith attended to support the cause, and signed autographs and danced with the crowd.[2]

Kate said in 1996 the band was "really trying to get it together and decide what the hell we were going to do."[3] That same year, Fred released another solo album. *Just Fred* saw him embrace his inner Iggy Pop, as he assembled a backing band of alt-rockers and brought in Steve Albini to produce. "I was in a weird space," said Fred. "The B-52s were working on something without me, so I said, 'Well, hell, I'm going to do something on my own.' Their thing never came about, but I committed to doing this solo album and I was in an angry mood."[4] He and old friend Richard Barone also put together a cover of Harry Nilsson's Coconut for a tribute album, and performed it live on Conan O'Brien. Fred, dressed in silver lamé pants, taps into an incendiary ruthlessness. His backing band wrings atonal skronk out of their guitars as the drummer keeps juicing the tempo. The song builds and builds before ending in an explosion of feedback and Fred dementedly screaming *Doctor!* in full rock mode.

Despite Fred's hurt feelings about the band, he did an interview around this time with Atlanta alternative rock station 99X, where he informed listeners that the B-52s, with Fred, were almost finished with their next album. "We're still working on songs sporadically and it should be out next year."[5] It wasn't. A year later, the Winter 1997 issue of the B-52s fanzine announced that Kate, Keith, and Cindy were now working on new music without Fred, as a "currently unnamed collaboration." By the end of the year, they were still no closer to an album, but had started calling themselves the B-53s.[6]

While they tried to figure out the B-52s' future, the band members made a *lot* of guest appearances, sometimes Fred, sometimes Kate, sometimes Cindy, sometimes Cindy and Kate together. Kate went to Japan and collaborated with Masahide Sakuma from the Plastics in an excellent band called NiNa.

Cindy and Keith Bennett had their first child in 1997. While Cindy took time to be with her newborn, Keith Strickland and Kate worked on some songs together. Old friend Jeremy Ayers contributed lyrics for a song called Sandbox Town that was "very Patsy Cline" according to Keith, but it has never surfaced.[7]

The entire group played a few shows that fall, including a corporate event on a US military aircraft carrier in New York City—because even when the B-52s do something normal, it ends up sounding surreal.

In 1998, the B-52s put out a greatest hits compilation called *Time Capsule: Songs for a Future Generation*. According to Keith, they did it "in order to buy some time to work on something else."[8] Two new songs, Debbie and Hallucinating Pluto, were taken from some of the abandoned sessions. Unfortunately, there's nothing particularly remarkable about either one. The songwriting, especially on the former, suffers from the same problems the band had on *Mesopotamia*. Too many ideas and competing melodies crammed into a song, where the good ideas (the chord change after *Debbie's coming in for a landing*) are quickly abandoned.

They toured to support the compilation, and played nearly 50 shows, including a 44-date summer tour co-headlining with the Pretenders that Kate called "The most sane tour we'd done."[9] Fred said at the time, "Any baggage the band had in the past is gone, so it's a real group effort."[10] These quotes suggest that previous tours had been insane and riddled with baggage. When asked how it felt to not be as popular, Fred replied, "I'm enjoying it now because I'm a much nicer person than I was then. It was just so hectic and crazy. I tasted my 15 minutes of fame and I enjoyed it, but I'm happy with where I am now."[11]

In 1999, Cindy took some time away from the band to have another child. Julee Cruise filled in for her while they toured. But when Paul McCartney asked the band to play a PETA benefit with him the following spring, Cindy was there. She also joined the band for the 5th annual Party Out of Bounds fundraiser, where they played a small club called the Athens Music Factory. For the occasion, they performed some songs they hadn't played in years, like 6060-842. The next night they came to Boneshakers and auctioned off B-52s memorabilia with Fred as the auctioneer. When someone bid $60 for a B-52s Fan Club comb, Fred joked, "Now it has our DNA on it and you can clone us."[12] The night raised $25,000.

In 2000, the B-52s played Atlanta's Gay Pride festival and drew 200,000 people. They also co-headlined another summer tour, this time with the Go-Go's and Psychedelic Furs. The B-52s bristled when people called it an "80s nostalgia" tour, but the accusation had a ring of truth.

In a heartbreaking turn of events that year, Fred's money manager, Dana Giacchetto, was arrested after embezzling money from a bunch of celebrities, including Fred, who was reportedly cheated out of "at least $339,000."[13] Giacchetto was sentenced to five years in prison, but was released after serving three. He eventually died, in 2016, at age 53, after a night of "heavy partying."[14]

The year 2001 saw more shows, and in 2002 Rhino put out an excellent double-CD compilation called *Nude on the Moon*, the cover of which, inexplicably, had a picture of the band clothed on the beach.[15] The band played a series of concerts to celebrate the 25th anniversary of their first show. One of them included an NYC show at Irving Plaza where Yoko Ono showed up to sing on Rock Lobster. This would be the first of many tours and album reissues to use the anniversary angle as a selling point. Fan club leader Mats Sexton self-published his book about the band that same year. Sadly out of print, *The B-52's Universe: The Essential Guide to the World's Greatest Party Band* is filled with pictures, contains a detailed gigography, and is essential for any B-52s fan.

The years continued to pass. The band played with Cher. They played with the Rolling Stones. They showed up on TV every now and then, playing some of their old songs. The audience always seemed to enjoy it. So did the band.

In 2006, Fred met Noah Brodie and Dan Marshall and formed the Superions, a dance-pop trio still going today that features Fred at his wackiest. Mike Turner, then manager of the Wuxtry Records in Athens, met Fred when the singer dropped into the store looking for some obscurities. Turner asked Fred to leave his list and come back in a week. After using his connections to track down almost all of the records, Fred was impressed. Turner also ran a local label called Happy Happy Birthday To Me (HHBTM) that put out a lot of Athens bands, and he threw some of his label's catalog in Fred's bag. "Fred was about to leave town," recalls Turner, "and he dropped by the store to say bye."

> I was out sick. So he got my number from the store and left this really long and nice voicemail with some of his favorite home remedies, and to say bye and thanks for finding the records for him. A few weeks later, after he had listened to a bunch of the label catalog I sent him home with, he called me up and asked if I'd be into doing a Superions record.[16]

The relationship has lasted for over ten years, and HHBTM has continued to release Superions records.

Funplex

By 2006, it had been 14 years since the last B-52s album. During that time, they had only managed to produce two songs, both of which went mostly unnoticed. If they hadn't liked being called a nostalgia act six years earlier, it was hard to argue any differently now. As Kate confided to an interviewer, "There comes a point where you're in danger of just becoming a retro act … unless you have a new record."[17] Keith also saw the writing on the wall:

> Well, if we're going to keep doing this, you know, we need new material, you know? And our fans have been very patient and very generous and—but they were beginning to sort of bang on the door, we want new songs, you know.[18]

The B-52s were going through a period of hipness again, being cited as influences by fashionable bands of the era like Scissor Sisters and The Gossip. They had also been credited with influencing the Olympia underground music scene of the 80s and 90s that spawned Beat Happening, Nirvana and Sleater-Kinney, all of whom professed a love for the B-52s. Energized by the recognition and name checks from newer bands, the B-52s got together in Atlanta to try and make another album. Could they make a record that people would care about? Could they write songs that they would enjoy playing? Keith brought a hard drive with some music he had recorded at his home in Key West, and they got to work.

The band operated within strictly defined individual roles—something that stood in contrast to their earlier, more fluid days. Keith wrote all the music, while the rest of the band came up with words and melodies. Keith's chord progressions remained straightforward and predictable, which placed limitations on the singers. This raises the question, rather than trot out one more A-C-D chord sequence, why not include the entire band in the process of creating the music? Maybe they felt set in their ways, and it was easier to work with everybody maintaining their comfortable and established roles. After 30 years in the B-52s, Keith described how the band's identity was stronger than the people who played in it:

> It's sort of like you fall into character and we've created this monster and it's very difficult sometimes to change the face of that monster and put on a different face. And you find yourself falling into that same groove and it

becomes very conscious I guess. And that comes from doing this for so long.[19]

Without a record label, the band paid for the sessions themselves, using money they had saved up from the previous two years of touring. When they were ready to record, they enlisted Steve Osbourne, who had produced New Order's 2001 comeback album *Get Ready*. The B-52s also brought in members of their touring band to play on the record. Former Waitresses bassist Tracy Wormworth had been with the band since 1992, and played on a few *Good Stuff* songs. Sterling Campbell and Zachary Alford split drumming duties, and Paul Gordon, a former member of New Radicals, played keyboards.

Ironically, the effort to sound contemporary makes *Funplex* sound somewhat dated now. The sparse production of *The B-52's* had made it sound timeless, but *Funplex* is coated in a glossy digital sheen that screams 2008. The B-52s had gone from sounding influenced by Andy Warhol to sounding influenced by the Dandy Warhols (at least in terms of production). Also, nothing on the album has the emotional pull of the songs on *Cosmic Thing* or *Bouncing Off the Satellites*.

Taking everything into account, *Funplex* has no right to be as good as it is. It's a delight, and probably the most fun B-52s record since the first album. Whatever creative alchemy existed between the four members resurfaced with a vengeance. Keith hadn't learned any new chord progressions in 16 years—Pump and Dancing Now are almost exactly the same song—but the band does more with his ideas this time, as *Funplex* adds hook after glorious hook into the mix. As a result, the album takes flight where *Good Stuff* crashed and burned.

The shift into the *Shake it to the last round* section of Hot Corner provides a melodic lift that was mostly missing on *Good Stuff*. It's not that Cindy is more valuable than Kate and Fred, just that the three voices and personalities complement each other so well that subtracting any one person from the mix weakens the band.

The first three songs on *Funplex* give equal time to all three vocalists. Leadoff track Pump is a dead ringer for LCD Soundsystem's North American Scum from the 2007 album *Sound of Silver*. That album had been a critical smash, and was a band favorite while they were working on *Funplex*.

Juliet of the Spirits' title echoes back to those Fellini parties Jeremy Ayers used to host back in Athens. Kate sings in a lower register here, but she combines with Cindy's voice to create new harmonic shapes. Deviant Ingredient is another under-acknowledged gem. The title alone sounds like something Prince should have thought of first, and the rest of the song—the rhyming *deviant ingredient* with *delirious experience*, and the slow, sensuous groove—is up there with his best work from this period.

Funplex's title track is the album's standout moment, as a trip to the mall becomes an attack on consumerism and how the mindless acquisition of goods will always break your heart. The song works because Fred, Kate, and Cindy don't write from a place of superiority or judgment. They're empathetic enough to convincingly tell the stories of the people in the mall, and use these stories to get their message across. Why sing about Marxist commodity fetishism when you can just find the moments where "pleasure" turns into "misery"? When Cindy takes on the persona of a "daytime waitress" at the Taco Tiki Hut, she still remembers her experience behind the counter at Kress well enough to tell a customer *Here's your stupid 7-Up*.

Fred combines his righteous anger with his sense of humor and depicts a mall cop beating up a shopper for wearing a peace t-shirt. That scenario wasn't a product of his imagination. In 2003, around the time the US invaded Iraq, a father and son were arrested at a mall outside Albany, NY after refusing to take off anti-war t-shirts they had bought at the mall, one of which simply read "peace on earth."[20]

The hypersexualized lyrics don't feel as goofy or forced. *Funplex* was the first B-52s album where Fred and Keith were publicly out, and the band seems to revel in this new freedom. When Fred sings *I am not an eroticist / I am a fully eroticized being / No more neuroses* at the end of Deviant Ingredient, it feels like a personal victory.

The album runs out of steam toward the end, with the last three songs sounding like afterthoughts. But in the well-worn genre of "aging musicians make comeback album that embraces current trends," *Funplex*, pulls off the trick as well as any band ever has. The last word on the album is party, and as it currently stands, that's the last recorded word from the B-52s.

Because the band didn't have a label and had insisted on paying for the sessions out of their own pockets, they were able to shop the record around. Keith said, "... we had it. And we thought, well let's check out some labels, we'll see. Eventually, Astralwerks ... heard it, and they just loved it, and they seemed to get it. It felt like a good fit."[21] It was a perfect match. Astralwerks, a subsidiary of EMI at the time, specialized in electronic and dance music, and had released important records by Chemical Brothers, Air, Basement Jaxx, and Hot Chip. *Funplex* came out on March 25, 2008, where it debuted at #11 on the album charts and sold 30,000 copies in its first week. Despite the high chart position and good reviews, the record didn't sell like the band hoped it would. Digital music and file sharing had caused record sales to crater at the beginning of the twenty-first century. "We made all of the money back and broke even," said Fred, conceding, "With downloads and piracy, it's going to be hard to do more albums."[22]

The digital revolution paid dividends though when the band went on tour that year, as Fred noticed the audiences were all familiar with the new songs. "[B]ecause of YouTube, they already know it," he said. "In the past, they used to clap politely, and then you'd play an older song and they'd go wild."[23] *Funplex* also turned out to be the #4 best-selling vinyl album in the US that year, as the medium was starting to make a resurgence.[24]

The album received generally positive reviews. No one hailed it as a masterpiece, but almost everyone was happy to see the B-52s back making records. Allmusic called *Funplex* "a good argument that they should get off the revival circuit and get back in the studio more often."[25] Critics also recognized the band's influence. Michaelangelo Matos observed in *AV Club*, "It's hard to imagine today's dance-rock landscape without the B-52s."[26]

The release of *Funplex* also coincided with a change in the band's written name, as the B-52s dropped the apostrophe and were no longer the B-52's, thus creating all kinds of problems for future biographers. When asked why they did it, Kate managed to give four different reasons in this quote, as well as a reason not to change it at all:

> It was not grammatically correct. It's not like a possessive. It just seemed superfluous. Actually, we were trying to modernize our logo. Then we realized it was so good, why change it? We just dropped the apostrophe because it's easier, and when you go on the web, it just simplifies things.[27]

In 2009, Gary Kurfirst died while vacationing in the Bahamas. He was 61. His legacy with the B-52s had its ugly moments, but he always worked hard, and he always wanted his bands to succeed.

The Wild Crowd in the Classic City

Funplex raised the band's profile and kicked off several years of touring. Highlights from this period include two shows the B-52s played in downtown Athens at the 2000 capacity Classic Center in 2011 and 2012. The first of these became a live album and a DVD called *With the Wild Crowd!* The shows gave people a chance to reflect on how Athens, and the band, had changed since that first B-52s show, and how it had stayed the same.

To paraphrase what Athens artist Paul Thomas said about the town back in 2005, "Cool things are always happening in Athens. It's just that sometimes *Spin* magazine writes about it and sometimes they don't." *Spin* may not be a print magazine anymore, but Athens is still standing. Back in 1977, the B-52s had taken what Athens had to offer—a radical social environment, cheap rent, a progressive art scene, and hip musical taste—and turned it into a band. In doing so, they inspired one of the most vital music scenes in America. In addition to Pylon and R.E.M., Athens has given us Method Actors, Pylon, Oh-Ok, Vic Chesnutt, Widespread Panic, Olivia Tremor Control, Neutral Milk Hotel, Elf Power, Drive-By Truckers, of Montreal, and those are just some of the best-known bands, the ones that, as Thomas would say, got written about in *Spin*.

For their Athens shows, the B-52s asked two lesser-known Athens bands to open, Casper & the Cookies in 2011, and Tunabunny in 2012. Cookies bassist Kay Stanton says, "I love that they take chances on these bands .... I mean how cool is that? How many bands are going to do that at that level?" But that was what the B-52s had always done, and what people like the Fans, Curtis Knapp, and Maureen McLaughlin had done for them. "They were so nice," recalls Stanton. Cookies singer/guitarist Jason NeSmith adds, "After we got off stage, we saw Kate in the loading dock after the show. She said something like, 'Really good set, guys.'"[28]

The authors of this book played the 2012 show as members of Tunabunny and had a similar experience as Casper & the Cookies. As an opening band, we were paid $250, provided with a dressing room, a cooler of beer and water. We ate the same food as the B-52s, in the same room, and were given spots on the guest list for friends and family. Keith, Cindy, Kate and Fred were all standing just off-stage when the set ended, and each made a point of thanking us for playing. Walking around the venue afterward, fans gave out hugs, and Bill Berry from R.E.M. complimented Tunabunny's drummer and invited the band to the after-party.

The generosity the B-52s showed to their two opening bands is rare for any headlining act, let alone a band 35 years into their career. Tunabunny were a small band, who had been written about in places like the *Village Voice* and NPR, but the show happened less than two weeks before the band flew to England for its first UK tour. After playing in front of 2000 people opening for the B-52s, the audiences in London looked a lot less intimidating. At its best, the Athens creative world has been a place without egos, and a place where those who find success are eager to return the gift.

The B-52s sounded great both nights, and the *Funplex* songs continued to get as big a cheer as the band's older ones. The night we played with them, when Keith said from the stage, "Ricky is here tonight," not one person in the room could have doubted him.

Artist Missy Kulik was in the balcony that night. A B-52s fan since she was 15 years old growing up outside of Pittsburgh, Kulik saw the band on MTV during the *Cosmic Thing* era and joined the B-52s fan club, run at the time by "Sue 52." The newsletters had a section where people could connect by writing letters to each other. "I probably had 50 to 60 pen pals in the 90s," she recalls. "That got me into zines."

> I would draw B-52s fan art … and send them to Sue 52 because I wanted her to print them. And every now and then the back page would be nothing but fan art. But I never got mine on there! I always wanted that. That was the height.[29]

After Kulik lost her job in 2002, some mutual friends who were part of the Elephant 6 community—a group of primarily Athens-based musicians and artists who gained international acclaim around the turn of the century—encouraged her to move to Athens. There, she became part of the local scene, playing music and making art. She also began drawing "Tofu Baby," a long-running comic strip in the pages of *Flagpole*:

> I was on unemployment, and Athens is the greatest place to be on unemployment. I think our rent split $600 three ways. It has changed. I remember meeting Paul Thomas [artist and proprietor of X-Ray Cafe] shortly after. [X-Ray] was a couple of waterfalls of books, and a handful of records. It was just a hangout place, and he would let us do the experimental music nights. He had a calendar, and you just came and wrote what you wanted to do.[30]

Missy was horrified to hear our critique of *Good Stuff.* In the interests of presenting a more fan-based point of view, we asked her to talk about why she liked the album. She began with the very first song, Tell It Like It T-I-Is:

> That's a fun song! Why wouldn't people like that song? Good Stuff—that's a good song! I think also, being a fan and learning that Cindy wasn't going to be in it … a lot of people dropped off. But I feel like Revolution Earth is such a beautiful song! I get chills thinking about it. Her vocals … I feel like those are beautiful lyrics too. I think Is That You Mo-Dean? is just a really funny song. Also the back and forth in this record is really good. This is a record I listen to when I'm waking up or feeling tired.

Liesl Dano has been involved with the B-52s starting in the early 90s editing a fanzine called *The B's Connection.* Dano helped organize the Party Out of Bounds fundraisers, and today oversees "B-52's: the Buzz," a B-52s Facebook group that functions as an online fan club. "The cool thing," says Dano about the site, "is being able to give fans a place to share their story, because everyone has a story about the B-52s. Some have waited a long time to find others who would appreciate it or understand."[31] The B-52s inspire a passionate loyalty among their fans, one that has always been reciprocated by the band. They have occasionally fielded questions online, and the archive of zines from the 80s and 90s is filled with interviews and contributions from the band. Keith has responded to questions on "the Buzz," and once shared several personal photos of him and Ricky for Issue #6 of *The B-52s United Fan Organization (UFO).*[32]

Still Having Fun

At the end of 2012, Keith announced that although he would remain a member of the B-52s, he wouldn't continue to tour with the group. In 2015, Kate released her first solo album, *Guitars and Microphones,* which featured collaborations with Sia and the Strokes' Nick Valensi. She also married Monica Coleman that year, who she had been dating since 2003. Fred gave the best man speech. Kate told Oprah that Coleman was the first woman she had ever been with, and that the relationship "seemed to me just very, very natural. I didn't think, 'Am I bisexual, am I a lesbian?' It just naturally happened. It didn't feel like bursting out of any closet."[33] In 2017, Cindy released a solo album on Kill Rock Stars entitled *Change.*

Neither record sounds much like the B-52s, but both suggest intriguing paths—both melodically and sonically—that would have made *Funplex* a stronger album. Knowing that Kate postponed *Guitars and Microphones* so the band could work on *Funplex* makes one wonder what she could have contributed to the band's album, given the opportunity. Meanwhile, Fred has continued to work with the Superions. Their 2010 holiday album *Destination … Christmas!* is a particular delight.

The band spent most of 2019 working on a book of their own, an oral history, that has yet to come out. Hopefully, one day it will. There will always be stories worth telling, and worth hearing, about the B-52s. "I'm pretty content," Fred said that year. "They're already booking shows for next year, so I guess they'll be wheeling me out onstage eventually."[34] At the time, Kate added, "I would never dream of doing it this long if I didn't still like them, and hanging out with them. We still have fun together. And we know when and what it has been like to NOT have fun."[35]

The worldwide COVID pandemic meant those shows had to be canceled, but in the spring of 2022, the B-52s, still consisting of Fred, Cindy, Kate, and a backing band, announced their farewell tour, though they made sure to emphasize that a farewell to touring did not necessarily mean a farewell to live performance.

In a *New York Times* interview that appeared a week before the tour began, Kate left open the possibility of future tours, saying, "Never say never," to which Fred curtly responded, "Never." When asked if the band members thought they had "contributed a lot to what people call the queering of American culture," Kate was quick to take credit. "We queered it," she said. "We done queered it."[36]

While it's unclear exactly who Kate meant by "we," it should include the many other people who have played a vital part in that struggle. Her use of the past tense felt jarring in 2022, as the past several years have seen a disturbing rise in anti-LGBTQ+ rhetoric, with many states passing anti-LGBTQ+ legislation. In the Supreme Court decision that year which struck down *Roe v. Wade*, Justice Clarence Thomas argued the court would be justified in using the same logic to take away the right to same-sex marriage. Far from being "done queered," America still has a long way to go. And if history has taught us anything, it's that as long as the forces of hatred and bigotry refuse to rest, those who believe people should have the freedom to love who they want can't rest either. In the beginning of 2023, the band issued a clear and forceful statement about the issue on social media.

> We, the B-52's, are deeply concerned about the numerous new bills that promote transphobia and discrimination against transgender individuals and drag artists, which have been introduced in the United States. We strongly denounce these bills and stand in solidarity with our LGBTQ+ community.
>
> It is unacceptable that in the 21st century, we are witnessing such blatant attempts to undermine the rights of individuals based on their gender identity and sexual orientation. These bills not only violate the fundamental human rights of the affected individuals but also perpetuate a toxic culture of hate and intolerance that has no place in our society.
>
> Join us in denouncing these bills and standing in support of our LGBTQ+ community. Together, let us work towards building a society that reflects our shared being and is truly, just, inclusive, and welcoming for all.
>
> With love,
> the B-52s

In a *New York Times* interview, Keith reflected on Ricky, over 50 years after they had first met, and nearly 30 years after Ricky's death. "Around 1983, Ricky bought one of the first Macintosh home computers, and he loved it. When I'm writing music at my computer now, using Logic Pro software, I always say, 'Gosh, Ricky would've loved this.' I often think about Ricky."[37]

Sadly, the opening bands chosen for the farewell tour, KC & the Sunshine Band and the Tubes, suggested that even the B-52s had come to see themselves as strictly entertainment. When asked if audiences would be treated to any surprises in the set list, Kate said, "Changing the set list is like Congress passing a bill; everybody wants their songs or their favorite songs to perform."[38] Despite the difficulty, the band managed to incorporate songs from *Good Stuff and Funplex* that hadn't been played in years. On January 10, 2023, the tour concluded in Athens. Georgia, nearly 46 years after the band played their first show at a house party a few miles away. At the end of the night, Keith Strickland joined the three other band members on stage to wave goodbye.

A month before the Athens show, the band announced they would play a pair of Las Vegas residencies in May and August of 2023.

As this book went to press, the band continued to work on a documentary produced by Fred Armisen and directed by Craig Johnson. The filmmakers have been given access to never-before-seen footage, including episodes of The Hell to Holler show, the Ricky Wilson-hosted fake TV show the band filmed in Mahopac, and it promises to be incredible.

The band still continues to talk about recording more songs with Keith. It may happen someday. It may not. For a group of people who have given nearly 50 years, and a huge chunk of their lives, to this thing called the B-52s, no one can argue they haven't earned the right to do things at their own pace. And after everything they have been through, that freedom can be considered a kind of victory.

Cindy's husband and Ricky's guitar tech, Keith Bennett has seen more B-52s shows than anybody, and after all this time, he still remains a fan:

> I don't know how many shows I've seen. I tried to figure it out one time, a thousand and something easy. There have been two that were kind of not-so-good. Most of them were spectacular. They kicked ass. They still do. There's nobody like them. You don't hear somebody else on the radio, and go, "I wonder if that's the B-52s."[39]

Follow Your Bliss

In 2016, Jeremy Ayers died unexpectedly following a seizure. In his obituary, local music writer Gordon Lamb wrote about the influence Ayers had on Athens from the beginning. "He remained closely associated and involved with nearly every subsequent arts movement in our city … and several generations of Athenian artists, musicians, writers and regulars counted him as a friend."[40] A memorial service was held at the Morton Theatre, adjacent to the B-52s' first practice space, where Cindy and Kate performed a version of 52 Girls in his honor with Kate on guitar. A painting of Ayers hangs today in The Grit, Athens' staple vegetarian restaurant.

Like most places in America, Athens has become a beiger, more gentrified place over the past 40 years. As downtown rents have continued to rise, quirky businesses have all but disappeared. And as housing costs have continued to rise, aspiring artists and musicians are forced to work more hours than they used to, leaving less time for creativity, and making it harder for bands to tour. Each year, it seems Athens becomes more and more of a playground for the obliviously wealthy, people who believe that culture is something you buy, not something you make, and that the more something costs the more value it has. Every time a music venue, or a 24-hour coffee spot, closes, an overpriced restaurant takes its place.

Despite all of this, places like The Grit still exist.[41] But it's difficult now to find the town's magic through sheer luck, by stumbling into the weird detritus of X-Ray Cafe, or an experimental show at Go Bar. But if the wild visionary beauty of Athens is harder to find than it used to be, that doesn't mean it isn't there. The 2019's and 2020's Ad-Verse Fest saw performers blur the line between music and performance art. The town's nascent hip-hop scene turned out Mariah Parker, a UGA doctoral student performing under the name Linqua Franqa. Parker transformed her music's radical politics into political office when she was elected County Commissioner in 2018.

The constant change that has fueled the town's creative scene means that what's true today doesn't have to be true tomorrow. The Athens music scene was created by iconoclasts, and it was created by people willing to take risks, to make something happen, anything to alleviate the boredom. Three years from now, someone might convert the abandoned cinema multiplex out by the mall into a live-work all-ages art space that features bands in one theater, experimental plays in another, and illegally streamed art films in yet another. Maybe they'll serve coffee and snacks to help make ends meet. Maybe it will trigger a creative renaissance in Athens, and once again people will make something that people in other places wish they could have. Although economic factors present the biggest obstacle, the only true limit is the town's imagination and collective desire.

Athens predecessors like Jeremy Ayers, Bill Green, Ravenstone, Julia Penelope Stanley, Bill Paul and Chris Rasmussen are just a few of the individuals that helped create the conditions where a band like the B-52s could happen. They, along with many others, pushed against the limits of what was possible in Athens. The B-52s found inspiration in the courage of those around them, and in turn, they inspired courage in others. To honor the spirit of the B-52s, and the legacy of Athens, one has to be willing to take risks, one has to be willing to provoke, and one has to be willing to dream the impossible.

The aftershocks of the B-52s are still being felt today. The band has existed, in various incarnations, for over 40 years, and have managed to remain true to the values they began with—ideas about sex, gender, fluidity, collaboration, and fun. The B-52s have embarrassed themselves on occasion (who among us hasn't), but they have never embarrassed their fans. If you went out and got a B-52s tattoo, the band has never done anything to make you regret it. They never supported a right-wing politician or spouted racist ignorance from the stage. They never got arrested for being physically violent or sexually assaulting anyone. They never found Jesus—or Satan. They have never trashed a hotel room or behaved like misogynist rockstar pigs. They have managed to conduct themselves with a dignity that is almost unheard of for a band of their stature.

Their story is something of a miracle. They have been both a great rock band as well as a great pop band. They have, despite their differences from mainstream culture, become a part of that culture. As individuals, the B-52s members grew up as outcasts. The Athens-area natives, particularly, were born into a life of low expectations and a drab future. Together, they forged something that gave them access to a life beyond anything they possibly could have imagined.

We can quibble about the Rock and Roll Hall of Fame, and how lesser bands than the B-52s have been anointed with that honor. We can quibble about their critical reputation, and how the discourse around the band doesn't do justice to their music. Ultimately, none of that matters. As the band enters its twilight years, their legacy is secure.

The B-52s have shone a light for people to follow. They have served as a brightly colored beacon for anyone who feels different, anyone who might be labeled a weirdo. We have used the word neon for this book because it describes the example they have set for others, and the incandescence they represent.

At the heart of the B-52s' music is a love for being alive that verges on the radical. They have managed to wring joy out of the unlikeliest subjects—abandonment, nuclear fission, and death, to name just a few. In the face of unspeakable tragedy, they continued to imagine utopia in their songs. The empathy in their music is bottomless; the humanity is endless. Their music will outlive us all.

Notes

1. Shapiro, "Change of Heart."
2. Sexton, *The B-52's Universe*, 112.
3. Ibid.
4. Fritch, "Q&A."
5. *B-Hive*, #7 Summer 1996, Mats Sexton B-52's memorabilia collection, Box 1, University of Georgia Libraries Special Collections.
6. *B-Hive*, #8 Winter1997, Mats Sexton B-52's memorabilia collection, Box 1, University of Georgia Libraries Special Collections.
7. Ibid.
8. *B-Hive*, Summer 1998 Issue 13, Mats Sexton B-52's memorabilia collection, Box 1, University of Georgia Libraries Special Collections.
9. Sexton, *The B-52's Universe*, 123.
10. Vaziri, "Q & A with Fred," 46.
11. Ibid.

12. Sexton, *The B-52's Universe*, 128.
13. Goldman, "Stung by Dana Giacchetto?"
14. New York Daily News, "Disgraced 'Stockbroker.'"
15. *Good Stuff* and *Whammy!* have the fewest songs represented, so we're not the only ones who like the other albums better. We would have substituted Big Bird though—as well as Topaz and Dirty Back Road—and cut Junebug, Follow Your Bliss, and Trism.
16. Mike Turner, email message to authors, October 29, 2019.
17. Norris, "B-52s, Bringing Back."
18. Norris, "B-52s, Bringing Back."
19. *B's Connection*, Summer 1998 Issue 13, Mats Sexton B-52's memorabilia collection, Box 1, University of Georgia Libraries Special Collections.
20. Democracy Now! "New York Man Arrested."
21. Harrison, "Q&A / Keith."
22. Nunn, "Fred Schneider."
23. Larsen, "B-52's Bring Fresh Sound."
24. Kreps, "Radiohead, Neutral Milk."
25. Jeffries, "B-52s, Funplex."
26. Matos, "B-52s: Funplex."
27. Bream, "Fun House."
28. Kay Stanton and Jason NeSmith in conversation with authors, October 13, 2019.
29. Missy Kulik in conversation with authors, October 27, 2019.
30. Ibid.
31. Email correspondence with authors, October 2019.
32. Mat Sexton's archive of these zines is housed at the University of Georgia Special Collections Library in Athens. The earliest one dates back to the early 80s, where in those pre-internet days you can read fans trying to figure out which band members are dating each other.
33. 2 Paragraphs, "B-52's Kate."
34. Rhodes, "Fred Schneider."
35. Amorosi, "Still Happy Together."
36. Tannenbaum, "The B-52s Say Farewell," AR-14.
37. Ibid.
38. Grow, "You Haven't Heard the Last," *Rolling Stone*.
39. Keith Bennett in conversation with authors, November 8, 2019.
40. Lamb, "R.I.P. Jeremy Ayers."
41. Between the acceptance of this manuscript and its publication, the Grit announced it would be closing permanently. The book's authors managed to take a picture of the painting of Jeremy Ayers that hung on the wall before they closed.

Bibliography

Books

Azerrad, Michael. *Come as You Are: The Story of Nirvana*. New York: Doubleday. 1994.

Bausum, Ann. *Viral: The Fight Against AIDS in America*. New York: Viking. 2019.

Brown, Rodger Lyle. *Party Out of Bounds*. Atlanta: Everthemore Books. 2003.

Bullock, Darryl W. *David Bowie Made Me Gay: 100 Years of LGBT Music*. New York: Overlook. 2017.

Carpenter, Bill. *Uncloudy Days: The Gospel Music Encyclopedia*. San Francisco: Backbeat Books. 2005.

Cateforis, Theo. *Are We Not New Wave?: Modern Pop at the Turn of the 1980s*. Ann Arbor: University of Michigan Press. 2011.

Chase, Clifford. Am I Getting Warmer? In *Heavy Rotation, Twenty Writers on the Albums that Changed Their Lives*, ed. Peter Terzian. New York: Harper Perennial. 2009.

Christgau, Robert. *Christgau's Record Guide, the '80s*. New York: Pantheon. 1990.

Colacello, Bob. *Holy Terror: Andy Warhol Close Up*. New York: Knopf. 2014, originally published 1990.

Considine, J.D. The B-52s. In *Rolling Stone Album Guide*, ed. Anthony DeCurtis and James Henke, with Holly George-Warren. New York: Random House. 1992.

Cusset, François. *French Theory: How Foucault, Derrida, Deleuze, & Co. Transformed the Intellectual Life of the United States*. Minneapolis: University of Minnesota. 2008.

DeCurtis, Anthony. *Rocking My Life Away*. Durham: Duke University Press. 1999.

S. Creney, B. A. Herron, *The Story of the B-52s*,
https://doi.org/10.1007/978-3-031-22570-3

Fletcher, Tony. *Remarks: The Story of REM.* New York: Bantam. 1990.

Frantz, Chris. *Remain in Love.* New York: St. Martin's Press. 2020.

Gendron, Bernard. *Between Montmartre and the Mudd Club: Popular Music and the Avant-Garde.* Chicago: University of Chicago Press. 2002.

Gumprecht, Blake. *The American College Town.* Amherst: University of Massachusetts. 2009.

Hager, Steven. *Art After Midnight: The East Village Scene.* New York: St. Martin's Press. 1996.

Hammond, Paul and Patrick Hughes. *Upon the Pun.* London: W.H. Allen. 1978.

Hennessy, Rosemary. *Profit and Pleasure: Sexual Identities in Late Capitalism.* New York: Routledge. 2000.

Hewitt, Christopher. *Political Violence and Terrorism in Modern America.* Westport, CT: Praeger Security International. 2005.

Hilburn, Robert. *Paul Simon: The Life.* New York: Simon & Schuster. 2018.

Hinson, Glenn. *Fire in My Bones: Transcendence and the Holy Spirit in African American Gospel.* Philadelphia: University of Pennsylvania Press. 2004.

Indiana, Gary. *Utopia's Debris.* New York: Basic Books. 2008.

Irvin, Jim (ed.). *The Mojo Collection: 4th Edition.* Edinburgh: Canongate Books. 2007.

Janovitz, Bill. *The Rolling Stones' Exile on Main Street.* New York: Bloomsbury Publishing USA. 2005.

Kauffman, L.A. *Direct Action: Protest and the Reinvention of American Radicalism.* London: Verso. 2017.

Lawrence, Tim. *Life and Death on the New York Dance Floor: 1980–1983.* Durham: Duke University. 2016.

Marcus, Greil. *Real Life Rock.* New Haven: Yale University Press. 2015.

Marks, Craig and Rob Tannenbaum. *I Want My MTV.* New York: Penguin. 2011.

Miller, James Andrew and Tom Shales. *Live from New York: The Complete, Uncensored History of Saturday Night Live as Told by Its Stars, Writers, and Guests.* New York: Little, Brown, and Co. 2002, 2014.

Moore, Thurston and Byron Coley. *No Wave.* New York: Abrams. 2008.

Morley, Paul. *Words and Music.* Athens: University of Georgia. 2005.

O'Dair, Barbara. *Trouble Girls: The Rolling Stone Book of Women in Rock.* New York: Random House. 1997.

Popoff, Martin. *The Clash: All the Albums, All the Songs.* Beverly, MA: Voyageur Press. 2018.

Powers, Ann. *Good Booty: Love and Sex, Black & White, Body and Soul in American Music.* New York: Harper Collins. 2017.

Reynolds, Simon. *Rip It Up and Start Again: Postpunk 1978–1984.* New York: Penguin Group. 2004.

Rodgers, Nile. *Le Freak: The Life and Times of Nile Rodgers.* New York: Spiegel & Grau. 2011.

Rombes, Nicholas. *Cultural Dictionary of Punk*. New York: Continuum. 2009.
Sears, James T. *Rebels, Rubyfruit, and Rhinestones: Queering Space the Stonewall South*. New Brunswick: Rutgers University Press. 2001.
Sedgwick, Eve Kosofsky. *Epistemology of the Closet*. Berkeley: University of California Press. 1990.
Sexton, Mats. *The B-52's Universe: The Essential Guide to the World's Greatest Party Band*. Minneapolis: Plan-B Books. 2002.
Shilts, Randy. *And the Band Played On*. New York: St. Martins. 1987.
Sicko, Mike. *Techno Rebels: The Renegades of Electronic Funk*. Detroit: Wayne State University Press. 2010.
Smith, Richard. *Seduced and Abandoned*. London: Cassell. 1995.
Stein, Seymour. *Siren Song: My Life in Music*. New York: St. Martin's. 2018.
Sullivan, Denise. *R.E.M.: Talk About the Passion, an Oral History*. Lancaster: Underwood-Miller. 1994.
Szwed, John F. *Space Is the Place: The Lives and Times of Sun Ra*. New York: Pantheon. 1997.
Thompson, Hunter S. *The Great Shark Hunt*. New York: Ballantine. 1979.
True, Everett. *Hey Ho Let's Go: The Story of the Ramones*. London: Omnibus. 2002.
Turner, Victor. *The Ritual Process: Structure and Anti-structure*. Cornell University Press. 1966.
Turner, Victor. *The Forest of Symbols*. Cornell University Press. 1967.
White, Charles. *The Life and Times of Little Richard: The Quasar of Rock*. New York: Harmony. 1985.
Womack, Ytasha L. *Afrofuturism*. Chicago: Lawrence Hill Books. 2013.
Youngquist, Paul. *A Pure Solar World: Sun Ra and the Birth of Afrofuturism*. Austin: University of Texas Press. 2016.

Periodicals and Web Content

2 Paragraphs, "B-52's Kate Pierson Says Falling in Love with a Woman 'Very Natural.'" October 14, 2016. https://2paragraphs.com/2016/10/b-52s-kate-pierson-says-falling-in-love-with-a-woman-very-natural/.
Agreeable, Mr. *Melody Maker*, July 16, 1994.
Alexander, Donnell. "Are Black People Cooler Than White People? Dumb Question." *Utne Reader*, Oct–Nov 1997.
Altman, Billy. "Hep Cats Wig Out." *Creem*, October 1979. *Athens Daily News*. "Obituary." October 16, 1985.
Amorosi, A.D. "The B-52s Kick Off 40th Anniversary Tour Still Happy Together." *Variety*, June 4, 2018. https://variety.com/2018/music/news/b-52s-40th-anniversary-interview-1202829528/.

Arnold, Jacob. "The B-52s Gave Chicago One Last Gift at Riot Fest." *Chicago Reader*, September 16, 2019. https://www.chicagoreader.com/chicago/riot-fest-b52s-house-new-wave-schneider-pierson-wilson.

Ayers, Anne. "Madonna Struts for Rain Forests." *USA Today*, May 25, 1989.

Barber, Lynden. "Wild Planet." *Melody Maker*, Aug 30, 1980.

Bartunek, CJ. "Dance Revolution '72." February 2, 2016. https://medium.com/thebigroundtable/dance-revolution-72-34d1e9089b5d.

Battaglio, Stephen. "Mahopac Neighbors Oppose Rezoning for Rock Band B52's." *Gannett Westchester Newspapers*, August 29, 1982.

Belew, Adrian, "Anecdote #606." Elephant Blog, March 28, 2007. http://elephant-blog.blogspot.com/2007/03/anecdote-606.html.

Bell, Roy. "RB 24: The Athens Art & Music Scene." Rabbit Box Storytelling. Mixcloud, 2014. https://www.mixcloud.com/rabbitbox/rb24-stories-from-the-athens-arts-music-scene-1975-to-1985-roy-bell/.

Bennett, Keith. "RB 24: The Athens Art & Music Scene." Rabbit Box Storytelling, Mixcloud, 2014a. https://www.mixcloud.com/rabbitbox/rb23-stories-from-the-athens-arts-music-scene-1975-to-1985-keith-bennett/.

Bennett, Kim Taylor. "We Talked to Pylon's Michael Lachowski Because He's a Legend." *Vice*, August 7, 2014b. https://www.vice.com/en_us/article/6w3vw6/we-talked-to-michael-lachowski-from-pylon-because-hes-a-legend.

Bibler, Michael P. "Water Skis and Dirty Back Roads: Reorienting the Deep South." *South*: volume xlviii, number 1, 11.

Billboard. "Billboard 200, Week of September 20, 1980." Accessed August 19, 2019. https://www.billboard.com/charts/billboard-200/1980-09-20.

Biography. "Kate Pierson." Last modified August 5, 2015. https://www.biography.com/people/kate-pierson-17178786.

Birch, Ian. "Dance Parties in Outer Space." *Melody Maker*, July 14, 1979.

Blashill, Pat. "52 Pickup." *Details*, August 1992.

Bordowitz, Hank. "The B-52's." *Reel to Real*, Vol 1. No. 5.

Brandt, Pamela. "The New Woman Sound Hits the Charts." *Ms.*, Sept. 1980.

Bream, Jon. "Fun House." *The Star Tribune*, June 8, 2008. http://www.startribune.com/fun-house/19583204/?c=y&page=2.

Brinklow, Adam L. "Rock Lobster Secrets: Seven Things You Probably Didn't Know About Aaron Fricke." *429*, October 31, 2013. http://fourtwonine.com/2013/10/31/3356-rock-lobster-secrets-seven-things-you-probably-didn-t-know-about-aaron-fricke/.

Brown, G. "B-52's Testing Edge of Social Activism." *The Denver Post*, October 27, 1992.

Carlin, Shannon. "The B-52s Kate Pierson on the Music that Made Her." *Pitchfork*, February 25, 2020. https://pitchfork.com/features/5-10-15-20/the-b-52s-kate-pierson-on-the-music-that-made-her.

Carson, Tom. *NY Rocker*, July 1979.
Carson, Tom. "B-52s' Take Off." *Village Voice*, June 12, 1978.
"Cases and Advocacy." GLAD, Accessed August 29, 2018. https://www.glad.org/cases/aaron-fricke-v-richard-b-lynch/.
Chandler, D.L. "Race Riots Explode in Georgia, Rock City of Augusta in 1970." *News One*, May 12, 2014. https://newsone.com/3009368/race-riots-augusta-ga/.
Che, Cathay. "52's Still Rockin' at 55." *The Advocate*, Feb 5, 2002.
Chin, Brian. "Disco File." *Record World*, Oct. 3, 1981.
Christgau, Robert. "Ain't Got No Home." *Village Voice*, October 23, 1978.
Clarke, Tina. "Serious Fun." *Music Express Magazine*, August 1992.
Cleary, David. "The B-52s Wild Planet." Allmusic. Accessed August 19, 2019. https://www.allmusic.com/album/wild-planet-mw0000202765.
Cohan, Brad. "America's (Other) Best Band: Pylon's Brilliant Punk Minimalism Lives On." *The Observer*, Jul 25, 2016. https://observer.com/2016/07/americas-other-best-band-pylons-brilliant-punk-minimalism-lives-on/.
Connelly, Christopher. "The B-52s." *Rolling Stone*, June 9, 1983a.
Connelly, Christopher. "David Byrne in Love." *Rolling Stone*, October 27, 1983b. https://www.rollingstone.com/music/music-news/byrne-in-love-66670/.
Corcoran, Penelope. "B's Wax." *Phoenix New Times*, Nov. 12–18, 1986.
Cott, Jonathan. "John Lennon: The Last Interview." Rolling Stone, December 23, 2010. https://www.rollingstone.com/music/music-news/john-lennon-the-last-interview-179443/.
Crawford, Robert. "B-52s' Cindy Wilson, Chris Shiflett Talk June Carter Cash, Sex Pistols." *Rolling Stone*, November 27, 2017. https://www.rollingstone.com/music/music-country/b-52s-cindy-wilson-chris-shiflett-talk-june-carter-cash-sex-pistols-125061/.
Dagostino, Scott. "Keith Strickland, The B-52s." March 5, 2008. https://scottdagostino.wordpress.com/2008/03/05/195/.
Dangerous Minds. "Frank Zappa, John Cage, Patti Smith & Others Celebrate William S. Burroughs at the Nova Convention." June 30, 2014. https://dangerousminds.net/comments/frank_zappa_john_cage_patti_smith_others_celebrate_william_s._burroughs_at.
Darling, Cary. "B-52 Pick-Up." *BAM*, December 10, 1986.
Democracy Now! "New York Man Arrested at Shopping Mall for Wearing 'Give Peace a Chance' T-Shirt: Over 150 Respond by Showing Up in Similar Shirts at the Mall." March 6, 2003, https://www.democracynow.org/2003/3/6/new_york_man_arrested_at_shopping.
Doyle, Tom. "Madonna Interview: MOJO." All About Madonna, March 1, 2015, originally published in *Mojo*, March 2015. http://allaboutmadonna.com/madonna-interviews/madonna-interview-mojo-march-2015.

Echazabal, Gabe. "Change Is Good: An Interview with Cindy Wilson of the B-52s." *Creative Loafing Tampa*, Jul 26, 2017. https://www.cltampa.com/music/interviews/article/20970524/change-is-good-an-interview-with-cindy-wilson-of-the-b52s.

Eldredge, Richard L. "Dancing on the Tables…" *Eldredge ATL* (blog), July 23, 2016. https://www.eldredgeatl.com/2016/07/23/dancing-on-the-tables-a-celebration-of-the-athens-atlanta-music-scene-starring-the-b-52s-the-fans-the-brains-glenn-phillips-and-some-act-named-r-e-m/.

Ellen, Mark. "B-52's: Beach Party on a Wild Planet." *NY Rocker*, November 1980.

Ellis, Rashaun. "Boybutante Is All Grown Up." *Flagpole*, April 9, 2014. https://flagpole.com/arts-culture/arts-culture-features/2014/04/09/boybutante-is-all-grown-up.

English, John. "Friends Remember Athens Artist Jeremy Ayers." *Flagpole*, November 2, 2016. https://flagpole.com/arts-culture/arts-culture-features/2016/11/02/friends-remember-athens-artist-jeremy-ayers.

EPA. "Luminous Processes, Inc. Athens, GA." Accessed August 15, 2019. https://cumulis.epa.gov/supercpad/SiteProfiles/index.cfm?fuseaction=second.Cleanup&id=0401841#bkground.

Felder, Rachel. "B-52's Organic and Static Free." *Alternative Press*, September 1989.

Ferrise, Pat. "Interview: Keith Strickland, of the B-52s: Putting It All Together." *Weeping Elvis*, April 28, 2012. http://www.weepingelvis.com/interview-keith-strickland-of-the-b-52s-putting-it-all-together.

Fritch, Matthew. "Q&A with Fred Schneider." *Magnet*, February 15, 2010. http://magnetmagazine.com/2010/02/15/qa-with-fred-schneider/.

"Gary Kurfirst: A Personal History." Accessed Sept 1, 2018. http://garykurfirst.com/history.html.

Georgia Historical Society. "Lt. Col. Lemuel Penn and the Civil Rights Act." Accessed October 12, 2019. https://georgiahistory.com/ghmi_marker_updated/lt-col-lemuel-penn/.

Ghansah, Rachel Kaadzi, "Watching the Stars: How Missy Elliott Became an Icon," *Elle*, June 2017, https://www.elle.com/culture/celebrities/a44891/missy-elliott-june-2017-elle-cover-story/.

Glueck, Grace. "'Far-Out Art' to Honor Carter Donated to Georgia Museum." *The New York Times*, December 16, 1976. https://www.nytimes.com/1976/12/16/archives/farout-art-to-honor-carter-donated-to-georgia-museum.html

Goldman, Andrew. "Who Was Stung by Dana Giacchetto? Talk to Fred Schneider of the B-52's." *Observer*, April 17, 2000. https://observer.com/2000/04/who-was-stung-by-dana-giacchetto-talk-to-fred-schneider-of-the-b52s/.

Goldman, Vivien. "Gary Kurfirst, Rock Promoter and Manager of the Talking Heads, Dies at 61." *The New York Times*, Jan 16, 2009. https://www.nytimes.com/2009/01/16/arts/16kurfirst.html.

Goldman, Vivien. "The Guide to Cult Status with those Wild! Wacky! B-52's!" *New Musical Express*, September 20, 1980. Rock's Backpages. Accessed October 16, 2018. http://www.rocksbackpages.com/Library/Article/the-guide-to-cult-status-with-those-wild-wacky-b-52s.

Goldstein, Toby. "Do You Dig The B-52s?" *Creem*, July 1982. Rock's Backpages. Accessed October 16, 2018. http://www.rocksbackpages.com/Library/Article/do-you-dig-the-b-52s.

Gosse, Van. "The B-52's Attack." *Village Voice*, Oct. 1, 1980.

Greenblatt, Leah. "The B-52s: The Stories Behind the Hit Songs." *Entertainment Weekly*. June 12, 2018. https://ew.com/music/b-52s-stories-behind-hit-songs/#channel-z-1989.

Groome, Carle VP. "The B-52's: Still Crashing the Party." *REFLEX*, July 28, 1999.

Gross, Jason. "Sun Ra: Space is the Place, Interview with John Szwee." *Perfect Sound Forever*. Aug. 1997. www.furious.com/perfect/sunra2.

Grow, Kory. "Love Shacks, Rock Lobsters and Nude Parties: The B-52's in Their Own Words." *Rolling Stone*, June 1, 2018. https://www.rollingstone.com/music/music-features/love-shacks-rock-lobsters-and-nude-parties-the-b-52s-in-their-own-words-627925/.

Grow, Kory. "You Haven't Heard the Last of the B-52s: America's Favorite Party Band Tries to Say Goodbye." May 28, 2022. rollingstone.com/music/music-features/b52s-kate-pierson-farewell-tour-interview-1357754/.

Gussow, Mel. "Stage: 'Vain Victory,' Campy Transvestite Musical Spectacle." *The New York Times*, August 25, 1971. https://www.nytimes.com/1971/08/25/archives/stage-vain-victory-campy-transvestite-musical-spectacle-show.html.

Haecker, Randal. "Bouncing About with the B-52's." *The University Star*, Nov. 11, 1986.

Haines, William. *Athens Observer*, April 13, 1978.

Ham, Jon. "Gay Students Try for Understanding." *The Red & Black*, Nov 10, 1971.

Hann, Michael. "'Everyone Is Welcome to the Party!': The B-52s on 40 Years of New Wave." *The Guardian*, July 16, 2019. https://www.theguardian.com/music/2019/jul/16/the-b-52s-kate-pierson-love-shack.

Harris, Will. "Kate Pierson of the B-52s." *AV Club*, November 1, 2011. https://music.avclub.com/kate-pierson-of-the-b-52s-1798228355.

Harrison, Heath. "B-52s Singer to Take Part in West Virginia Music Hall Induction." *Ironton Tribune*, December 14, 2017. irontontribune.com/2017/12/14/b-52s-singer-to-take-part-in-west-virginia-music-hall-induction.

Harrison, Shane. "Q&A / Keith Strickland of the B-52s: 'Just Really a Happy Experience'." *Atlanta Journal-Constitution*, March 25, 2008.

Hart, Ron. "The B-52's 'Cosmic Thing' at 30." *Billboard*, June 28, 2019. https://www.billboard.com/articles/columns/rock/8518005/the-b-52s-cosmic-thing-album.

Helmore, Edward. "They Wanted to Be as Big as the Beatles…" *The Guardian*, April 8, 2016. https://www.theguardian.com/music/2016/apr/08/the-ramones-legacy-queens-museum-new-york-exhibit.

Henke, James. "Interview: The B-52's." *Rolling Stone*, December 11, 1980. https://rollingstone.com/music/music-features/interview-the-b-52s-113100/.

HIV.GOV. "A Timeline of HIV and AIDS." Accessed September 30, 2019. https://www.hiv.gov/hiv-basics/overview/history/hiv-and-aids-timeline.

Hochman, Steve and Mary Herczog. "AIDS and Rock: Sound of Silence." *Rolling Stone*, April 30, 1992.

Hochswender, Wood. "The Jungle Is Given a Certain Cachet." *New York Times*, May 26, 1989.

Hodgson, Peter. "Interview: Keith Strickland of the B-52s." *i heart guitar* (blog), November 11, 2011. http://iheartguitarblog.com/2011/11/interview-keith-strickland-of-the-b-52s.html.

Hogan, Kathy and Miriam Pace. "Students React to Jeans Poll." *The Red & Black*, May 3, 1975.

Holden, Stephen. "The B-52s American Graffiti." *Village Voice*, August 13, 1979.

Holden, Stephen. "Rock-and-Roll: Set by B-52's at the Forest Hills Stadium." *The New York Times*, August 7, 1983. https://www.nytimes.com/1983/08/07/arts/rock-and-roll-set-by-b-52-s-at-the-forest-hills-stadium.html.

Holland, Maggie, and Savannah Sicurella. "Confronting UGA's History of Blackface and Racism on Campus from the Past 70 Years" *The Red & Black*, April 4, 2019. https://www.redandblack.com/uganews/confronting-uga-s-history-of-blackface-and-racism-on-campus/article_79d20eda-567f-11e9-bdf2-a3b6b1d7f6ba.html.

Horn, Mark C. "The B-52s' Cindy Wilson: Still Cosmic After All These Years." *Echomag*, August 12, 2019. https://echomag.com/the-b-52s-cindy-wilson/.

Howe, Desson. "The Flintstones." *The Washington Post*, May 27, 1994. http://www.washingtonpost.com/wp-srv/style/longterm/movies/videos/theflintstonespghowe_a0b05e.htm.

Huff, Christopher A. "Student Movements of the 1960s." *New Georgia Encyclopedia*, accessed June 1, 2020. http://www.georgiaencyclopedia.org/articles/history-archaeology/student-movement-1960s.

Hunt, Jon. "Gays Hold Dance." *Athens Banner-Herald & The Daily News*, March 12, 1972.

Hutcherson, Kim. "Producer Danny Beard Reflects on Georgia's Unique Musical Tradition." *Decaturish*, March 23, 2015. https://decaturish.com/2015/03/producer-danny-beard-reflects-on-georgias-unique-music-tradition/.

Inglis, Sam. "Recording & Remixing Roxy Music's Avalon." *Sound on Sound*, August 2003. https://www.soundonsound.com/people/recording-remixing-roxy-musics-avalon.

Isler, Scott. "The B-52's: Sixties Going on Eighties." *Rolling Stone*, October 4, 1979.

Isler, Scott. "The Devil Went Down to Georgia," *Trouser Press*, Dec. 1980.

Jeffries, David. "The B-52s, Funplex." *Allmusic*. https://www.allmusic.com/album/funplex-mw0000498036.

Jipson, Arthur. "Why Athens? Investigations into the Site of an American Music Revolution." *Popular Music and Society*, Volume 18, 1994, Issue 3.

Kael, Pauline. "Three Cheers." *The New Yorker*, November 26, 1984. https://web.archive.org/web/20160304123806/http://www.davidbyrne.com/archive/film/Stop_Making_Sense/s_m_s_press/s_m_s_pauline_kael_nyer.php.

Kandel, Steve. "The B-52s' Arcade Fire." *SPIN*, November 2010.

Kass, Sarah. "B-52's Whirlwind." *B-Side*, Dec 89/Jan 90.

Katz, Robin. "Chic: Perfection in Planning." *Smash Hits* (1979). Rock's Backpages. Accessed August 21, 2018. http://www.rocksbackpages.com/Library/Article/chic-perfection-in-planning.

Kent, Nick. "The B-52s, Fashiøn: Lyceum, London." *New Musical Express*, July 14, 1979. Accessed August 27, 2018. http://www.rocksbackpages.com/Library/Article/the-b-52s-fashin-lyceum-london.

"Klaus Nomi," George Dubose works, 2003, http://www.george-dubose.com/klausnomi.html.

Kozak, Roman. "Rock'n'Rolling." *Billboard*, Sept 9, 1981.

Kreps, Daniel. "Radiohead, Neutral Milk Hotel, Help Vinyl Sales Almost Double In 2008." *Rolling Stone*, January 8, 2009. https://www.rollingstone.com/music/music-news/radiohead-neutral-milk-hotel-help-vinyl-sales-almost-double-in-2008-252602/.

La Ganga, Maria L. "The First Lady Who Looked Away…" *The Guardian*, Mach 11, 2016. https://www.theguardian.com/us-news/2016/mar/11/nancy-ronald-reagan-aids-crisis-first-lady-legacy.

Lamb, Gordon. "Art Rocks Athens Documents Classic City Creativity." *Flagpole*, May 21, 2014. https://flagpole.com/arts-culture/arts-culture-features/2014/05/21/art-rocks-athens-documents-classic-city-creativity.

Lamb, Gordon. "Beyond, Beyond and Then Some." *Flagpole*, February 8, 2012. https://flagpole.com/music/music-features/2012/02/08/beyond-beyond-and-then-some.

Lamb, Gordon. "R.I.P. Artist and Athens Scene Fixture Jeremy Ayers." *Flagpole*, Oct 24, 2016. https://flagpole.com/blogs/culture-briefs/posts/r-i-p-athens-artist-jeremy-ayers.

Larsen, Peter. "The B-52's Will Bring a Fresh Sound to Anaheim." *Orange County Register*, May 9, 2008. https://www.ocregister.com/2008/05/09/the-b-52s-will-bring-a-fresh-sound-to-anaheim/.

LaSalle, Mick. "B-52s Are Airborne Again." *San Francisco Chronicle*, July 31, 1989.

Leland, John. "Twilight of a Difficult Man: Larry Kramer and the Birth of AIDS Activism." *The New York Times*, May 29, 2017. https://www.nytimes.com/2017/05/19/nyregion/larry-kramer-and-the-birth-of-aids-activism.html.

Lepidus, Harold. "B52's Born Under a Good Sign." *Boston Rock*, No. 40.

Levy, Joe. "How Bob Dylan Made Rock History On 'Highway 61 Revisited.'" *Rolling Stone*, August 30, 2016. https://www.rollingstone.com/music/music-features/how-bob-dylan-made-rock-history-on-highway-61-revisited-249576/.

Lott, Tim. "The B-52s: I Belong to Dada." *Record Mirror*, July 14, 1979. Rock's Backpages. Accessed August 21, 2018. http://www.rocksbackpages.com/Library/Article/the-b-52s-i-belong-to-dada.

Loud, Lance. "B-52 Bummer." *The Advocate*, June 28, 1994.

Magnuson, Ann and Kenny Scharf. "New York City's Club 57…" *Interview*, October 13, 2017. interviewmagazine.com/culture/new-york-citys-club-57-will-have-its-moment-in-the-spotlight.

Malins, Steve. "Shiny Hippy People." *VOX*, August 1992.

Martens, Joel. "Fred Schneider, It's a Cosmic Thing." *Rage*, July 7, 2017. http://www.ragemonthly.com/2017/07/07/the-b-52s/.

Matos, Michaelangelo. "The B-52s: Funplex." *AV Club*, March 24, 2008. https://music.avclub.com/the-b-52s-funplex-1798203978.

Matthews, Dan. "Fred Schneider." *Classic City Live!*, May 15–21, 1991.

maureenmc2000. "The Athens, Ga./NYC Axis: This Is Where It All Began." *Daiquiris on Call*, Tumblr, January 27, 2013a. https://maureenmc2000.tumblr.com/post/41663852236/the-athens-ga-nyc-axis-this-is-where-it-all.

maureenmc2000. "Remembering Lester." *Daiquiris on Call*, Tumblr, April 11, 2013b. https://maureenmc2000.tumblr.com/post/47707692856/remembering-lester.

Mieses, Stanley. "B-52s: Bouffant Bop." *Melody Maker*, January 13, 1979.

Mieses, Stanley. "Caught in the Act." *Melody Maker*, December 23, 1978.

Mizek, Steve. "A Not So Brief History of Electro, Part One," *Reverb LP* (blog), May 10, 2018. https://lp.reverb.com/articles/a-not-so-brief-history-of-electro-by-steve-mizek-part-i.

Moody, Paul. "The Radical Jazz Activist Who Worshipped Aliens." *AnOther Magazine*, December 11, 2017. http://www.anothermanmag.com/life-culture/10097/sun-ra-the-radical-jazz-activist-who-worshipped-aliens.

Moore, Keith. "Southern Comfort: The B-52's Relive Their Past Lives." *Request*, February 1990.

Morgan, Adam. "Interview: Fred Schneider of the B-52's." *Surviving the Golden Age*, February 2, 2010. http://survivingthegoldenage.com/interview-fred-schneider-of-the-b-52s/.

Morris, Gina. "B's Bomb? Blowing Sky High." *NME*, February 27, 1992.

New York Daily News. "Disgraced 'Stockbroker to the Stars' Dana Giacchetto Dead After Hard Night of Partying." June 13, 2016. https://www.nydailynews.com/entertainment/gossip/confidential/disgraced-stockbroker-stars-dana-giacchetto-dies-article-1.2671892.

The New York Times. "Family in AIDS Case Quits Florida After House Burns." Aug. 30, 1987.

The New York Times. "Poll Indicates Majority Favor Quarantine for AIDS Victims." December 20, 1985. https://www.nytimes.com/1985/12/20/us/poll-indicates-majority-favor-quarantine-for-aids-victims.html.

The New York Times. "200 Seized in Athens." May 16, 1970. https://www.nytimes.com/1970/05/16/archives/200-seized-in-athens.html.

The New York Times. "U. of Georgia Eases Rules on Curfews and Drinking." July 20, 1968. https://www.nytimes.com/1968/07/20/archives/u-of-georgia-eases-rules-on-curfews-and-drinking.html?searchResultPosition=1.

"New Wave." *Allmusic*, Accessed October 12, 2018. https://www.allmusic.com/style/new-wave-ma0000002750.

Norris, Michele. "The B-52s, Bringing Back the Party." *All Things Considered (NPR)*. April 10, 2008. https://www.npr.org/transcripts/89528959?storyId=89528959.

Norton, Mark J. "Surpriiiise, Your Mom Likes the B-52's." *Creem*, December 1980.

Nunn, Jerry. "Fred Schneider." *Chicago Pride*. August 24, 2009. https://chicago.gopride.com/news/interview.cfm/articleid/145696.

Nurse, Donna Bailey. "Ursula K. Le Guin: The Crossover Artist." *Black Iris*, January 29, 2018. http://www.blackiris.co/new-blog-36/.

Ocamb, Karen. "Larry Kramer's Historic Essay: AIDS at 30." Bilerico Report. http://bilerico.lgbtqnation.com/2011/06/larry_kramers_historic_essay_aids_at_30.php, first published in the *New York Native*, Issue 59, March 14–27, 1983.

Parker, Lyndsey. "The B-52's' Fred Schneider on RuPaul's Pre-Fame …" *Yahoo! Entertainment*, March 30, 2017. https://www.yahoo.com/entertainment/the-b-52s-fred-schneider-on-rupauls-pre-fame-love-shack-cameo-he-got-the-line-dance-going-204218086.html.

Pat Irwin Music. "The B-52's—Good Stuff." Accessed September 29, 2019. https://patirwinmusic.com/portfolio-item/the-b-52s-good-stuff/.

Paulson, Dave. "The B-52s, Nashville Symphony Join Forces." *The Tennessean*, Feb 2, 2016. https://www.tennessean.com/story/entertainment/music/2016/02/02/b-52s-nashville-symphony-join-forces/79708862/.

Pennock, Tom. "The B-52s on Rock Lobster: 'There's Not Any Songs Like It!'." *Uncut*, August 27, 2018. https://www.uncut.co.uk/features/b-52s-rock-lobster-theres-not-songs-like-104998.

People. "Rock Hudson." December 23, 1985. https://people.com/archive/rock-hudson-vol-24-no-26/.

Phipps, Keith. "Random Rules: Keith Strickland of the B-52s." *AV Club*, April 21, 2008. https://music.avclub.com/random-rules-keith-strickland-of-the-b-52s-1798213772.

Pond, Steve. "Backstage at the US Festival: It's Only Rock & Roll." *Rolling Stone*, October 14, 1982. https://www.rollingstone.com/music/music-news/backstage-at-the-us-festival-its-only-rock-roll-86656/.

Pond, Steve. "Murmur." *Rolling Stone*, May 26, 1983. https://www.rollingstone.com/music/music-album-reviews/murmur-104268/.

Rachel, T. Cole. "Cindy Wilson on creating the world you want to be in." *The Creative Independent* (blog), January 17, 2017. https://thecreativeindependent.com/people/cindy-wilson-on-creating-the-world-you-want-to-be-in/.

Rambali, Paul. "The B-52s: Hot Pants Cold Sweat And A Brand New Beehive Hair Do." *New Musical Express,* June 9, 1979. Rock's Backpages. Accessed August 21, 2018.

The Red & Black. "SGA Election Extra—Comparative Look at Platforms." April 16, 1974.

Reines, Roz. "Planet of the Wild Dolls." *Melody Maker*, Nov 8, 1980.

Reinolds, Christine. "Escape From New York Tour Draws Small Crowds." *Tulsa World*, July 22, 1990. https://www.tulsaworld.com/archive/escape-from-new-york-tour-draws-small-crowds-tom-tom/article_b54e5cb4-9f2a-582b-acec-a05471253429.html.

Reyes-Kulkarni, Saby. "The B-52s' Fred Schneider and Cindy Wilson Reflect on 40 Weird, Wonderful Years." *Bandcamp Daily*, September 11, 2017. https://daily.bandcamp.com/2017/09/11/cindy-wilson-fred-schneider-interview/.

Rhodes, Wendy. "Fred Schneider on the B-52's Early Struggles: 'My Voice Was Considered Commercial Radio Poison.'" *Miami New Times*, August 20, 2019. https://www.miaminewtimes.com/music/things-to-do-in-miami-the-b-52s-at-the-broward-center-august-29-2019-11245463.

Richardson, Derek. "Silliness with A Cutting Edge: The B-52's Regain Their Stride." *Record*, September 1983.

Rockwell, John. "B-52's, Rock Band from Georgia." *The New York Times*, June 3, 1978.

Rockwell, John. "The Fans Rock Imaginatively on Impressive Instrumentals." *The New York Times*, January 15, 1977. https://www.nytimes.com/1977/01/15/archives/the-fans-rock-imaginatively-on-impressive-instrumentals.html.

Rockwell, John. "The Pop Life." *The New York Times*, July 13, 1979.

Rogers, Ray. "Reviews." *Spin*, n.d.

Rose, Cynthia. "The B-52's: Hair Today Gone Tomorrow?" *New Musical Express*, January 3, 1981. Rock's Backpages. Accessed October 16, 2018. http://www.rocksbackpages.com/Library/Article/the-b-52s-hair-today-gone-tomorrow.

Rotter, Joshua. "The B-52s at 40, still dancing that mess around." *48 Hills*, August 7, 2019. https://48hills.org/2019/08/the-b-52s-at-40/.

Runtagh, Jordan. "The B-52s at 40: An Oral History of Their Awesomely Bizarre Beach Party Breakthrough 'Rock Lobster.'" *People*, May 29, 2018. https://people.com/music/the-b-52s-rock-lobster-oral history/.

Sandall, Robert. "B-52s: The Love Shack Shakes Again." Daily Telegraph, April 3, 2008. Rock's Backpages. Accessed October 16, 2018. http://www.rocksbackpages.com/Library/Article/b-52s-the-love-shack-shakes-again.

Sanderlin, Phil. "Diamond Lil Highlights Affair." *The Red & Black*, March 22, 1972.

Savage, Jon. "The B-52s: *B-52s* (Island)." *Melody Maker*, June 30, 1979. Accessed August 27, 2018. http://www.rocksbackpages.com/Library/Article/the-b-52s-ib-52si-island.

Sawyer, Miranda. "The Public Has a Right to Art…" *The Guardian*, June 2, 2019. https://www.theguardian.com/artanddesign/2019/jun/02/public-has-right-to-art-keith-haring-tate-liverpool-exhibition.

Schoemer, Karen. "Beehives and Ballyhoo." *Spin*, March 1990.

Schoemer, Karen. "Recordings: At Home in the Top 40 and Still Full of Kitsch." *The New York Times*, December 31, 2019. https://www.nytimes.com/1989/12/31/arts/recordings-at-home-in-the-top-40-and-still-full-of-kitsch.html.

Schultz, Barbara. "Classic Tracks." *Mix*, July 2012.

Scrudato, Ken. "BlackBook Interview: The B-52s' Fred Schneider on 40 Years of Making 'Surreal' Music." Black Book, May 24, 2018. https://bbook.com/arts-culture/blackbook-interview-the-b-52s-fred-schneider-on-40-years-of-making-surreal-music/.

Sexton, Mats. "B-Hive Fanzine." Spring/Summer 1997.

Shapiro, Eileen. "Fred Schneider—The B-52s Appearing at Summer Stage …" *Get Out!*, September 9, 2019. https://getoutmag.com/fred-schneider-the-b-52s-appearing-at-summer-stage-in-central-park-september-24/.

Shapiro, Gregg. "Change of Heart: An Interview with Cindy Wilson of the B-52s." *Wisconsin Gazette*, June 1, 2018. https://www.wisconsingazette.com/entertainment/change-of-heart-an-interview-with-cindy-wilson-of-the/article_82462636-65ae-11e8-a057-3fead4976479.html.

Shearer, Lee. "Life Uncertain for Gays Here." *The Athens Observer*, November 13, 1980.

Sigerson, David. "B52s on Target at New Club." *Melody Maker*, March 24, 1979.

Simadis, Valerie. "Cosmic Thing: An Interview with Cindy Wilson of the B-52's." *Please Kill Me*, December 5, 2017. https://pleasekillme.com/interview-cindy-wilson-b-52s/.

Simels, Steve. "The B-52's." *Stereo Review*, October 1979.

Siskel, Gene. "'Flintstones' As Much Fun as Watching a Stone Age." *Chicago Tribune*. May 27, 1994. https://www.chicagotribune.com/news/ct-xpm-1994-05-27-9405270142-story.html.

Smith, Roberta. "Right Where She Belongs." *The New York Times*. April 2, 2021.

Sokol, Brett. "Club 57, Late-Night Home of Basquiat and Haring, Gets a Museum-Worthy Revival." *The New York Times,* October 26, 2017. https://www.nytimes.com/2017/10/26/arts/design/club-57-museum-of-modern-art.html.

Southern Garage Bands. "Ravenstone." Accessed August 12, 2019. https://southerngaragebands.com/ravenstone.html.

Specter, Michael. "Public Nuisance." *The New Yorker*, May 13, 2002. https://www.newyorker.com/magazine/2002/05/13/public-nuisance.

Spitz, Marc. "Return of the Rock Lobsters." *The New York Times*, March 16, 2008, AR24.

"Steve Rabolvsky, '79." *1300 Elmwood*, Winter, 2011. http://1300elmwood.buffalostate.edu/winter-2011/steve-ralbovsky-79.

Suwak, Jeff. "Cindy Wilson of the B-52s." Songfacts, August 1, 2019. https://www.songfacts.com/blog/interviews/cindy-wilson-b52s.

Swanson, Dave. "When the Toronto Heatwave Festival Tried To Be The 'New Wave Woodstock.'" *Diffuser*, August 23, 2013. http://diffuser.fm/toronto-heatwave-anniversary/.

Swenson, John. "Frank Zappa: America's Weirdest Rock Star Comes Clean." *High Times* (1980), reprinted in Rock's Backpages. Accessed October 16, 2018, http://www.rocksbackpages.com/Library/Article/frank-zappa-americas-weirdest-rock-star-comes-clean.

Tannenbaum, Rob, "The B-52's Say Farewell to the Road," Aug. 14, 2022.

Taylor, John Martin. "The B-52s and Me." *Hoppin; John's* (blog), February 16, 2008. https://hoppinjohns.net/?p=263.

"Teenage Jesus & The Jerks, Chronology." Undated, http://www.fromthearchives.com/ll/chronology1.html.

Thomas, Bryan. "'Monster': Fred Schneider's MTV-Banned Video …" Night Flight, February 29, 2016, http://nightflight.com/monster-fred-schneiders-mtv-banned-video-featured-a-rare-cameo-by-celebrated-nyc-drag-queen-legend-ethyl-eichelberger/.

"Tom Tom Club." Lecture hosted by Benji B, posted December 22, 2014. http://www.redbullmusicacademy.com/lectures/tom-tom-club.

Trakin, Roy. "Steven Stanley: "Youth Sound." *Musician*, November 1983. Rock's Backpages. Accessed October 16. 2018, http://www.rocksbackpages.com/Library/Article/steven-stanley-youth-sound.

True, Everett. "Singles." *Melody Maker*, July 9, 1994.

Vaziri, Aidin. "Q & A with Fred Schneider of B-52's." *The San Francisco Chronicle*, July 26, 1998.

Ware, Tony. "Athens, GA: Freak Beat." *XLR8R*, August 17, 2019. https://www.xlr8r.com/features/athens-ga-freak-beat-1.

Warhol Stars. "Jackie Curtis' Vain Victory." Warholstars.org. Accessed August 11, 2019. https://warholstars.org/vain-victory-3.html.

Watching the Wheels. "Jukebox Hero 1: Queens of Noise." April 13, 2017. https://watchingthewheelsdad.net/tag/joan-jett/.

Whitall, Susan. "Heatwave Festival: Crouching Towards Bowmanville or Elvis: What Happened?" *Creem*, November 1980. Rock's Backpages. Accessed October 16, 2018. http://www.rocksbackpages.com/Library/Article/heatwave-festival-crouching-towards-bowmanville-or-elvis-what-happened.

Wilde, Jon. "B-52's: The Band that Refused to Die." *Melody Maker*, April 7, 1990.

Wilkinson, Roy. "Wig Wam Bam!" *Sounds*, August 8, 1987.

Williams, Alex. "Glenn O'Brien, Writer and Editor Who Gained Fame with Warhol, Dies at 70." *The New York Times*, April 7, 2017.

Yarbrough, Jeff. "Rock Hudson: On Camera and Off." *People*, August 12, 1985. https://people.com/archive/cover-story-rock-hudson-on-camera-and-off-vol-24-no-7/.

YouTube. "The B-52's—Guiding Light." Accessed September 3, 2019a. https://www.youtube.com/watch?v=ffB2rqz4HfQ.

YouTube. "B52s Kate Pierson Interview | The US Festival of 1982." Accessed September 2, 2019b. https://www.youtube.com/watch?v=fmCRnXbQug4.

YouTube. "Keith Strickland on 'It Gets Better'." January 21, 2011. https://www.youtube.com/watch?v=-YnsYrYqYEA.

Archival and Other Materials

Azerrad, Michael. *Nude on the Moon: The B-52s Anthology*. The B-52's. Rhino Records. R2 78357. 2002. Compact disc. Liner notes.

The B's Connection. Issue #12, July 1993. Mats Sexton B-52's memorabilia collection, Box 1, University of Georgia Libraries Special Collections.

"The B-52's Only Official Correspondence Club." Dec 1991/Jan 1992. Mats Sexton B-52's memorabilia collection, Box 1, University of Georgia Libraries Special Collections.

B-Hive, #7, Summer 1996. Mats Sexton B-52's memorabilia collection, Box 1, University of Georgia Libraries Special Collections.

B-Hive, #8, Winter 1997. Mats Sexton B-52's memorabilia collection, Box 1, University of Georgia Libraries Special Collections.

B-Hive, Spring/Summer 1997. Mats Sexton B-52's memorabilia collection, Box 1, University of Georgia Libraries Special Collections.

B-Hive, Summer 1998, Issue 13. Mats Sexton B-52's memorabilia collection, Box 1, University of Georgia Libraries Special Collections.

The B-52's United Fans Organization, Issues #9 and #10. Mats Sexton B-52's memorabilia collection, Box 1, University of Georgia Libraries Special Collections.

CGE Mouthpiece, April 14, 1974, Box 1, LGBT Resource Records, UA17-009 University of Georgia Libraries Special Collections.

De Muir, Harold. "An Interview with Fred Schneider and Keith Strickland of the B-52's." Unknown title, January 28, 1987. Mats Sexton B-52's memorabilia collection, ms 4110, Book 6, University of Georgia Libraries Special Collections.

Hawkins, Robert J. Reprint of review of San Diego Sports Arena show. Unidentified newspaper (likely *San Diego Union-Tribune*). *B's Connection*, Issue #10, November/December 1992, Mats Sexton B-52's memorabilia collection, Box 1, University of Georgia Libraries Special Collections.

Henderson, Kim. "I Never Thought AIDS Could Touch Me." Unidentified newspaper, Jan 28, 1990. Box 1, LGBT Resource Records, UA17-009 University of Georgia Libraries Special Collections.

Hester, Conoly. "Are AIDS Cases Under-reported in NE Georgia?" Unidentified newspaper. Box 1, LGBT Resource Records, UA17-009 University of Georgia Libraries Special Collections.

Hester, Conoly. "When Loved One has AIDS." Unidentified newspaper. March 10, 1988, Box 1, LGBT Resource Records, UA17-009 University of Georgia Libraries Special Collections.

Interview with Dany Johnson "Club 57." *The World of Keith Haring*. Soul Jazz Records. SJRLP444. 2019. LP. Liner notes

M. Louise McBee from the Office of the Dean in UGA Division of Student Affairs to Dean O. Suthern Sims, Nov 11, 1971, Box 1, LGBT Resource Records, UA17-009 University of Georgia Libraries Special Collections.

Owen, Frank. "Flying High: The B-52's Strike Back." Uncredited magazine, Mats Sexton B-52's memorabilia collection, ms 4110, Book 8, University of Georgia Libraries Special Collections.

Queer Weekly, June 21, 1992, reprinted in *B-Hive*, Spring/Summer 1997, Mats Sexton B-52's memorabilia collection, Box 1, University of Georgia Libraries Special Collections.

Testimony in Court Case Re: Dance, March 10, 1972, Box 1, LGBT Resource Records, UA17-009 University of Georgia Libraries Special Collections.

University of Georgia Libraries Special Collections. Mats Sexton B-52's memorabilia collection, Box 1.

University of Georgia Libraries Special Collections. University of Georgia Ephemera Collection, UA85-001, Box 77, Folder 42.
"WSB-TV Newsfilm Clip of Governor Lester Maddox Blaming His Generation For the Current Social Unrest as Students Protesting Kent State, Georgia, 1970 May 13," WSB-TV newsfilm collection, reel 1639, 7:54/09:03, Walter J. Brown Media Archives and Peabody Awards Collection, The University of Georgia Libraries, Athens, Ga, as presented in the Digital Library of Georgia, http://dlg.galileo.usg.edu/crdl/do:ugabma_wsbn_59642.

Index[1]

[1] Note: Page numbers followed by 'n' refer to notes.

S. Creney, B. A. Herron, *The Story of the B-52s*,
https://doi.org/10.1007/978-3-031-22570-3